ALGORITHMS
AND
DATA STRUCTURES

ALGORITHMS
AND
DATA STRUCTURES

Design, Correctness, Analysis

Jeffrey H. Kingston

University of Sydney

**ADDISON-WESLEY
PUBLISHING
COMPANY**

Sydney · Wokingham, England · Reading, Massachusetts
Menlo Park, California · New York · Don Mills, Ontario
Amsterdam · Bonn · Singapore · Tokyo · Madrid · San Juan

Cover designed by Crayon Design
Typeset by Times Graphics
Printed and bound in Singapore

First printed 1990.

National Library of Australia Cataloguing in Publication Data
Kingston, Jeffrey H. (Jeffrey Howard).
  Algorithms and data structures : design, correctness, analysis.

  Bibliography.
  Includes index.
  ISBN 0 201 41705 7.

  1. Algorithms. 2. Data structures (Computer science).
  I. Title.

005.1

Library of Congress Cataloging-in-Publication Data
Kingston, Jeffrey H.
   Algorithms and data structures : design, correctness, analysis
Jeffrey H. Kingston.
     p.   cm.
   ISBN 0-201-41705-7
   1. Data structures (Computer science) 2. Algorithms. I. Title.
QA76.9.D35K524   1990
005.7'3--dc20

                                                      90-163
                                                      CIP

Preface

This book is intended as a text for a one-semester second or third year course on algorithms and data structures. It aims to present the central topics of the subject, coherently organized, with emphasis more on depth of treatment than on broad survey.

My motive in choosing depth over breadth was a desire to involve the student by making all the material fully accessible. For example, an average complexity analysis is the best way to justify the use of Quicksort, but since this is not easy to perform, some preparation in analysis techniques is needed. Similarly, the correctness of Dijkstra's algorithm is not clear, and it requires a proof using loop invariants. Thus are we led naturally to depth of treatment.

I have retained the traditional organization by application area for most of the book (Chapters 6–10). This brings together alternative solutions to the various problems, and makes manifest to the student the general scope of the subject in a way that a text structured around design or analysis techniques cannot do. Chapters 1–4 are devoted to techniques: correctness, analysis, the use of abstract data types, and algorithm design.

Finding the right level of treatment for correctness is difficult. Proofs of correctness are essential for some of the graph algorithms of Chapter 10, and the presentation of even quite simple algorithms can be improved by giving their loop invariants; but a formal treatment including predicate transformers would easily fill an entire book. I have compromised, using informal arguments to establish formal invariants, and including an introductory chapter that could be assigned as reading.

By counting the number of times that a characteristic operation is performed, the analyses give quite precise results, without excessive detail. Amortized complexity, an unusual feature of this book, is the key to some exciting new data structures – notably Fibonacci heaps, which lead to an optimal implementation of Dijkstra's algorithm.

Abstract data types have helped greatly in organizing the subject matter, both by classifying and specifying data structures, and by removing them from the algorithms. They permeate the book, and there are whole chapters devoted to the implementation of three important ones: the symbol table, the priority queue, and the disjoint sets structure.

For algorithm design, the usual list of strategies is presented, and the reader is invited to consider applying each to the problem at hand. Backtracking and branch-and-bound have been omitted, since they are most often applied to NP-hard and artificial intelligence problems that lie outside the scope of this text.

As I wrote this book, I perceived a need for a more systematic classification of iterative algorithms than is usually given. To this end, I have identified two distinctive kinds of loop invariant, the first occurring in such trivial algorithms as summing an array and insertion sort, and the second in more subtle algorithms, including the greedy algorithms. This classification is presented in Section 4.2.

The book is entirely self-contained in its treatment of correctness, analysis of algorithms (except basic probability theory), data abstraction, and algorithm design. Some knowledge of the kind usually imparted in a second programming course is assumed: familiarity with a Pascal-like programming language, linked structures, and recursion.

Executable Modula-2 code is given in nearly all cases; it has been compiled and tested. The major technical issue in choosing a programming language for presenting this material must be the degree of support provided for data abstraction. Modula-2 has the necessary modules and opaque types; regrettably, the absence of type inheritance, generic modules, procedure name overloading, and function value dereferencing leads to some loss of generality or readability in some programs.

Specific attributions are given throughout the text. More generally, I am indebted to a number of previous authors, especially to Aho *et al.* (1983) for my choice of subject areas, as well as many of the individual topics; to Tarjan (1983), whose monograph provided a model for my organization, and some of its most interesting material; and to Knuth (1973a, b) for general inspiration, as well as most of the analyses in Chapters 5–8.

Several people generously gave their time during the development of the book at Sydney University. Greg Ryan carefully read the manuscript; Stephen Russell and John Gough assisted with Modula-2; and Bryden Allen, Greg Butler, Norman Foo, and Alan Fekete gave reviews and advice. My thanks also to my thesis supervisor, Allan Bromley, for his encouragement over the years.

This book has grown from courses taught while visiting the University of Iowa in 1984–7, and, in a general way, owes much to my colleagues there, especially Donald Alton, Keith Brinck, and Douglas Jones, and to the congenial environment I found at Iowa. Accordingly, I dedicate the book with gratitude to my many American friends.

Contents

Preface   v

Chapter 1 Algorithm Correctness   1

    1.1   Problems and Specifications   1
    1.2   Recursive Algorithms   2
    1.3   Iterative Algorithms   4
         Exercises   9

Chapter 2 Analysis of Algorithms   13

    2.1   Characteristic Operations and Time Complexity   13
    2.2   Recursive Algorithms   16
    2.3   Iterative Algorithms   21
    2.4   Evaluating Efficiency, and the O-notation   26
         Exercises   28

Chapter 3 Data Abstraction   36

    3.1   Abstract Data Types   36
    3.2   Lists, Stacks, and Queues   40
    3.3   Correctness of ADT Implementations   43
    3.4   Analysis of ADT Implementations   47
    3.5   Amortized Analysis   50
         Exercises   55

Chapter 4 Algorithm Design   62

    4.1   The Design Process   62
    4.2   Incremental Algorithms   64
    4.3   Divide-and-Conquer   66
    4.4   Dynamic Programming   71
         Exercises   77

Chapter 5 Properties of Binary Trees   82

    5.1   Definitions   82

5.2   Height and Path Length   83
5.3   Skew Trees and Complete Trees   85
5.4   Huffman Trees   88
        Exercises   92

Chapter 6   Symbol Tables   **96**

6.1   Specification   96
6.2   Linked Lists   97
6.3   Locality of Reference and Self-adjusting Lists   98
6.4   Binary Search Trees   103
6.5   Analysis of Binary Search Tree Insertions   105
6.6   Splay Trees   110
6.7   B-trees   116
6.8   Hashing   122
6.9   Choosing a Symbol Table Implementation   126
        Exercises   127

Chapter 7   Priority Queues   **142**

7.1   Specification   142
7.2   Heap-ordered Trees   144
7.3   The Heap   147
7.4   Heapsort   149
7.5   Binomial Queues   153
7.6   Fibonacci Heaps   156
7.7   Choosing a Priority Queue Implementation   163
        Exercises   164

Chapter 8   Sorting   **175**

8.1   Insertion Sorting   176
8.2   Selection Sorting   181
8.3   Merging and Mergesort   182
8.4   Quicksort   187
8.5   Radix Sorting   190
8.6   Choosing a Sorting Algorithm   193
        Exercises   194

Chapter 9   Disjoint Sets   **202**

9.1   Specification   202
9.2   The Galler–Fischer Representation   206
9.3   Union by Size   208
9.4   Path Compression   210
        Exercises   216

Chapter 10   Graph Algorithms   **219**

   10.1   Definitions   220
   10.2   Specification and Representation   221
   10.3   Relations and Digraphs   223
   10.4   Directed Acyclic Graphs   228
   10.5   Shortest Paths and Breadth-first Search   236
   10.6   Depth-first Search   245
   10.7   Strongly Connected Components   248
   10.8   Biconnectivity   250
   10.9   Minimum Spanning Trees and Kruskal's Algorithm   254
   10.10   Prim's Algorithm   261
   10.11   The Travelling Salesperson Problem   267
         Exercises   272

Chapter 11   Lower Bounds   **284**

   11.1   Models of Computation   285
   11.2   Adversary Bounds   286
   11.3   Decision Trees   288
   11.4   Entropy   292
   11.5   Transformations   297
         Exercises   301

Recommended Further Reading   **304**

References   **305**

Index   **309**

Chapter 1

Algorithm Correctness

There are several good reasons for studying the correctness of algorithms, for example, to improve the quality of the programs we write, or of the languages we use. But the reasons for doing it here, in this book, are as follows.

First, some algorithms are so mysterious as to defy intuition. To understand these algorithms formal methods must be used.

Second, although it is true that every algorithm depends for its correctness on specific properties of the problem at hand, there must also be a strategy for putting those properties to work. To prove an algorithm correct is to reveal this strategy; it can then be used in comparisons with other algorithms, and in the development of new algorithms.

The study of correctness, as we will go about it, is known as *axiomatic semantics*, and it is principally owing to Floyd (1967) and Hoare (1969). It is possible, using the methods of axiomatic semantics, to prove that a program is correct as rigorously as one can prove a theorem in logic. This will not be attempted here, because it is an entire subject in itself (Dijkstra, 1976; Gries, 1981); instead, a less rigorous approach will be taken which is compatible with the fully rigorous one, but which is more appropriate to our aims of understanding, comparing, and developing algorithms.

1.1 Problems and Specifications

A *problem* is a general question to be answered, usually possessing several *parameters*. A problem is specified by describing the form we expect the parameters to take and the question we ask about them. For example, the *minimum-finding problem* is 'S is a set of numbers. What is a minimum element of S?' It has one parameter, S.

1

An *instance* of a problem is an assignment of values to the parameters. For example, '$S = \{5, 2, 6, 9\}$' is an instance of the minimum-finding problem.

An *algorithm* for a problem is a step-by-step procedure for taking any instance of the problem and producing a correct answer for that instance. If several answers are equally correct, as often happens, the algorithm is free to produce any one. An algorithm is *correct* if it is guaranteed to produce a correct answer to every instance of the problem.

Specifying a problem can be a difficult task in itself, because there is a need for great precision. For example, the empty set has no minimum element, so the specification given above for the minimum-finding problem is flawed. A good way to state a specification precisely is to give two Boolean expressions, or *conditions*: the first, called the *precondition*, states what may be assumed to be true initially; the second, called the *postcondition*, states what is to be true about the result. For example, the minimum-finding problem could be specified like this:

Pre: S is a finite, non-empty set of integers
Post: m is a minimum element of S.

We could write (there exists $x \in S$ such that $m = x$) **and** (for all $x \in S$, $m \leq x$) to express more formally what it means for m to be a minimum element of S. By assuming that all instances are non-empty, we are saying that we don't care what an algorithm for this problem does if it is given the empty set. It is the user's responsibility to supply only instances in accord with the precondition.

1.2 Recursive Algorithms

Newcomers to recursion are often confused by the apparent circularity of the method: to solve a problem, first solve the problem. But it is misleading to view recursion in this way; rather, one *instance* is solved by solving one or more different, and smaller, instances. When proving that a recursive algorithm finds the correct solution to some instance, we therefore need to assume that it finds correct solutions to these smaller instances, and this suggests immediately that we should use induction on the size of the instance to prove correctness.

As a first example, consider the problem of calculating $n!$, whose specification is

(* *Pre*: n is an integer such that $n \geq 0$ *)
$x := Factorial(n)$;
(* *Post*: $x = n!$ *)

The convention of including the conditions as comments in a program fragment at the points where they should be true has been adopted. The usual recursive algorithm for this problem is

```
procedure Factorial(n: integer): integer;
begin
  if n = 0 then
    return 1;
  else
    return n*Factorial(n − 1);
  end;
end Factorial;
```

and its proof of correctness is as follows:

Theorem 1.1:   For all integers $n \geq 0$, $Factorial(n)$ returns $n!$.

Proof: by induction on n.

Basis step: $n = 0$. Then the test $n = 0$ succeeds, and the algorithm returns 1. This is correct, since $0! = 1$.

Inductive step: The inductive hypothesis is that $Factorial(j)$ returns $j!$, for all j in the range $0 \leq j \leq n - 1$. It must be shown that $Factorial(n)$ returns $n!$. Since $n > 0$, the test $n = 0$ fails and the algorithm returns $n*Factorial(n - 1)$. By the inductive hypothesis, $Factorial(n - 1)$ returns $(n - 1)!$, so $Factorial(n)$ returns $n \times (n - 1)!$, which equals $n!$.   ■

Notice that the proof is only possible because the recursive call is given a smaller instance than the original, so that the inductive hypothesis may be applied to it. Also, the theorem says nothing about the behaviour of $Factorial(n)$ for $n < 0$, and in fact the algorithm never halts for these n.

The second example is the *binary search algorithm*. Its goal is to determine whether a number x is present in the sorted array $A[a..b]$:

```
(* Pre: a ≤ b + 1 and A[a..b] is a sorted array *)
found := BinarySearch(A, a, b, x);
(* Post: found = x ∈ A[a..b] and A is unchanged *)
```

Binary search first compares x with the middle element of the array, $A[mid]$. If $x < A[mid]$, it must lie in the left half of the array if it is present at all; if $x > A[mid]$, it must lie in the right half. The algorithm is naturally expressed recursively:

```
procedure BinarySearch(var A: AType; a, b: integer; x: KeyType):
boolean;
var mid: integer;
begin
  if a > b then return false;
  else
    mid := (a + b) div 2;
    if    x = A[mid] then return true;
    elsif x < A[mid] then return BinarySearch (A, a, mid − 1, x);
    else                      return BinarySearch (A, mid + 1, b, x);
    end;
  end;
end BinarySearch;
```

A has been made a **var** parameter for efficiency's sake; its value does not change. The proof of correctness is by induction on the size of the array $A[a..b]$:

Theorem 1.2: For all $n \geq 0$, where $n = b - a + 1$ equals the number of elements in the array $A[a..b]$, *BinarySearch*(A, a, b, x) correctly returns the value of the condition $x \in A[a..b]$.

Proof: by induction on n.

Basis step: $n = 0$. The array is empty, so $a = b + 1$, the test $a > b$ succeeds, and the algorithm returns **false**. This is correct, because x cannot be present in an empty array.

Inductive step: $n > 0$. The inductive hypothesis is that, for all j such that $0 \leq j \leq n - 1$, where $j = b' - a' + 1$, *BinarySearch*(A, a', b', x) correctly returns the condition $x \in A[a'..b']$. From the calculation $mid := (a + b)$ **div** 2 it may be concluded that $a \leq mid \leq b$. If $x = A[mid]$, clearly $x \in A[a..b]$ and the algorithm correctly returns **true**. If $x < A[mid]$, since A is sorted it may be concluded that $x \in A[a..b]$ if and only if $x \in A[a..mid - 1]$. By the inductive hypothesis, this second condition is returned by *BinarySearch*(A, a, $mid-1$, x). The inductive hypothesis does apply, since $0 \leq mid-1) - a + 1 \leq n - 1$. The case $x > A[mid]$ is similar, and so the algorithm works correctly on all instances of size n. ∎

1.3   Iterative algorithms

In this section the technique used to prove the correctness of an algorithm containing a **while** loop is explained. The following algorithm, which determines the sum of the elements of $A[a..b]$, will be used as the first example:

(* *Pre*: $a \leq b + 1$ *)
$i := a;\ sum := 0;$
while $i \neq b + 1$ **do**
  $sum := sum + A[i];$
  $i := i + 1;$
end;

(* *Post*: $sum = \displaystyle\sum_{j=a}^{b} A[j]$ *)

As usual, the precondition and postcondition are included as comments at the points where they should be true. Note that, by definition, $A[a..a - 1]$ denotes an empty array whose sum is 0, and this algorithm calculates this empty sum correctly.

The key step in the proof of correctness is the invention of a condition, called the *loop invariant* of the algorithm, which is supposed to be true at the beginning and end of each iteration of the **while** loop. By the 'beginning of an iteration' is meant the moment just before the boolean test at the top of the loop is executed.

There may be several loop invariants, such as **true** or (in the example above) $a \leq b + 1$; but to be useful a loop invariant must capture the relationship among the variables that change in value as the loop progresses. The loop invariant for the algorithm above is $sum = \Sigma_{j=a}^{i-1} A[j]$, which expresses the relationship between the variables *sum* and i; the reader may easily verify intuitively that this condition holds at the beginning and end of each iteration.

For the record, and as a model for the more difficult proofs in later sections of this book, here is a proof that the condition really is a loop invariant:

Theorem 1.3:   (Loop invariant of summing algorithm) At the beginning of the kth iteration of the summing algorithm above, the condition $sum = \Sigma_{j=a}^{i-1} A[j]$ holds.

Proof: by induction on k.

Basis step: $k = 1$. At the beginning of the first iteration, the initialization statements clearly ensure that $sum = 0$ and $i = a$. Since $0 = \Sigma_{j=a}^{a-1} A[j]$, the condition holds.

Inductive step: The inductive hypothesis is that $sum = \Sigma_{j=a}^{i-1} A[j]$ at the beginning of the kth iteration. Since it has to be proved that this condition holds after one more iteration, it is also assumed that the loop is not about to terminate, that is, that $i \neq b + 1$. Let *sum'* and i' be the values of *sum* and i at the beginning of the $(k + 1)$st iteration. We are required to show that $sum' = \Sigma_{j=a}^{i'-1} A[j]$. Since $sum' = sum + A[i]$, and $i' = i + 1$, we have

$$sum' = sum + A[i]$$

$$= \sum_{j=a}^{i-1} A[j] + A[i]$$

$$= \sum_{j=a}^{i} A[j]$$

$$= \sum_{j=a}^{i'-1} A[j],$$

and so the condition holds at the beginning of the $(k + 1)$st iteration. ∎

Establishing the loop invariant is invariably the hard part of the proof, but there are two easier steps remaining. First of all, the postcondition must be shown to hold at the end. Consider the last iteration of the loop in the summing algorithm. At the end of it, the loop invariant holds, as we have shown. Then the test $i \neq b + 1$ is made, fails, and execution passes to the point after the loop. Clearly, at that moment the condition

$$sum = \sum_{j=a}^{i-1} A[j] \text{ and } i = b + 1$$

holds. But

$$sum = \sum_{j=a}^{i-1} A[j] \text{ and } i = b + 1$$

$$\Rightarrow sum = \sum_{j=a}^{b} A[j]$$

which is the desired postcondition; so that *Post* has been shown to hold when the algorithm terminates. Notice that this conclusion could not have been reached so simply if $i \leq b + 1$ had been used as the condition at the top of the loop. In general, just after the completion of the execution of the loop 'while B ...', with loop invariant I, the condition I and not B holds, and it is necessary to prove that this implies *Post*.

The final step is to show that there is no risk of an infinite loop. The method of proof is to identify some integer quantity that is strictly increasing (or decreasing) from one iteration to the next, and to show that when this becomes sufficiently large (or small) the loop must terminate.

For the summing algorithm, i is strictly increasing, and when it reaches $b + 1$ the loop must terminate. Note that this argument depends on i being no greater than $b + 1$ initially; in other words, the condition $a \leq b + 1$ must be true initially in order for termination to be guaranteed.

To summarize, then, the steps required to prove that the iterative algorithm

> (* *Pre* *)
> . . .
> **while** B **do**
>   . . .
> **end**;
> (* *Post* *)

is correct are as follows:

(1) Guess a condition I.

(2) Prove by induction that I is a loop invariant.

(3) Prove that I **and not** $B \Rightarrow Post$.

(4) Prove that the loop is guaranteed to terminate.

With practice, a clear intuitive understanding of the correctness of an algorithm will lead immediately to the loop invariant. Remember that it involves all the variables whose values change within the loop, but that it expresses an unchanging relationship among those variables. It must also contain complete information about what the algorithm has achieved.

For example, the loop invariant $sum = \sum_{j=a}^{i-1} A[j]$ makes good intuitive sense. It simply says that, at the beginning of each iteration, sum contains the sum of all the values examined so far.

Some good guidance on the general form of the loop invariant may be obtained from $Post$, since I must satisfy I **and not** $B \Rightarrow Post$, where B and $Post$ are known. Indeed, it is good policy to take $Post$ and generalize it in some way to obtain I. For example, in the summing algorithm above, I is just $Post$ with b replaced by $i - 1$. This simple relationship ensures that the condition I **and not** $B \Rightarrow Post$ is readily proven.

At the other extreme, check that the initialization statements establish I. If they do, and I **and not** $B \Rightarrow Post$, it is probably worthwhile to proceed with the main part of the induction.

Correctness of binary search. This section will be concluded with a study of the correctness of the following non-recursive binary search algorithm:

```
procedure BinarySearch(var A: AType; a, b: integer; x: KeyType):
boolean;
var i, j, mid: integer;
    found: boolean;
begin
    (* Pre: a ≤ b + 1 and A[a] ≤ ... ≤ A[b] *)
    i := a; j := b; found := false;
    while (i ≠ j + 1 and not found do
        mid := (i + j) div 2;
        if   x = A[mid] then found := true;
        elsif x < A[mid] then j := mid − 1;
        else                   i := mid + 1;
        end;
    end;
    (* Post: found = x ∈ A[a..b] *)

    return found;
end BinarySearch;
```

From the discussion of the recursive binary search algorithm in Section 1.2, it is fairly evident that the loop invariant should state that $x \in A[a..b]$ if and only if $x \in A[i..j]$. This takes care of the variables i and j.

The harder question is how to bring *found* and *mid* into the loop invariant, especially since *mid* is undefined at the beginning of the first iteration. Perhaps the best way to handle these two is to imagine another version of the algorithm in which the index of x is actually returned if found. For this version, *found* $\Rightarrow (a \le mid \le b$ **and** $x = A[mid])$ must be added to the postcondition, and this immediately suggests that it be included in the loop invariant:

$(x \in A[a..b]$ if and only if $x \in A[i..j])$
and (*found* $\Rightarrow (a \le mid \le b$ **and** $x = A[mid]))$

The initialization $i := a; j := b; found :=$ **false**; clearly establishes this invariant. At termination the loop invariant and $i = j + 1$ **or** *found* both hold. If *found* is true, the loop invariant tells us that $a \le mid \le b$ **and** $x = A[mid]$, so we must have $x \in A[a..b]$; on the other hand, if *found* is false, then $i = j + 1$ and so $x \notin A[i..j]$ and therefore $x \notin A[a..b]$. Thus the postcondition holds. The rest of the proof is left as an exercise; it is quite similar to the argument used to prove that the recursive binary search algorithm was correct.

EXERCISES

1.1   Consider the following recursive algorithm:

> **procedure** $g(n$: **integer**): **integer**;
> **begin**
>   **if** $n \leq 1$ **then**
>   **return** n;
>   **else**
>   **return** $5*g(n - 1) - 6*g(n - 2)$;
>   **end**;
> **end** g;

Prove by induction on n that $g(n)$ returns $3^n - 2^n$ for all $n \geq 0$.

1.2   Prove that the specification

> (* *Pre*: $a \leq b + 1$ *)
> *SelectionSort*(A, a, b);
> (* $A[a] \leq A[a + 1] \leq \ldots \leq A[b]$ *)

is satisfied by the procedure

> **procedure** *SelectionSort*(**var** A: *AType*; a, b: **integer**);
> **var** i: **integer**;
> **begin**
>   **if** $a = b + 1$ **then**
>   (* *do nothing* *)
>   **else**
> $i := MinIndex(A, a, b)$;
>   **if** $i \neq a$ **then**
> $Swap(A[i], A[a])$;
>   **end**;
>   *SelectionSort*$(A, a + 1, b)$;
>   **end**;
> **end** *SelectionSort*;

You may assume that *MinIndex*(A, i, j) returns the index of a minimum element of the non-empty array $A[i..j]$, and that *Swap*$(A[i], A[j])$ swaps the two indicated elements.

1.3   The specification given for *SelectionSort* in the preceding question is satisfied by the following procedure:

```
procedure Unexpected(var A: AType; a, b: integer);
var i: integer;
begin
  for i := a to b do
    A[i] := 0;
  end;
end Unexpected;
```

Tighten up the specification so that only genuine sorting algorithms satisfy it.

1.4 Prove that the following algorithm is correct with respect to the given precondition and postcondition:

```
(* Pre: a ≤ b and x ∈ A[a..b] *)
i := a;
while x ≠ A[i] do
  i := i + 1;
end;
(* Post: a ≤ i ≤ b and x ∉ A[a..i − 1] and x = A[i] *)
```

1.5 Prove that the following algorithm is correct with respect to the given precondition and postcondition. Use the postcondition as a guide when guessing the loop invariant.

```
(* Pre: true *)
i := a; found := false;
while (i ≤ b) and not found do
  found := A[i] = x;
  i := i + 1;
end;
(* Post: (found      ⇒ (a ≤ i − 1 ≤ b and x = A[i − 1]) and
         (not found ⇒ x ∉ A[a..b])                          *)
```

1.6 The following algorithm for evaluating the polynomial $a_0 + a_1 x + \ldots + a_{k-1} x^{k-1}$ at the point $x = x_0$, is named after William G. Horner:

```
type Poly = array [0..k − 1] of integer;

procedure Horner(a: Poly; x0: integer): integer;
var i, total: integer;
begin
  total := 0;
  for i := k − 1 to 0 by −1 do
    total := a[i] + total*x0;
  end;
  return total;
end Horner;
```

Find the loop invariant of this algorithm and prove it correct.

1.7 In addition to finding if $x \in A[a..b]$, the following iterative version of binary search finds the index of the place where x lies, or, if x is not present, the index of the place just to the left of x's place in the ordering:

```
procedure BinarySearch(var A: AType; a, b: integer;
x: KeyType; var pos: integer): boolean;
var i, j, mid: integer;
  found: boolean;
begin
  (* Pre: a ≤ b + 1 and A[a] ≤ ... ≤ A[b] *)
  i := a; j := b; found := false;
  while (i ≠ j + 1) and not found do
    mid := (i + j) div 2;
    if x = A[mid] then found := true;
    elsif x < A[mid] then j := mid − 1;
    else                i := mid + 1;
    end;
  end;
  if found then pos := mid; else pos := j; end;
  (* Post: (found       ⇒ a ≤ pos ≤ b and A[pos] = x) and
           (not found ⇒ a − 1 ≤ pos ≤ b and
           ( for all k s.t. a ≤ k ≤ pos, A[k] < x) and
           ( for all k s.t. pos + 1 ≤ k ≤ b, x < A[k]) ) *)
  return found;
end BinarySearch;
```

Prove that this algorithm is correct. Your first task is to determine what must be true just after the loop terminates in order for the final **if** statement to establish *Post*.

1.8 *The bill-splitting problem* (J.McCormack). A group of N people living in a shared household receive a bill for M cents. They want to split the bill N ways as fairly as possible, given that fractions of one cent are not allowed. The following algorithm is proposed:

```
m := M;
for n := N to 1 by −1 do
  r := m div n;
  WriteInt(r, 4);
  m := m − r;
end;
```

Does it always work?

1.9 *Tail recursion elimination.* Recursion is a powerful tool for expressing algorithms, and it is used extensively throughout this book. However, when a recursive algorithm is heavily used in a production system, it may be worthwhile to tune it by eliminating some or all of the recursive calls. In general, recursion elimination requires that the runtime stack be replaced by an explicit stack appearing in the algorithm; but, in the case where there is only one recursive call, and it is the last statement in the body of the procedure, the recursion can be replaced with a simple loop. This case is known as *tail recursion*. In general, the tail-recursive procedure

> **procedure** *TailRec*(*x*: *InsuranceType*): *ResultType*;
> **var** *y*: *InstanceType*;
>   *r*: *ResultType*;
> **begin**
>   **if** *B*(*x*) **then**
>   *r* := *C*(*x*);
>   **else**
>   *y* := *D*(*x*);
>   *r* := *TailRec*(*y*);
>   **end**;
>   **return** *r*;
> **end** *TailRec*;

has identical effect to the non-recursive procedure

> **procedure** *NonRec*(*x*: *InstanceType*): *ResultType*;
> **var** *y*: *InstanceType*;
>   *r*: *ResultType*;
> **begin**
>   **while not** *B*(*x*) **do**
>   *y* := *D*(*x*);
>   *x* := *y*;
>   **end**;
>   *r* := *C*(*x*);
>   **return** *r*;
> **end** *NonRec*;

where $B(x)$, $C(x)$ and $D(x)$ are any functions of the appropriate type (**boolean**, *ResultType* and *InstanceType* respectively). Prove this assertion by showing that if $r := TailRec(x)$ satisfies the specification

> (* *Pre*: *f*(*x*) *)
> *r* := *TailRec*(*x*);
> (* *Post*: *g*(*r*) *)

then so does $r := NonRec(x)$.

1.10 Eliminate tail recursion from the *SelectionSort* procedure given in Exercise 1.2.

Chapter 2

Analysis of Algorithms

The speed of computation has increased so much over the last thirty years that it might seem that efficiency in algorithms is no longer important. But, paradoxically, efficiency matters more today than ever before. The obvious reason why this is so is that our ambition has grown with our computing power. Virtually all applications of computing – the simulation of continuous systems, high-resolution graphics, and the interpretation of physical data, for example – are demanding more speed.

The more subtle, and more important reason is as follows. The time that many algorithms take to execute is a non-linear function of the size of their input, and this can greatly reduce their ability to benefit from increases in speed. For example, consider an algorithm that sorts n numbers into increasing order in n^2 steps. Suppose computing speed can be increased by a factor of 10 000. In the time that it used to take to execute n^2 steps, $10\,000n^2 = (100n)^2$ steps can now be executed. Thus, only 100 times as many numbers can be sorted. Two of the potential four orders of magnitude improvement have been lost to an inefficient algorithm.

Another example is the multiplication of integers. It takes longer to perform one 64-bit multiplication than it does to perform two 32-bit multiplications, as far as anyone knows.

The faster computers run, the more needed are efficient algorithms to take advantage of their power. The field of computer science which studies efficiency is known as *analysis of algorithms*.

2.1 Characteristic Operations and Time Complexity

Consider the following algorithm, which finds the index of a minimum element of the non-empty array $A[a..b]$:

```
procedure MinIndex(var A: AType; a, b: integer): integer;
var i, m: integer;
begin
  m := a;
  for i := a + 1 to b do
    if A[i] < A[m] then
      m := i;
    end;
  end;
  return m;
end MinIndex;
```

How long does $MinIndex(A, 1, n)$ take to execute? The answer depends on the particular implementation (that is, computer and compiler) used and on the size of the array, n. Since our interest is in the algorithm itself, and not in a particular implementation of it, these two factors need to be separated. In general, this is done by choosing some *characteristic operation* that the algorithm performs repeatedly, and defining the *time complexity*, $T(n)$, of an algorithm to be the number of characteristic operations it performs when given an input of size n.

For example, if $m := a$ is chosen as the characteristic operation for $MinIndex(A, 1, n)$, then $T(n) = 1$, since the operation is performed exactly once. Or, if it is decided to take the comparison $A[i] < A[m]$ as the characteristic operation, then $T(n)$ is the number of times the body of the loop is executed. It is not hard to see that this is $T(n) = n - 1$, since $A[m]$ is compared with the $n - 1$ numbers $A[2..n]$. Finally, if $m := i$ is chosen as the characteristic operation, $T(n)$ could be anything from 0 to $n - 1$, depending on the values in the array. This value dependence is considered below.

One way to choose among these answers is to refer to some particular implementation. Suppose it takes p microseconds to execute the body of the **for** loop once, and q microseconds to execute the initialization and return parts. Then the execution time is $p(n - 1) + q$, which is $pT(n) + q$ microseconds if the second complexity function is chosen. A characteristic operation and its corresponding complexity function are called *realistic* if the execution time with respect to some implementation is bounded by a linear function of $T(n)$. By choosing a realistic characteristic operation, the inherent complexity $T(n)$ is neatly separated from the implementation-dependent details p and q. The choice of a realistic characteristic operation is almost always so obvious that it will rarely be justified; in principle the analysis could be done for every possible operation and the largest answer taken.

Now consider this algorithm for determining whether x is an element of $A[a..b]$:

```
procedure LinearSearch (var a: AType; a, b, x: integer): boolean;
var i: integer;
   found: boolean;
begin
   i := a; found := false;
   while (i ≤ b) and not found do
      found := A[i] = x;
      i := i + 1;
   end;
   return found;
end LinearSearch;
```

The time complexity of $LinearSearch(A, 1, n, x)$ depends on the value of x and on the contents of the array. There are two questions to be asked:

(1) Over all instances of size n, what is the maximum time the algorithm takes to execute? This is its *worst-case time complexity*, $W(n)$.
(2) Over all instances of size n, what is the average time the algorithm takes to execute? This is its *average time complexity*, denoted $A(n)$.

More formally, suppose algorithm P accepts k different instances of size n. Let $T_i(n)$ be the time complexity of P when given the ith instance, for $1 \le i \le k$, and let p_i be the probability that this instance occurs. Then

$$W(n) = \max_{1 \le i \le k} T_i(n)$$

$$A(n) = \sum_{i=1}^{k} p_i T_i(n).$$

Exercise 2.2 shows that $A(n) \le W(n)$, with equality if and only if $T_1(n) = T_2(n) = \ldots = T_k(n)$, assuming all the probabilities are non-zero.

Average complexity analysis is complicated by the need to find a suitable assignment of values to the probabilities p_i. In one sense, any values would do, but if the result is to be useful the values must reflect the conditions under which the algorithm will be used – a vague and subjective requirement. For some problems, no consensus on suitable probabilities has been reached (for example, graph problems).

$W(n)$ and $A(n)$ will now be determined for $LinearSearch(A, 1, n, x)$, choosing $x = A[i]$ as the characteristic operation. Two reasonable assumptions about the probabilities are: (a) the probability that x will be found somewhere in the array is a constant, p; and (b) if x is present, it is equally likely to be found at any position in the array.

Although $LinearSearch(A, 1, n, x)$ has an infinite number of instances, they fall into just $k = n + 1$ classes. If $x = A[i]$, the algorithm

Table 2.1

i	Instance	p_i	$T_i(n)$
1	$x = A[1]$	p/n	1
2	$x = A[2]$	p/n	2
	$\cdots$		
i	$x = A[i]$	p/n	i
	$\cdots$		
n	$x = A[n]$	p/n	n
$n+1$	$x \notin A[1..n]$	$1-p$	n

will determine this and stop after comparing x with $A[1]$, $A[2]$, ..., $A[i]$; that is, after performing i characteristic operations. Since the probability p of x being present is spread equally among the n cases $x = A[1]$, $x = A[2]$, ..., $x = A[n]$, each must have probability p/n. If x is not present, we compare x with all n elements before stopping. This is all summarized in Table 2.1.

From Table 2.1 it is clear that $LinearSearch(A, 1, n, x)$ has a worst-case complexity of $W(n) = n$ comparisons. This occurs when $x = A[n]$, and when x is not present. The average complexity is

$$
\begin{aligned}
A(n) &= \sum_{i=1}^{n+1} p_i T_i(n) \\
&= \sum_{i=1}^{n} p_i T_i(n) + p_{n+1} T_{n+1}(n) \\
&= \sum_{i=1}^{n} \frac{p}{n} i + (1-p)n \\
&= \frac{p(n+1)}{2} + (1-p)n
\end{aligned}
$$

For example, if $p = 1$ the algorithm will scan about halfway along the array on average.

2.2 Recursive Algorithms

It was shown in Section 1.2 that the correctness of a recursive algorithm is proved by induction on n, the size of its input. This assumed that the recursive calls were correct; no investigation of them was needed.

A similar strategy often applies to the analysis of a recursive algorithm. Since, for all n, $T(n)$ is the time complexity of the algorithm

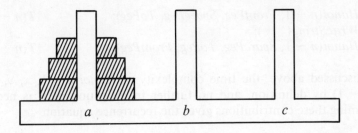

Figure 2.1

when given an input of size n, a recursive call of size $n/2$, say, has time complexity $T(n/2)$; no further investigation of it is needed. Just as the algorithm is defined in terms of itself, this approach will lead to an expression for $T(n)$ in terms of itself: a *recurrence equation* for $T(n)$, which must then be solved.

For example, consider the *Towers of Hanoi* problem, defined as follows. There are three pegs, labelled a, b, and c. On peg a there is a stack of n discs, each with a hole in the middle to accommodate the peg. As Figure 2.1 shows, the discs increase in size towards the bottom of the peg. The problem is to transfer the stack of discs to peg c, one disc at a time, in such a way as to ensure that no disc is ever placed on top of a smaller disc.

Here is a well-known algorithm for the Towers of Hanoi problem:

```
procedure Hanoi(n: integer; FromPeg, ToPeg, SparePeg: char);
begin
   if n > 0 then
      Hanoi(n − 1, FromPeg, SparePeg, ToPeg);
      WriteString(" Move the top disc from peg "); Write(FromPeg);
      WriteString(" to peg "); Write(ToPeg); WriteLn;
      Hanoi(n − 1, SparePeg, ToPeg, FromPeg);
   end;
end Hanoi;
```

Incidentally, it is good policy to make the base of recursive algorithms as low as possible. In the case of *Hanoi*, it makes sense to move zero discs from one peg to another. This policy invariably leads to simpler algorithms and it is the one employed in this book.

Let $T(n)$ be the time complexity of *Hanoi*(n, x, y, z), when the characteristic operation is the printing of one line. Clearly, $T(0) = 0$ because the test $n > 0$ fails and nothing is printed. For larger n, the following statements are executed and costs incurred:

$Hanoi(n-1, FromPeg, SparePeg, ToPeg)$;	$T(n-1)$
$WriteString(\dots)$;	1
$Hanoi(n-1, SparePeg, ToPeg, FromPeg)$;	$T(n-1)$

As discussed above, the time complexity of $Hanoi(n-1, x, y, z)$ is $T(n-1)$ by definition, and no further investigation of it is needed. Summing these contributions gives the recurrence equation

$$T(0) = 0$$
$$T(n) = 2T(n-1) + 1$$

for $T(n)$. (By convention the second line is taken to apply only when $n \geq 1$, since the first line handles $n = 0$.) This recurrence equation defines $T(n)$ for all n: $T(1) = 2T(0) + 1 = 1$, then $T(2) = 2T(1) + 1 = 3$, and so on. The analysis could end now, but a formula for $T(n)$ that does not have $T(n-1)$ on the right hand side is preferable. Such a formula is said to express $T(n)$ in *closed form*, and the process of deriving a closed form expression for $T(n)$ is called *solving* the recurrence equation.

Of the variety of techniques for solving recurrence equations, only the simplest will be needed in this book: *repeated substitution*. Since the formula $T(n) = 2T(n-1) + 1$ holds for all $n \geq 1$, $n-1$ may be substituted for n to obtain $T(n-1) = 2T(n-2) + 1$ for all $n \geq 2$. Similarly, $T(n-2) = 2T(n-3) + 1$. Therefore

$$\begin{aligned} T(n) &= 2T(n-1) + 1 \\ &= 2[2T(n-2) + 1] + 1 \\ &= 2[2[2T(n-3) + 1] + 1] + 1 \\ &= 2^3 T(n-3) + 2^2 + 2^1 + 2^0 \end{aligned}$$

(provided $n \geq 3$), expanding the brackets in a way that elucidates the emerging pattern. If this substitution is repeated i times, it clearly gives

$$T(n) = 2^i T(n-i) + 2^{i-1} + 2^{i-2} + \dots + 2^0$$

($n \geq i$). Induction on i could be used to prove this, but this is rarely necessary. By choosing i as large as possible, the base of the recurrence equation can be used to eliminate T from the right hand side: if $i = n$, then $T(n-i) = T(0) = 0$. Hence

$$\begin{aligned} T(n) &= 2^n 0 + 2^{n-1} + 2^{n-2} + \dots + 2^0 \\ &= \sum_{i=0}^{n-1} 2^i \\ &= 2^n - 1 \end{aligned}$$

applying the standard formula for the sum of a geometric progression. This completes the analysis of *Hanoi*.

There are cases where the information needed for an analysis is in the data, not the code. Consider this algorithm for the inorder traversal of a binary tree:

```
procedure InorderTraversal(root: ptr);
begin
    if root ≠ nil then
        InorderTraversal(root^.leftchild);
        Visit(root);
        InorderTraversal(root^.rightchild);
    end;
end InorderTraversal;
```

where *Visit(root)* stands for some operation to be performed at each node in the tree, such as printing its contents. The term *inorder* is a reminder that the root is visited in between the traversal of its left subtree and its right subtree. Other possibilities are *preorder* (visit the root first) and *postorder* (visit the root last).

We choose *Visit(root)* as our characteristic operation. It is performed once for each node in the tree being traversed, so $T(n) = n$, where n is the number of nodes in the tree. For want of a better term, this will be called the *global structure* approach to analysis. The global structure over which the algorithm travels is identified, and the number of characteristic operations is related to the size of the structure.

Analysis of binary search.   This section closes with an example which shows how to deal with the practical difficulties and complications that often hinder analyses. The binary search algorithm, which was proved correct in Section 1.2, determines whether x is present in the sorted array $A[a..b]$:

```
procedure BinarySearch(var A: AType; a, b: integer; x: KeyType):
boolean;
var mid: integer;
begin
    if a > b then return false;
    else
        mid := (a + b) div 2;
        if   x = A[mid] then return true;
        elsif x < A[mid] then return BinarySearch(A, a, mid − 1, x);
        else                  return BinarySearch(A, mid + 1, b, x);
    end;
    end;
end BinarySearch;
```

Since the array size is roughly halved after each comparison between x and $A[mid]$, and since an array of length n can be halved only about $\log_2 n$ times before reaching a trivial length, the worst-case complexity of $BinarySearch(A, 1, n, x)$ is about $\log_2 n$.

A more precise analysis can be made using recurrence equations. One comparison between x and $A[mid]$ (with a three-way outcome) is taken as the characteristic operation. Let $T(n)$ be the time complexity of $BinarySearch(A, 1, n, x)$. Then the algorithm sets mid to $\lfloor (n + 1)/2 \rfloor$[†], and examination of the program text reveals that

$$T(0) = 0$$
$$\begin{aligned}
T(n) &= 1 && \text{if } x = A[mid]\\
&= 1 + T(\lfloor (n + 1)/2 \rfloor - 1) && \text{if } x < A[mid]\\
&= 1 + T(n - \lfloor (n + 1)/2 \rfloor) && \text{if } x > A[mid]
\end{aligned}$$

Although it is sometimes possible to solve messy recurrence equations like this one, in general it is better to make some assumptions which simplify the task. The first step in simplifying this recurrence is to eliminate the floor function, which is done by restricting n to values of the form $n = 2^k - 1$, where k is a non-negative integer. This choice ensures that the array always breaks symmetrically into two equals pieces plus middle element:

$$2^k - 1$$

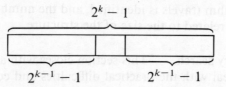

$$2^{k-1} - 1 \qquad 2^{k-1} - 1$$

Algebraically this is $\lfloor (n + 1)/2 \rfloor = \lfloor (2^k - 1 + 1)/2 \rfloor = 2^{k-1}$ for $k \geq 1$, giving

$$T(0) = 0$$
$$\begin{aligned}
T(2^k - 1) &= 1 && \text{if } x = A[mid]\\
&= 1 + T(2^{k-1} - 1) && \text{if } x < A[mid]\\
&= 1 + T(2^{k-1} - 1) && \text{if } x > A[mid]
\end{aligned}$$

This is now simplified further by considering only the worst case, which by inspection occurs (for example) when the test $x = A[mid]$ always fails:

[†] The notation $\lfloor x \rfloor$, 'floor of x' is used for the greatest integer less than or equal to x; the result of an integer division of one positive number by another is always truncated in this way. Similarly, $\lceil x \rceil$, 'ceiling of x', is the smallest integer greater than or equal to x.

$$W(0) = 0$$
$$W(2^k - 1) = 1 + W(2^{k-1} - 1).$$

This may now be solved by repeated substitution:

$$
\begin{aligned}
W(2^k - 1) &= 1 + W(2^{k-1} - 1) \\
&= 1 + [1 + W(2^{k-2} - 1)] \\
&= 1 + [1 + [1 + W(2^{k-3} - 1)]] \\
&= \cdots \\
&= i + W(2^{k-i} - 1)
\end{aligned}
$$

($i \le k$), and letting $i = k$ gives $W(2^k - 1) = k + W(0) = k$. But now $2^k - 1 = n$, and $k = \log_2(n + 1)$, so finally

$$W(n) = \log_2(n + 1)$$

(for $n = 2^k - 1$), which concludes this analysis of binary search.

Although it might seem that the restriction to values of n of the form $2^k - 1$ weakens the result, in practice this does not matter very much: $W(n)$ is a monotone increasing function of n, and hence the formula given is a good approximation even when n is not of the form $2^k - 1$ (Exercise 2.15). In Exercise 5.8 it is shown that $W(n) = \lceil \log_2(n + 1) \rceil$ for arbitrary n.

2.3 Iterative Algorithms

Just as recursive algorithms lead naturally to recurrence equations, so iterative algorithms lead naturally to formulas involving summations.

The simplest iterative algorithms to analyse are those containing only **for** loops. The technique is based on the observation that, in the code fragment

```
for i := a to b do
    S;
end;
```

the statement S is executed $b - a + 1$ times, provided that $a \le b + 1$. In particular, if $a = b + 1$, S is executed zero times. (This also applies when counting downwards from b to a.)

Analysis of an algorithm containing nested **for** loops generally begins with the innermost loop. Consider, for example, this algorithm for adding two matrices $A[1..n, 1..m]$ and $B[1..n, 1..m]$ together:

```
for i := 1 to n do
  for j := 1 to m do
    C[i, j] := A[i, j] + B[i, j];
  end;
end;
```

The addition $A[i, j] + B[i, j]$ is taken as the characteristic operation. First, the complexity of

```
for j := 1 to m do
  C[i, j] := A[i, j] + B[i, j];
end;
```

is clearly m additions, by the observation above. This reduces the problem to analysing the outer loop, which now has the form

```
for i := 1 to n do
  ⟨perform m additions⟩
end;
```

During each of the n iterations of the outer loop, m additions are performed, giving a total of $W(n, m) = nm$ additions overall.

In some algorithms, the cost of the inner loop depends on the value of the index variable of the outer loop, and this complicates the analysis a little. Consider this algorithm for sorting the elements of the array $A[a..b]$ into non-decreasing order:

```
procedure BubbleSort(var A: AType; a, b: integer);
var i, j: integer;
begin
  for i := b to a by −1 do
    for j := a + 1 to i do
      if A[j − 1] > A[j] then
        Swap(A[j − 1], A[j]);
      end;
    end;
  end;
end BubbleSort;
```

It works by 'bubbling' the largest entry up to $A[b]$, the second largest to $A[b − 1]$, and so on. The outer loop's invariant is '$A[a..b]$ contains a permutation of its original contents, and $A[i + 1..b]$ contains the $b − i$ largest entries, in sorted order.'

Now take the comparison $A[j - 1] > A[j]$ as the characteristic operation, and analyse the cost of *BubbleSort*$(A, 1, n)$. As before, begin by considering the inner loop in isolation:

```
for j := 2 to i do
  if A[j − 1] > A[j] then
    Swap(A[j − 1], A[j]);
  end;
end;
```

where $a + 1$ has been replaced by 2. Applying the observation about **for** loops, the operation $A[j - 1] > A[j]$ is performed $i - 1$ times, so that the problem reduces to analysing

```
for i := n to 1 by −1 do
  ⟨perform i − 1 comparisons⟩
end;
```

where b has been replaced by n and a by 1. Clearly, the total cost is $(n - 1) + (n - 2) + \ldots + 0$, so

$$T(n) = \sum_{i=1}^{n} (i - 1) = \frac{n(n - 1)}{2}$$

By comparison with other sorting algorithms studied in Chapter 8, *BubbleSort* is highly inefficient.

Incidentally, it is firm policy in this text to produce algorithms that work correctly on the smallest possible input. It makes sense to sort an empty array (that is, an array of length zero); accordingly, this version of *BubbleSort* is well defined when $a = b + 1$, and the analysis is correct too.

As with recursive algorithms, sometimes the information needed for the analysis is in the data, not the code. In such cases the global structure method already introduced in the previous section is needed: identify the global structure, and relate $T(n)$ to its size.

For example, consider the non-recursive implementation of the inorder traversal of a binary tree, as presented in Figure 2.2 (the recursive version was analysed in Section 2.2). The idea is to proceed from the first node of the traversal to its successor, to the next successor, and so on. Parent pointers are needed in addition to the usual left child and right child links. If x has a right child, its successor in the inorder traversal is

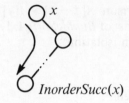

$InorderSucc(x)$

If x has no right child, its successor is

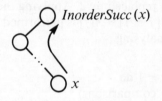

$InorderSucc(x)$

If $Visit(x)$ is chosen as the characteristic operation, then immediately $T(n) = n$, the number of nodes in the tree. But it is not clear that this choice is realistic, because $Visit(x)$ does not lie inside the inner loops of the code of Figure 2.2.

Another characteristic operation, which *is* realistic, is the *edge-traverse*. An edge-traverse is the movement of the algorithm's attention across one link, which in this example could be by any one of the operations $y := y^\wedge.leftchild$, $y := y^\wedge.rightchild$, or $y := y^\wedge.parent$. Examination of examples like

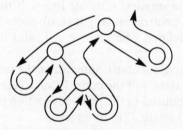

shows that every link is traversed exactly twice: once on the way down, and once on the way back. The final traverse out of the root is ignored. If $n \geq 1$, there are $n - 1$ edges in an n-node binary tree (Exercise 5.1), so $T(n) = 2(n - 1)$. Note that the algorithm treats $n = 0$ as a special case, and accordingly the same must be done in the analysis: $T(0) = 0$.

```
procedure InorderInit(x: ptr): ptr;
var y: ptr;
begin
  y := x;
  while y^.leftchild ≠ nil do
    y := y^.leftchild;
  end;
  return y;
end InorderInit;

procedure InorderSucc(x: ptr): ptr;
var y: ptr;
begin
  y := x;
  if y^.rightchild ≠ nil then
    y := y^.rightchild;
    while y^.leftchild ≠ nil do
      y := y^.leftchild;
    end;
  else
    while (y^.parent ≠ nil) and (y^.parent^.rightchild = y) do
      y := y^.parent;
    end;
    y := y^.parent;
  end;
  return y;
end InorderSucc;

procedure InorderTraversal(root: ptr);
var x: ptr;
begin
  if root ≠ nil then
    x := InorderInit(root);
    while x ≠ nil do
      Visit(x);
      x := InorderSucc(x);
    end;
  end;
end InorderTraversal;
```

Figure 2.2 Non-recursive inorder traversal of a binary tree. Type *ptr* is a pointer to a record containing *leftchild*, *rightchild*, and *parent* pointers.

2.4   Evaluating Efficiency, and the *O*-notation

A number of algorithms have been analysed, but so far no opinions expressed about their efficiency. Consider the Towers of Hanoi algorithm, for example, whose worst-case time complexity was shown in Section 2.2 to be $W(n) = 2^n - 1$ lines of output. Is this an efficient algorithm?

Clearly, the Towers of Hanoi algorithm is not efficient. When given the small instance $n = 10$, the algorithm produces 1023 lines of output; when given the instance $n = 20$, it produces 1 048 575 lines.

Even if its time complexity was $W(n) = 2^n - 100$, or $W(n) = 2^n/100$, the Towers of Hanoi algorithm would still be inefficient. General assessment of an algorithm's efficiency does not depend very strongly on constant factors in the time complexity function, unless they are unusually large or small. What is important is the general form of the function, in this case 2^n.

Similarly, when two algorithms for the same problem are compared, the general form of their complexity functions is usually sufficient to determine which is best. For example, compare linear search, of worst-case time complexity $W(n) = n$ comparisons, with binary search, of worst-case time complexity $W(n) = \log_2(n + 1)$ comparisons.

If this comparison is considered unfair, since more work is done in binary search per comparison than is done in linear search, implementation-dependent constants can first be added so as to express the complexities in microseconds. The result might be $W(n) = n + 3$ microseconds for linear search, and $W(n) = 5\log_2(n + 1) + 16$ microseconds for binary search, say. Figure 2.3 is a graph of these two functions. It can be seen that for $0 \le n \le 40$, linear search is superior to binary search; for larger n, binary search becomes dramatically more efficient.

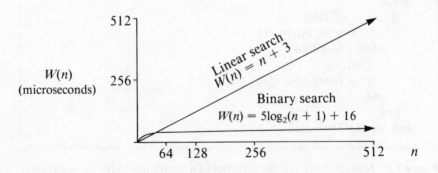

Figure 2.3

   The crossover point is rather sensitive to the values of the constant factors, but the superiority of binary search for large n is not, since it is well known that for any positive constants a, b, c, and d, the quotient

$$\frac{a\log_2(n + 1) + b}{cn + d}$$

approaches 0 as n increases. That is, even without knowing the values of the constant factors, it can be concluded that binary search is superior for sufficiently large n; and unless some exceptionally large constant factors are present, binary search would be preferred for this reason.

   A convenient way to express the general form of a function is provided by the *O-notation*. For example, the time complexity of binary search is $O(\log n)$, pronounced 'big oh of $\log n$', meaning that it has the general form of $\log n$. The term *asymptotic time complexity* is also used here.

   More precisely, the notation $O(f(n))$, appearing in a formula, stands for a quantity x_n which may not be explicitly known but which is known to satisfy $|x_n| \le M \,|\, f(n)\,|$, for $n \ge n_0$, where M and n_0 are fixed constants. For example,

$$\lceil \log_2(n + 1) \rceil = O(\log_2 n)$$

because x_n may be taken equal to $\lceil \log_2(n + 1) \rceil$, with $|x_n| \le 2\,|\log_2 n|$ for all $n \ge 2$. Incidentally, the formula $\log_a n = \log_b n / \log_b a$ shows that the base of a logarithm is irrelevant inside O, so it is usually omitted.

   The equation $g(n) = O(f(n))$ says that $g(n)$ is no larger than a constant times $f(n)$, for sufficiently large n. The notation $g(n) = \Omega(f(n))$, 'big omega of $f(n)$', will be used to mean that $g(n)$ is no smaller than a constant times $f(n)$, for sufficiently large n. Finally, $g(n) = \Theta(f(n))$, 'big theta of $f(n)$', can be written when $g(n) = O(f(n))$ and $g(n) = \Omega(f(n))$.

   Note that the statement $W(n) = O(f(n))$ does not prohibit $W(n)$ from being of smaller order than $f(n)$. Since assurances that an algorithm will not take more than a certain time are of prime interest, this is usually sufficient; but, if a more precise statement is wanted, then $W(n) = \Theta(f(n))$ may be used to say that $W(n)$ is of the same order as $f(n)$. Also observe that the statement $W(n) = \Omega(f(n))$ does not mean that every instance takes at least on the order of $f(n)$ time to solve; rather, it means that for all n there exists an instance which takes this long. For example, the complexity of linear search is $\Omega(n)$, since when x is not found the entire list must be searched; but there are instances of arbitrarily large size which require only $O(1)$ time: those where x is present at the front of the list.

   Problems for which $O(n\log n)$ algorithms exist are said to be *feasible*, meaning that large instances of them can be solved. Problems for which

Table 2.2

Complexity (microseconds)	Largest instance solvable in one second	Largest instance solvable in one day	Largest instance solvable in one year
$W(n) = n$	$n = 1\ 000\ 000$	$n = 86\ 400\ 000\ 000$	$n = 31\ 536\ 000\ 000\ 000$
$W(n) = n\log_2 n$	$n = 62\ 746$	$n = 2\ 755\ 147\ 514$	$n \simeq 798\ 160\ 978\ 500$
$W(n) = n^2$	$n = 1000$	$n = 293\ 938$	$n = 5\ 615\ 692$
$W(n) = n^3$	$n = 100$	$n = 4\ 421$	$n = 31\ 593$
$W(n) = 2^n$	$n = 19$	$n = 36$	$n = 44$

all algorithms are $\Omega(a^n)$ are *infeasible*, because even on the fastest computing equipment available today, or in the foreseeable future, only small instances will be able to be solved. The feasibility of problems with intermediate complexities, such as $O(n^2)$ and $O(n^3)$, will depend on the size of the instance that must be solved. This is illustrated in Table 2.2, which shows the largest instance which can be solved in a given time, for various complexity functions.

EXERCISES

2.1 Using the formal definitions of $W(n)$ and $A(n)$ given in Section 2.1, prove that $A(n) \leq W(n)$.

2.2 Assuming that all the p_i are non-zero, show that $A(n) = W(n)$ if and only if $T_1(n) = \cdots = T_k(n)$.

2.3 Consider the following algorithm for the linear search of a sorted array $A[a..b]$. The algorithm employs a *sentinel*: it adds x to the end of A before commencing, so as to simplify the search.

```
procedure SortedSearch(A: AType; a, b: integer; x: KeyType):
boolean;
var i: integer;
begin
    A[b + 1] := x;
    i := a;
    while A[i] < x do
        i := i + 1;
    end;
    return (i ≤ b) and (x = A[i]);
end SortedSearch;
```

(a) Choose a characteristic operation. Construct a table of cases for the analysis, similar to the table given in Section 2.1. What is the worst-case complexity of *SortedSearch*(A, 1, n, x)?

(b) Making reasonable assumptions about the probabilities of the cases, find the average complexity of *SortedSearch*(A, 1, n, x).

2.4 Consider the following algorithm for finding the index of a minimum element of $A[a..b]$:

```
procedure MinIndex(var A: AType; a, b: integer): integer;
var m: integer;
begin
  if a = b then
    m := a;
  else
    m := MinIndex(A, a + 1, b);
    if A[a] < A[m] then
      m := a;
    end;
  end;
  return m;
end MinIndex;
```

(a) Show that, if $T(n)$ is the number of comparisons of the form $A[a] < A[m]$ made by *MinIndex*(A, 1, n), then

$$T(1) = 0$$
$$T(n) = 1 + T(n - 1).$$

(b) Solve this recurrence by repeated substitution. How does the performance of this version of *MinIndex* compare with the one given in Section 2.1?

(c) What is the average number of times that the operation $m := a$ will be performed, counting recursive calls? (*Hint*: it will be performed only when $A[a]$ is a minimum element of $A[a..b]$. What is a reasonable probability to assign to this event?)

2.5 The following version of binary search is often preferred because it has a two-way rather than a three-way branch, and so is more amenable to efficient compilation. It assumes that the array to be searched is non-empty.

```
procedure BinarySearch(var A: AType; a, b: integer;
x: KeyType): boolean;
var mid: integer;
begin
  if a = b then
    return x = A[a];
  else
    mid := (a + b) div 2;
    if x ≤ A[mid] then
      return BinarySearch(A, a, mid, x);
    else
      return BinarySearch(A, mid + 1, b, x);
    end;
  end;
end BinarySearch;
```

Analyse this algorithm, taking as your measure of complexity the number of comparisons between x and elements of A.

2.6 The *Fibonacci numbers* are defined by the recurrence equation

$$F(0) = 0$$
$$F(1) = 1$$
$$F(n) = F(n - 1) + F(n - 2)$$

For example, the first few terms of the sequence are 0, 1, 1, 2, 3, 5, 8, 13, 21, 34, 55, ... Unfortunately, the recurrence equation cannot be solved by repeated substitution; a more advanced technique, the use of generating functions, is required. Prove by induction on n that

$$\phi^{n-2} \leq F(n) \leq \phi^{n-1}$$

for all $n \geq 2$, where $\phi = (1 + \sqrt{5})/2 \simeq 1.618\,033\,9$. You should begin by showing that $\phi^2 = \phi + 1$, and use this identity to prove the result.

2.7 Consider the following algorithm for calculating $F(n)$, as defined in the previous question:

```
procedure Fib(n: integer): integer;
begin
  if n ≤ 1 then
    return n;
  else
    return Fib(n - 1) + Fib(n - 2);
  end;
end Fib;
```

Choosing the statement **return** n as your characteristic operation, show that $T(n) = F(n + 1)$, and use the previous question to conclude that $T(n) = \Theta(\phi^n)$.

2.8 *Euclid's algorithm.* The following algorithm, for finding the greatest common divisor of two positive integers, is similar to one given by Euclid:

> **procedure** *gcd*(n, m: **integer**): **integer**;
> **begin**
>   **if** $m = 0$ **then return** n;
>   **else return** *gcd*(m, n **mod** m);
> **end** *gcd*;

Its correctness follows from a simple theorem in number theory that we will not give here.

(a) Show that the number of **mod** operations performed by this algorithm is given by the recurrence equation

$$T(n, 0) = 0$$
$$T(n, m) = 1 + T(m, n \bmod m)$$

and solve this for the special case of the Fibonacci numbers defined in the previous question; that is, for $n = F(k + 1)$ and $m = F(k)$.

(b) Show that, for all integers n and m such that $n \geq m > 0$,

$$n + m \geq \frac{3}{2}(m + n \bmod m).$$

(*Hint*: let $n = am + b$ where $a \geq 1$ and $0 \leq b < m$, and consider the fraction $(n + m)/(m + n \bmod m)$.)

(c) Use (b) to prove by induction on m that

$$T(n, m) \leq \log_{3/2}(n + m)$$

provided $n \geq m > 0$.

2.9 Solve the following recurrence equations where c is a constant. When necessary, you may assume that $n = 2^k$.

(a) $T(0) = 1$
   $T(n) = cT(n - 1)$

(b) $T(0) = 1$
   $T(n) = nT(n - 1)$

(c) $T(1) = 1$
   $T(n) = 1 + T(\lfloor n/2 \rfloor)$

(d) $T(1) = 1$

$T(n) = 1 + 2T(\lfloor n/2 \rfloor)$

(e) $T(1) = 0$

$T(n) = c\lceil \log_2 n \rceil + T(\lceil n/2 \rceil)$

(f) $T(1) = 0$

$T(n) = \lceil n\log_2 n \rceil + T(\lceil n/2 \rceil)$

2.10 Show that the solution to the two-dimensional recurrence equation

$T(n, 0) = 1$

$T(0, m) = 1$

$T(n, m) = T(n - 1, m) + T(n, m - 1)$

is

$$T(n, m) = \binom{n + m}{n}.$$

2.11 Consider the following algorithm for multiplying two n by n matrices:

type *Matrix* = **array** $[1..n]$, $[1..n]$ **of integer**;

```
procedure MatrixMultiply(var A, B, C: Matrix);
var i, j, k: integer;
begin
  for i := 1 to n do
    for j := 1 to n do
      C[i, j] := 0;
      for k := 1 to n do
        C[i, j] := C[i, j] + A[i, k] *B[k, j];
      end;
    end;
  end;
end MatrixMultiply;
```

If the characteristic operation is one multiplication of matrix elements, what is the complexity of *MatrixMultiply* as a function of n?

2.12 Consider the following algorithm for sorting the array $A[a..b]$ into non-decreasing order:

```
procedure StraightSelectionSort(var A: AType; a, b: integer);
var i, j, m: integer;
begin
  for i := a to b − 1 do
    m := MinIndex(A, i, b);
    if i ≠ m then
      Swap(A[i], A[m]);
    end;
  end;
end StraightSelectionSort;
```

Taking as your measure of complexity one comparison between elements of A[a..b], as occurs within *MinIndex*, what is the complexity of this algorithm?

2.13 Consider the following algorithm for finding both the index of a minimum element and the index of a maximum element of the array A[a..b]. Procedure *Odd* returns true when its argument is an odd number.

```
procedure MinMax(A: AType; a, b: integer; var min, max: integer);
  var i: integer;
begin
  if Odd(b − a + 1) then
    min := a;
    max:= a;
    i  := a + 1;
  elsif A[a] < A[a + 1] then
    min := a;
    max:= a + 1;
    i  := a + 2;
  else
    min := a + 1;
    max:= a;
    i  := a + 2;
  end;
  while i < b do
    if A[i] < A[i + 1] then
      if A[i]    < A[min] then min := i; end;
      if A[i + 1] > A[max] then max := i + 1; end;
    else
      if A[i + 1] < A[min] then min := i + 1; end;
      if A[i]    > A[max] then max := i; end;
    end;
    i := i + 2;
  end;
end MinMax;
```

(a) Explain how this algorithm works, clearly indicating the differences between the odd and even cases. Then give a formal loop invariant.

(b) Analyse $MinMax(A, 1, n, min, max)$ for arbitrary $n \geq 1$, using one comparison between elements of A as the characteristic operation, and show that its time complexity is

$$T(n) = \lceil 3n/2 \rceil - 2$$

Recall that $\lceil x \rceil$ ('ceiling of x') means the smallest integer greater than or equal to x. (*Hint*: consider the cases n even and n odd separately.)

2.14 The following algorithm is a standard part of most text editors. It searches for the first occurrence of the string (that is, array of characters) $B[1..m]$ within the string $A[1..n]$, returning the index where B begins if found. The value $limit = n - m + 1$ is the rightmost place in A where B could possibly begin.

```
procedure StringSearch(A, B: String; n, m: integer; var start:
integer): boolean;
var found: boolean;
    i, j, limit: integer;
begin
  found := false; limit := n − m + 1; start := 0;
  while not found and (start < limit) do
    start := start + 1;
    i := start; j := 1;
    while (j ≠ m + 1) and (A[i] = B[j]) do
      i := i + 1;
      j := j + 1;
    end;
    found := j = m + 1;
  end;
  return found;
end StringSearch;
```

How many times is the comparison $A[i] = B[j]$ performed in the worst case? Note that in Modula-2, this test will only be performed after the test $j \neq m + 1$ succeeds.

2.15 Prove, by induction on n, that the function $W(n)$ defined by

$$W(0) = 0$$
$$W(n) = 1 + W(\lfloor (n + 1)/2 \rfloor - 1)$$

is monotone non-decreasing, that is, that $W(n) \leq W(n + 1)$ for all n. You may assume that $\lfloor x \rfloor$ is a monotone non-decreasing function of x.

2.16 Suppose you have 1 hour of computer time each evening to run a certain program. You find that the hour is exactly long enough for your program to process an input of size $n = 1\,000\,000$. Then your employer buys a computer which runs 100 times faster than the old one. How large an input will your program handle in 1 hour now, if its complexity $T(n)$ is (for some constants k_i)

(a) $k_1 n$
(b) $k_2 n \log_{10} n$
(c) $k_3 n^2$
(d) $k_4 n^3$
(e) $k_5 10^n$

2.17 Use the formal definition of the O-notation to prove that

$$a_0 + a_1 n + a_2 n^2 + \ldots + a_k n^k = O(n^k)$$

2.18 Does $2^n = \Theta(3^n)$?

Chapter 3

Data Abstraction

As programs become larger, it becomes harder to be sure that they are correct. It has been found that this complexity (not to be confused with time complexity) can best be managed by splitting the program into small, coherent pieces, understanding each piece, and understanding how the pieces fit together.

The algorithms in this book are all rather small, so there will be little need for this technique. There is one application for it, however: to separate data structures from algorithms. Consider an algorithm for sorting a set of numbers by repeatedly extracting the smallest remaining number until none is left. It is clear that this will work, even without specifying what data structure is used to represent the set. This separation of data structure from algorithm allows the study of each in isolation, and provides a valuable way to organize and simplify. The concept is called *data abstraction*.

3.1   Abstract Data Types

Modern programming languages provide a variety of means for structuring data: arrays, records, and pointers being the principal ones. Before fixing on any such concrete representation, however, it is better to take a more abstract view.

Accordingly, the concept of a mathematical entity, not tied to any particular representation, is the right place to begin. Here are some standard examples:

(1) A *set*, as in mathematics, is a collection of zero or more entries. An entry may not appear more than once. A set of n entries may be denoted $\{a_1, a_2, \ldots, a_n\}$, but the position of an entry has no significance.

36

(2) A *multiset* is a set in which repeated elements are allowed. For example, {5, 7, 5, 2} is a multiset. Multisets are generally easier to deal with than sets, since checking for duplicates is expensive.

(3) A *sequence* is an ordered collection of zero or more entries, denoted $\langle a_1, a_2, \ldots a_n \rangle$. The position of an entry in a sequence is significant; for example, the fifth entry, or the successor of a given entry, may be referred to.

(4) A *graph* $G = \langle V, E \rangle$ is a set V of *vertices* (nodes) and a set E of *edges* (arcs, links), i.e. two-element subsets of V. This definition excludes self-loops (edges from a vertex to itself) and parallel edges (two edges connecting the same two vertices). For example,

$$V = \{a, b, c, d\}$$

$$E = \{\{a, d\}, \{d, c\}, \{a, c\}\}$$

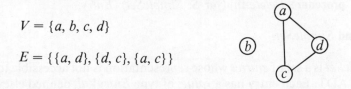

The reader may extend this list to include, for example, directed graphs, complex numbers, and matrices.

When one of these entities is used in an algorithm, certain operations are performed on it. For example, the algorithm might do insertions and membership tests on a set. This observation leads naturally to the concept of an *abstract data type* (*ADT*): a mathematical entity together with some operations defined on it.

The importance of the abstract data type concept was recognized only relatively recently, but it has been implicitly used since the beginning of modern computing history. The mathematical entity *integer*, for example, with the operations addition, subtraction, negation, multiplication, division, and the comparisons, has always been at the heart of computing machinery, and it provides a good illustration of the advantages to be gained from recognizing and specifying ADTs. First, users of *integer* never need concern themselves with the implementation of the operations: they know what the operations do, and can use them effectively without ever knowing what electronic circuitry is being employed. Second, the implementor of *integer* (in this case a hardware designer) is free to experiment with different implementations, such as carry-lookahead adders, fast multiplication circuits, and so on. All that matters is that the right result be returned. By providing a clean interface between use and implementation, the ADT separates the two and clarifies the task of both.

The formal notation for an ADT declaration used in this book is the *definition module* construct from Modula-2. For example, here is a very simple ADT which is based on the set:

```
definition module SimpleSet;

type Entry;

procedure New(val: EntryVal): Entry;
procedure ValueOf(x: Entry): EntryVal;
procedure Update(x: Entry; val: EntryVal);

type SimpleSet;

procedure Initialize(var S: SimpleSet);
procedure Empty(S: SimpleSet): boolean;
procedure Insert(x: Entry; var S: SimpleSet);
procedure DeleteAny(var S: SimpleSet): Entry;

end SimpleSet.
```

SimpleSet is a set of *entries* whose representation is not accessible to users of the ADT. Each entry has a *value*, of type *EntryVal*, defined elsewhere. The *New* operation creates a new entry with the specified value; *ValueOf* returns the value of an entry; and *Update* modifies the value of an entry.

Ideally, *Entry* would be defined as an ADT in its own right, and sometimes this is possible, but in general the need to allocate an appropriate amount of memory for an entry when executing *New* (including space for fields used to link entries together into sets) requires that *Entry* and *SimpleSet* be defined together.

The operation *Initialize(S)* sets *S* to empty; the operation *Empty(S)* tests whether *S* is empty. *Insert(x, S)* adds *x* to *S*; *DeleteAny(S)* deletes and returns an arbitrary element of *S*. Notice how this ADT can be used without knowing whether it is implemented using an array, linked list, or whatever.

There are many other examples of ADTs, ranging from **boolean** with operations **and**, **or**, and **not**, all the way up to databases. Chapters 6, 7, and 9 are concerned with some other standard ADTs.

An example of the use of ADTs.   This section closes with an example which demonstrates why ADTs are useful.

Given an array of n numbers, $A[1..n]$, consider the problem of determining the k largest elements, where $k \le n$. For example, if A contains $\{5, 3, 1, 9, 6\}$, and $k = 3$, then the result is to be $\{5, 9, 6\}$.

The following algorithm will not be justified in any detail, since that is not the purpose here, but it does solve the problem. The algorithm scans the array from left to right, remembering the k largest numbers it has seen so far. These numbers are kept in decreasing order in an array $M[1..k]$:

```
for i := 1 to k do
  j := i − 1;
  while (j > 0) and (A[i] > M[j]) do
    M[j + 1] := M[j];
    j := j − 1;
  end;
  M[j + 1] := A[i];
end;

for i := k + 1 to n do
  if A[i] > M[k] then
    j := k − 1;
    while (j > 0) and (A[i] > M[j]) do
      M[j + 1] := M[j];
      j := j − 1;
    end;
    M[j + 1] := A[i];
  end;
end;
```

It is difficult to follow the logic of this algorithm, because its structure is obscured by low-level details.

Now consider applying data abstraction to this algorithm. Abstractly, M is a multiset of numbers. What are the operations? It must be possible to initialise M to empty, and to insert a new number into M. In the second loop, a minimum element of M is required, and subsequently this element must be deleted. If we assume the existence of an ADT with these operations, the algorithm becomes

```
Initialize(M);
for i := 1 to k do
  Insert(New(A[i], 0), M);
end;
for i := k + 1 to n do
  if A[i] > KeyOf(FindMin(M)) then
    x := DeleteMin(M);
    Insert(New(A[i], 0), M);
  end;
end;
```

(For a reason that will become clear in a moment, M has been made into a set of entries, each with a *key* equal to $A[i]$ for some i, and a *value*, which in this example is redundant and is always 0. The operation $KeyOf(x)$ returns the key of entry x.)

There are two major reasons for preferring this version to the other.

First, it makes clear the structure of the algorithm by hiding away irrelevant details. Second, the purpose of M is now much clearer: it is an ADT which provides the operations *Initialize*, *Insert*, *FindMin*, and *DeleteMin*. In this case, the operations are standard ones from the priority queue ADT of Chapter 7. Thus an efficient implementation of M may be taken off the shelf; the result is not only a clearer algorithm, but also a more efficient one.

3.2   Lists, Stacks, and Queues

This section is devoted to a family of ADTs which are based on the sequence. Its most general member is an ADT that will be called the *list*:

> **definition module** *List*;
>
> **type** *Entry*;
>
> **var** *NilEntry*: *Entry*;
> **procedure** *New*(*v*: *EntryVal*): *Entry*;
> **procedure** *GetEntryVal*(*x*: *Entry*; **var** *val*: *EntryVal*);
> **procedure** *SetEntryVal*(*x*: *Entry*; *val*: *EntryVal*);
>
> **type** *List*;
>
> **procedure** *Initialize*(**var** *L*: *List*);
> **procedure** *Empty* (*L*: *List*): **boolean**;
> **procedure** *FirstEntry*(*L*: *List*): *Entry*;
> **procedure** *NextEntry*(*x*: *Entry*; *L*: *List*): *Entry*;
> **procedure** *MakeList*(*x*: *Entry*): *List*;
> **procedure** *Append*(*L1*, *L2*: *List*): *List*;
> **procedure** *Delete*(*x*: *Entry*; **var** *L*: *List*);
>
> **end** *List*.

Procedure *Initialize*(*L*) initializes *L* to the empty list; *Empty*(*L*) tests whether *L* is empty. For traversing a list, *FirstEntry*(*L*) returns the first entry of list *L*, and *NextEntry*(*x*, *L*) returns the entry of *L* that is the successor of *x*. Both operations return *NilEntry* if the specified entry does not exist, which makes the traversal code very simple:

```
x := FirstEntry(L);
while x ≠ NilEntry do
    Visit(x);
    x := NextEntry(x, L);
end;
```

The operation *MakeList*(*x*) returns a list containing *x* as its only entry. *Append*(*L*1, *L*2) joins lists *L*1 and *L*2 end to end, and returns the result; the values of *L*1 and *L*2 are undefined afterwards. These two operations may be used together to add an entry to the back of a given list, like this:

$$L := Append(L, MakeList(x));$$

and similarly to add an entry to the front of a list. Finally, *Delete*(*x*, *L*) deletes entry *x* from list *L*. Other operations, for example, to insert an entry just before or after a specified entry, could be added. This ADT is very frequently used; for example, a text editor uses an extension of it to maintain its sequence of lines.

The usual implementation employs a *doubly linked list* of entries: each entry *x* contains pointers $x^\wedge.predecessor$ and $x^\wedge.successor$ to its predecessor and successor in the list. The list as a whole is represented by a pointer to its first entry; for example, the list $L = \langle x_1, x_2, \ldots, x_n \rangle$ has representation:

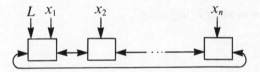

Notice that the first and last entries are linked together to form a circle; this clever arrangement simplifies the code and permits efficient access to the back of the list. *NilEntry* and the empty list are both nil pointers.

A complete implementation of this ADT, using doubly linked lists as described, appears in Implementation Module 3.1.

The list is a very convenient ADT, but there are times when the full complement of its operations is not needed, and some saving of space or time in the implementation is desired. There are a variety of possibilities, but only the two most common ones will be studied here. The first is the *stack*:

definition module *Stack*;

    type *Stack*;

    procedure *Initialize*(**var** *S*: *Stack*);
    procedure *Empty*(**var** *S*: *Stack*): **boolean**;
    procedure *Push*(*x*: *Entry*; **var** *S*: *Stack*);
    procedure *Pop*(**var** *S*: *Stack*): *Entry*;

end *Stack*.

Initialize and *Empty* are as before. The operation *Push*(*x*, *S*) adds an entry to the front of the stack, and so it is equivalent to the list operations *S* := *Append*(*MakeList*(*x*), *S*). The operation *x* := *Pop*(*S*) deletes and returns the first entry of the stack; it is equivalent to the sequence of list operations *x* := *FirstEntry*(*S*); *Delete*(*x*, *S*).

The reader may verify that a stack can be implemented using a singly linked list of entries, terminated by a nil pointer:

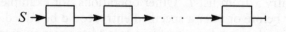

It is also possible to store the entries in adjacent positions of an array, thereby avoiding pointers altogether. This simplicity of implementation, and the stack's intimate connection with recursion (which will not be explored here), make it the most frequently encountered specialized list ADT.

The second specialized list is the *first-in-first-out* (*fifo*) *queue*:

definition module *FifoQueue*;

    type *Entry*;

    procedure *New*(*v*: *EntryVal*): *Entry*;
    procedure *GetEntryVal*(*x*: *Entry*; **var** *val*: *EntryVal*);
    procedure *SetEntryVal*(*x*: *Entry*; *val*: *EntryVal*);

    type *FifoQueue*;

    procedure *Initialize*(**var** *Q*: *FifoQueue*);
    procedure *Empty*(*Q*: *FifoQueue*): **boolean**;
    procedure *FirstEntry*(*Q*: *FifoQueue*): *Entry*;
    procedure *Enqueue*(*x*: *Entry*; **var** *Q*: *FifoQueue*);
    procedure *Dequeue*(**var** *Q*: *FifoQueue*): *Entry*;
    procedure *Append*(*Q*, *R*: *FifoQueue*): *FifoQueue*;

  end *FifoQueue*.

The operation *Enqueue*(*x*, *Q*) adds entry *x* to the back of the fifo queue *Q*, equivalently to the list operations *Q* := *Append*(*Q*, *MakeList*(*x*)). The operation *Dequeue*(*Q*) deletes and returns the entry at the front, equivalently to the list operations *x* := *FirstEntry*(*Q*); *Delete*(*x*, *Q*). This means that entries emerge in the order they were added, which accounts for the description 'first-in-first-out'.

Append is not normally considered to be part of this ADT, but it has been included for the convenience of the radix sort algorithm of Section 8.5. This ADT will also be used in Section 8.3 when merging lists, and in Section 10.5 as an aid to the breadth-first traversal of a graph.

FifoQueue can be implemented efficiently as a circularly linked list of entries, accessed by a pointer to the last entry:

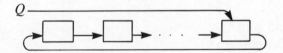

An empty list is represented by a nil pointer. See Implementation Module 3.2 for this implementation.

It is also possible to implement the fifo queue (excluding *Append*) without any pointers, by storing the entries in consecutive positions of a circular array, provided an upper limit on the size of the queue is accepted.

This section has merely scratched the surface of the variations that are possible on list operations and their implementations. One that has been avoided is the use of a *header*: a node at the front of the list that does not correspond to any entry. Headers often simplify coding by removing the nil-pointer case; on the other hand, if many small lists are created and appended, effort is wasted allocating and deallocating headers. There seems little to gain by studying many such variants.

3.3   Correctness of ADT Implementations

Abstract data types simplify programs by hiding the details of their implementations. If an ADT is specified abstractly, then algorithms which use it will be easier to prove correct. On the other hand, a proof of correctness for an ADT implementation must be done at the concrete level. To connect these two levels, some new ideas are needed.

An ADT will be specified by giving a precondition and postcondition for each of its operations. These conditions may refer only to the abstract entity (set, sequence, or whatever) on which the ADT is based; in this way they are made independent of any implementation. For example, the *SimpleSet* ADT of Section 3.1, which is based on the multiset, has the following abstract specification:

(* *Pre*: **true** *)
Initialize(*S*);
(* *Post*: $S' = \{\}$ *)

```
(* Pre: true *)
e := Empty(S);
(* Post: e = (S = { }) and S' = S *)

(* Pre: true *)
Insert(x, S);
(* Post: x' = x and S' = S ∪ {x} *)

(* Pre: S ≠ { } *)
x := DeleteAny(S);
(* Post: x ∈ S and S' = S − {x} *)
```

Here S' refers to the value of S after the call is completed, so that, for example, the postcondition $S' = S \cup \{x\}$ means that the new value of the multiset S equals the old value with x added. Notice that the specification gives no hint of how the ADT is implemented.

Some operations, such as *Append* for lists, destroy their parameters. In such cases the postcondition must state that these parameters are now undefined.

In general, there will be an ADT with its accompanying abstract specification, and a concrete implementation of the ADT, and the task will be to prove that the implementation satisfies the specification. For example, a proof might be required that the following implementation of *SimpleSet* is correct:

```
const Max = 255;

type SimpleSet = pointer to
record
  size:    [0..Max];
  entries: array [1..Max] of Entry;
end;

procedure Initialize(var S: SimpleSet);
var p: SimpleSet;
begin
  Allocate(p, SIZE(p^));
  S := p;
  S^.size := 0;
end Initialize;

procedure Empty(S: SimpleSet): boolean;
begin
  return S^.size = 0;
end Empty;
```

```
procedure Insert(x: Entry; var S: SimpleSet);
begin
  if S^.size = Max then
    Error("SimpleSet.Insert: S is full");
  else
    S^.size := S^.size + 1;
    S^.entries[S^.size] := x;
  end;
end Insert;

procedure DeleteAny(var S: SimpleSet): Entry;
begin
  if S^.size = 0 then
    Error("SimpleSet.DeleteAny: S is empty");
  else
    S^.size := S^.size − 1;
    return S^.entries[S^.size + 1];
  end;
end DeleteAny;
```

There is a systematic way to go about this (Liskov and Guttag, 1986). The first step is to give a condition, called the *representation invariant*, denoted $I(S)$, which is true if and only if S is a valid concrete value of the abstract type. For the implementation of *SimpleSet* just given,

$$I(S) = \text{for all } i \text{ such that } 1 \le i \le S^.size, S^.entries[i] \text{ is well-defined.}$$

It is customary to leave out things that the compiler checks, such as that S is of type *SimpleSet* and $S^.size \ge 0$; they are implicitly assumed. This example is quite simple, merely ruling out garbage values for the entries; in other cases, $I(S)$ could prohibit duplicates, or define a complex data structure. The condition is *invariant* in the sense of being true throughout the lifetime of S.

The second step is to define, for all concrete values S satisfying $I(S)$, what the corresponding abstract value is. This is done by giving an *abstraction function* $A(S)$, which maps the concrete value S to its corresponding abstract value. (There can be only one such abstract value, otherwise the implementation would be ambiguous.) The abstraction function for the *SimpleSet* implementation is

$$A(S) = \{S^.entries[i] \mid 1 \le i \le S^.size\}$$

That is, the abstract value corresponding to the concrete value S is a multiset containing $S^.entries[1..S^.size]$.

$I(S)$ and $A(S)$ are an integral part of any ADT implementation; in fact, they are defined before any code is written. So it can be assumed from now on that every ADT implementation comes equipped with its representation invariant and abstraction function.

The third step in proving an ADT implementation correct is to make its specification concrete in the following way. First, replace all references to S, S' etc. by $A(S), A(S')$, and so on; this just makes explicit that the values are abstract ones. Next, whenever an operation uses a variable S, add $I(S)$ to its precondition; and whenever it produces a value S', add $I(S')$ to its postcondition. This will be justified in a moment; the result is a *concrete specification*. For example, the concrete specification of *Insert* is:

(* *Pre*: $I(S)$ *)
Insert(x, S);
(* *Post*: $I(S')$ **and** $A(S') = A(S) \cup \{x\}$ *)

The fourth and final step is to prove the correctness of each operation with respect to its concrete specification. For the *Insert* operation, such a proof might run (in outline) as follows. By the precondition $I(S)$, it is known that $S^\wedge.entries\ [1..S^\wedge.size]$ is well defined, say with abstract value $A(S) = \{x_1, \ldots, x_n\}$. The statements of *Insert* clearly add x to the end of S, producing a new value S' which satisfies $I(S')$ and has abstract value

$$A(S') = \{x_1, \ldots, x_n, x\} = A(S) \cup \{x\}$$

So *Insert*'s postcondition holds afterwards.

Incidentally, the call to *Error* in *Insert* represents a failure of the implementation to meet the specification, which says nothing about an upper limit on the size of a *SimpleSet*. Rather than complicate the specification to no useful purpose, it is better to hide this implementation-dependent limit and terminate with an error message if it is exceeded. Strictly speaking, the proofs must say 'if no error messages are generated, then the ADT implementation is correct'.

The addition of $I(S)$ to the preconditions will now be justified, arguing inductively as follows. Assume that $I(S)$ holds for all values S in existence before the mth call begins. If the operation is used correctly, its abstract precondition also holds. It follows that its concrete precondition holds. The operation has been proved correct, so its concrete postcondition holds afterwards. This postcondition includes $I(S')$ for all S'. An ADT may be accessed only by its own operations, so no values change between the end of the mth call and the beginning of the $(m + 1)$st. Therefore $I(S)$ holds for all S just before the $(m + 1)$st operation begins.

There are two ways in which this argument can fail: if an S is declared and not initialized to a value satisfying $I(S)$, and if an operation is called at a time when its abstract precondition does not hold. It is good practice to protect ADT implementations by checking preconditions as has been done in *DeleteAny*, if this can be done efficiently.

3.4   Analysis of ADT Implementations

Abstract data types were originally developed to protect data structures from invalid access, so it is natural that they should be valuable aids to correctness. But they are equally valuable in analysis, particularly of data structures.

Consider an implementation of an ADT with operations $P_1, P_2, \ldots,$ P_v. Each operation's implementation is an algorithm, and so may be analysed in the usual way; the result is a sequence of functions $W_1(n)$, $W_2(n)$, $\ldots, W_v(n)$, which together constitute the *worst-case complexity of the ADT implementation*. The parameter n is always taken to be the size of the ADT at the moment the operation is called.

The difficulty of assigning meaningful probabilities to the instances, already noted in Section 2.1, becomes acute here. With one exception, the analysis of the chained hash table in Section 6.8, average complexity analyses of ADT implementations will not be attempted in this book.

For example, consider the priority queue ADT as an example:

   definition module *PriQueue*;

      type *PriorityQueue*;

      procedure *Initialize*(**var** *Q*: *PriorityQueue*);
      procedure *Empty*(*Q*: *PriorityQueue*): **boolean**;
      procedure *Insert*(*x*: *Entry*; **var** *Q*: *PriorityQueue*);
      procedure *FindMin*(**var** *Q*: *PriorityQueue*): *Entry*;
      procedure *DeleteMin*(**var** *Q*: *PriorityQueue*): *Entry*;

   end *PriQueue*.

A priority queue is a set of entries, each containing a key and a value; the size of the ADT is taken to be the size of this set. *Initialize* initializes the set to empty; *Insert* adds an entry; *FindMin* returns an entry with minimum key; and *DeleteMin* deletes and returns an entry with minimum key.

A simple linked list may be used to implement this ADT, with the entries either sorted into increasing order by key, or left unsorted. Inser-

Table 3.1

	Unsorted linked list	Sorted linked list
Initialize	$O(1)$	$O(1)$
Empty	$O(1)$	$O(1)$
Insert	$O(1)$	$O(n)$
FindMin	$O(n)$	$O(1)$
DeleteMin	$O(n)$	$O(1)$

tion into an unsorted list is trivial, but finding a minimum entry requires a search; the opposite is true for the sorted list. So the worst-case complexities of these two implementations are as given in Table 3.1.

When analysing an algorithm which makes use of an ADT, the total cost of all the calls to the ADT's implementation must be calculated. The most common method of doing this is as follows.

Suppose the algorithm makes a total of $m = m_1 + m_2 + \ldots + \overset{.}{m_v}$ calls to the ADT: m_1 to the P_1 operation, m_2 to P_2, etc., arbitrarily intermixed. Number these calls from 1 to m in the order they occur, and let t_i be the actual complexity of the ith call, for $1 \leq i \leq m$. The size of the ADT will vary over the course of the sequence of calls. Let n_{i-1} be the size of the ADT just before the ith call, and let

$$n = \max_{1 \leq i \leq m} n_{i-1}.$$

Then, if the ith call is a P_j operation, $t_i \leq W_j(n_{i-1})$, and so the total cost can be estimated as

$$\sum_{i=1}^{m} t_i \leq \sum_{i=1}^{m} W_j(n_{i-1})$$

$$\leq \sum_{i=1}^{m} W_j(n)$$

$$= m_1 W_1(n) + \ldots + m_v W_v(n)$$

assuming that the W_j are monotone non-decreasing. Note that n here represents the maximum ADT size over the whole sequence of calls, whereas when $W_j(n)$ is quoted for operation P_j it refers to the ADT size at the moment P_j is called.

It often happens that a different characteristic operation must be chosen for analysing each operation, so that $W_1(n)$ may count comparisons, $W_2(n)$ may count additions, and so on. In such cases one should multiply by implementation-dependent constants before adding these functions* together, or equivalently, report the result as $O(m_1 W_1(n) + \ldots + m_v W_v(n))$.

For example, here is an algorithm (already introduced in Section 3.1) for finding the k largest elements of an array $A[1..n]$:

```
Initialize(M);
for i := 1 to k do
    Insert(New(A[i], 0), M);
end;
for i := k + 1 to n do
    if A[i] > KeyOf(FindMin(M)) then
        x := DeleteMin(M);
        Insert(New(A[i], 0), M);
    end;
end;
```

The analysis of this algorithm is not difficult. In the worst case, the test $A[i] > KeyOf(FindMin(M))$ always succeeds, and one call to *Initialize* is performed, n calls to *Insert*, $n - k$ calls to *FindMin*, and $n - k$ calls to *DeleteMin*. The maximum ADT size is k.

Therefore, if the unsorted linked list is used to implement the priority queue, the total cost of all the calls will be

$$O(1 \times 1 + n \times 1 + (n - k) \times k + (n - k) \times k) = O(nk).$$

If the sorted linked list is used, the total complexity is

$$O(1 \times 1 + n \times k + (n - k) \times 1 + (n - k) \times 1) = O(nk)$$

so that there is nothing to choose between these two implementations. On the average, however, the test $A[i] > KeyOf(FindMin(M))$ is likely to fail most of the time, so that there will be many more *FindMin* calls than insertions and deletions, assuming k is small. Since the sorted linked list provides $O(1)$ complexity for *FindMin*, it is preferred for use with this algorithm.

This example teaches two important lessons. First, only the worst-case complexity of an ADT implementation need be known in order to analyse an algorithm which uses it; the details of the implementation are irrelevant. Second, a variety of implementations may easily be tried to see which is best for a given algorithm. Indeed, the extra step may even be taken of designing the ADT implementation with certain complexity goals in mind (for example, an $O(1)$ *FindMin*). This design strategy has been called *balancing* (Aho et al., 1974).

3.5 Amortized Analysis

The method just given for analysing algorithms employing ADTs usually works well. However, as will be seen in a moment, there are cases where the results it produces are wildly pessimistic. The unravelling of this phenomenon will lead to an alternative method called *amortized analysis*, and beyond it to a principle of data structure design with a wealth of applications.

Perhaps the simplest example where worst-case analysis proves unsatisfactory is offered by the following ADT, which is a stack with the ability to pop k entries at once, as is needed by some parsing algorithms:

> **definition module** *ParserStack*;
>
> **type** *Entry*;
>
> **type** *ParserStack*;
>
> **procedure** *Initialize*(**var** *S*: *ParserStack*);
> **procedure** *ExamineTop*(**var** *S*: *ParserStack*): *Entry*;
> **procedure** *Push*(*x*: *Entry*; **var** *S*: *ParserStack*);
> **procedure** *Pop*(*k*: **integer**; **var** *S*: *ParserStack*);
>
> **end** *ParserStack*.

The implementation is a linked list of entries, like the one discussed in Section 3.2.

Working through the worst-case analysis of this ADT implementation, the complexity of *Push*(*x*, *S*) is clearly $O(1)$, but *Pop*(*k*, *S*) requires k pointer operations, and so, since k could be as large as the size of the stack, its worst-case complexity is $O(n)$. The total complexity of a sequence of m_1 calls to *Push* and m_2 calls to *Pop* will be $O(m_1 + m_2 n)$.

That is the standard argument; now consider the following *ad hoc* argument. More entries cannot be popped off the stack than were pushed onto it, so the total cost of pops cannot exceed the total cost of pushes. Therefore, the total cost of any sequence of m_1 calls to *Push* and m_2 calls to *Pop* is $O(m_1)$ in the worst case.

The standard analysis was not wrong; it delivered an upper bound on the total complexity which was much larger than it needed to be. This happened because the analysis failed to notice that a sequence of worst-case pops is impossible: after one worst-case pop, the stack is empty and a second worst-case pop cannot happen.

In order to tighten up the analysis, it turns out that the susceptibility of the state of an ADT implementation to expensive operations must be measured. (The state of an ADT implementation is its configuration at some moment in time – its size, shape, the values it contains, etc.) This is done by associating with each possible state S a real number $\Phi(S)$, called the *potential of S*, chosen so that the more susceptible a state is, the higher its potential. For example, it would be reasonable to let the potential of a parser stack be the number of entries it contains, because a large stack is susceptible to expensive pops, and a small one is not.

Consider now a sequence of m calls to an ADT, and let t_i be the actual complexity of the ith call, as usual. Define the *amortized complexity* a_i of the ith call by

$$a_i = t_i + \Phi(S_i) - \Phi(S_{i-1})$$

where S_{i-1} is the state of the ADT just before the ith call is begun, and S_i is the state of the ADT just after it has finished. Now,

$$\sum_{i=1}^{m} t_i = \sum_{i=1}^{m} [a_i - \Phi(S_i) + \Phi(S_{i-1})]$$

$$= \sum_{i=1}^{m} a_i - \Phi(S_m) + \Phi(S_0)$$

$$\leq \sum_{i=1}^{m} a_i$$

assuming Φ is chosen so that $\Phi(S_m) \geq \Phi(S_0)$. The total amortized complexity is an upper bound for the total actual complexity, and the potentials cancel out.

Consider, then, an ADT with operations $P_1, P_2, \ldots, P_v$, and a sequence of $m = m_1 + m_2 + \ldots + m_v$ calls to the ADT: m_1 to P_1, m_2 to P_2, etc., arbitrarily intermixed. Let $W_{\Phi j}(n)$ be the maximum, over all instances of P_j of size n, of the amortized complexity of the instance. (Contrast this with $W_j(n)$, which is the maximum over the same instances of the actual complexity.) Now, if the ith operation in the sequence is P_j, then $a_i \leq W_{\Phi j}(n_{i-1})$, where n_{i-1} is the ADT size just before the ith call begins, and so

$$\sum_{i=1}^{m} t_i \leq \sum_{i=1}^{m} a_i$$

$$\leq \sum_{i=1}^{m} W_{\Phi j}(n_{i-1})$$

$$\leq \sum_{i=1}^{m} W_{\Phi j}(n)$$

$$= m_1 W_{\Phi 1}(n) + \ldots + m_v W_{\Phi v}(n)$$

Table 3.2

i	Operation	S	$\Phi(S)$	t_i	a_i
	Initialize		0		
1	Push(a, S)	a	1	1	2
2	Push(e, S)	$a\,e$	2	1	2
3	Push(f, S)	$a\,e\,f$	3	1	2
4	Pop$(2, S)$	a	1	2	0

assuming that the $W_{\Phi j}(n)$ are monotone. So amortized bounds are just as good for bounding the total cost of a sequence of operations as worst-case bounds are; and they may be smaller if Φ is carefully chosen. The sequence of functions $W_{\Phi 1}(n)$, $W_{\Phi 2}(n)$, ..., $W_{\Phi v}(n)$ is called the *amortized complexity* of the ADT implementation.

Choosing a potential function $\Phi(S)$ is a matter of experience and trial-and-error. For the *ParserStack* example above, the size of the stack is a good choice for $\Phi(S)$. If every operation sequence begins with an empty stack, the condition $\Phi(S_m) \geq \Phi(S_0)$ always holds. Table 3.2 is a typical trace of the ADT implementation.

In general, for a push, $t_i = 1$, $\Phi(S_i) - \Phi(S_{i-1}) = 1$ (the size of the stack increases by exactly 1), so that $a_i = 2$. For $Pop(k, S)$, $t_i = k$, $\Phi(S_i) - \Phi(S_{i-1}) = -k$ (the stack size decreases by k), so $a_i = 0$. The total complexity of any sequence of m_1 pushes and m_2 pops is therefore $O(m_1 \times 2 + m_2 \times 0) = O(m_1)$.

As this example shows, an amortized analysis spreads the cost of an occasional expensive operation among nearby calls, like accounting methods which spread the cost of a single large purchase over several years. This is the origin of the term 'amortization'. Amortized analysis is due to Tarjan (1985); he mentions that its formulation using potential functions is by D. Sleator.

There is a useful trick for simplifying amortized analyses by breaking the operations into small stages and analysing each stage. Consider the ith operation. It has actual complexity t_i, amortized complexity a_i, and it takes the ADT from state S_{i-1} to state S_i. Now suppose some intermediate states reached by the ADT within the course of the operation can be identified; call them S_1', S_2', ..., S_{k-1}', and let $S_{i-1} = S_0'$ and $S_i = S_k'$. Let t_j' be the actual cost incurred in moving from S_{j-1}' to S_j', for $1 \leq j \leq k$; clearly, the actual complexity of the whole operation is the sum of these numbers:

$$t_i = \sum_{j=1}^{k} t_j'.$$

The amortized complexity of each stage can be defined in the usual way:

$$a_j' = t_j' + \Phi(S_j') - \Phi(S_{j-1}')$$

and thus

$$
\begin{aligned}
\sum_{j=1}^{k} a_j' &= \sum_{j=1}^{k} [\, t_j' + \Phi(S_j') - \Phi(S_{j-1}') \,] \\
&= \sum_{j=1}^{k} t_j' + \Phi(S_k') - \Phi(S_0') \\
&= t_i + \Phi(S_i) - \Phi(S_{i-1}) \\
&= a_i.
\end{aligned}
$$

The amortized complexity of the whole operation is equal to the sum of the amortized complexities of its stages. For example, this approach could have been used to break *Pop*(*k*, *S*) into *k* pops of a single element, each of amortized complexity 0.

This section concludes with an amortized analysis of the traversal of a binary tree in inorder, using an ADT whose operations are

    procedure *InorderInit*(*x*: *BinaryTree*): *Node*;
    procedure *InorderSucc*(*x*: *Node*): *Node*;

as defined in Figure 2.2 on page 25. This example leads to a less intuitive potential function than the previous one.

As discussed in Section 2.3, a suitable characteristic operation to choose when analysing these operations is the edge-traverse, of the form $y := y^\wedge.leftchild$, $y := y^\wedge.rightchild$, or $y := y^\wedge.parent$. Although a single *InorderInit* or *InorderSucc* operation could require up to $n - 1$ edge-traverses, it was shown in Section 2.3 that the full sequence of one *InorderInit* followed by n *InorderSucc* operations, required to traverse the tree, take a total of only $2(n - 1)$ edge-traverses, which is much less than the $O(n^2)$ result of a crude worst-case analysis. Since this is just the kind of situation that amortized analysis is designed for, it is worthwhile to look for a potential function which leads to an amortized complexity of $O(1)$ per operation.

The state of the ADT at any moment is clearly equal to the binary tree being traversed, plus a distinguished node x: the place that the traversal has reached. Only x changes over the course of one call to *InorderSucc*:

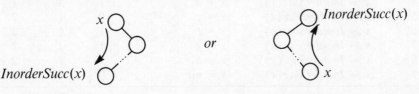

The potential function must cancel completely the cost of traversing down to the left or up to the left, since otherwise the resulting amortized bounds could not be $O(1)$. After some trial and error, then, this leads to the following. Define the *rank* of node x, $r(x)$, by setting the rank of the root to 0 and applying

$$r(x^\wedge.leftchild) = r(x) - 1$$
$$r(x^\wedge.rightchild) = r(x) + 1$$

at each node recursively. For example, the following tree has ranks written inside its nodes:

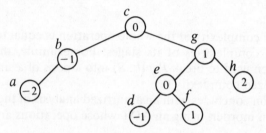

Define $\Phi(S)$ to be the rank of the distinguished node, or 0 initially and finally.

Now an edge-traverse of the form $x := x^\wedge.leftchild$ has actual complexity 1, but since $r(x^\wedge.leftchild) = r(x) - 1$, there is a compensating decrease of 1 in potential, leaving an amortized complexity of 0. Similarly, an edge-traverse from a right child to its parent also has an amortized complexity of 0.

Tracing the traversal of the tree above, and calculating the amortized complexity of each operation gives Table 3.3.

Table 3.3

i	Operation	S	$\Phi(S)$	t_i	a_i
		$x = \text{nil}$	0		
1	$x := InorderInit(T)$	$x = a$	-2	2	0
2	$x := InorderSucc(x)$	$x = b$	-1	1	2
3	$x := InorderSucc(x)$	$x = c$	0	1	2
4	$x := InorderSucc(x)$	$x = d$	-1	3	2
5	$x := InorderSucc(x)$	$x = e$	0	1	2
6	$x := InorderSucc(x)$	$x = f$	1	1	2
7	$x := InorderSucc(x)$	$x = g$	1	2	2
8	$x := InorderSucc(x)$	$x = h$	2	1	2
9	$x := InorderSucc(x)$	$x = \text{nil}$	0	2	0

Every *InorderSucc* operation except the last one has an amortized complexity of 2, and it is easy to see why this must be so. Consider the operation

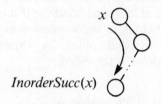

The edge-traverse $x := x^\wedge.rightchild$ has actual complexity 1, and causes a potential increase of 1, for an amortized complexity of 2. The leftward-moving edge-traverses have amortized complexity 0, as already shown. Since the sum of the amortized complexities of the edge-traverses equals the amortized complexity of the operation, the amortized complexity of this type of *InorderSucc* operation is 2.

It is easy to check that the upward-moving kind of *InorderSucc* also has an amortized complexity of 2 (except the last one, which has an amortized complexity of 0); and the amortized complexity of *InorderInit* is always 0. It follows that the total complexity of the traversal is exactly $2(n - 1)$ edge-traverses.

EXERCISES

3.1   Give a formal specification of the ADT *List* which accords with the informal description given in Section 3.2. Pay particular attention to the operations which may return *NilEntry*.

3.2   *Least-recently-used page replacement.* Virtual memory systems create an illusion of an unlimited main memory space by keeping pages (1024-byte segments of memory) on disk and moving them into main memory as needed. If main memory is full, some other page must be swapped out, and a good candidate is the least recently used page. Show how a linked list of pages can be used to keep track of which page is least recently used at any time.

3.3 *Find-the-mouse.* Modern high-resolution display screens generally have *windows*: rectangular areas of the screen, each with the ability to carry out tasks independently of the others. There is a background window covering the whole screen, and windows may partly or totally hide it or other windows. Thus, every point on the screen lies inside at least one window; if it lies in several windows, it is deemed to belong to the window that is currently hiding the other windows at that point. A variety of commands for rearranging windows is provided:

definition module *WindowModule*;

    type *Window*;

    procedure *NewWindow*(*x, y, xsize, ysize*: **integer**): *Window*;
    procedure *BringToTop*(*w*: *Window*);
    procedure *ChangeWindow*(*w*: *Window*; *x, y, xs, ys*: **integer**);
    procedure *DeleteWindow*(*w*: *Window*);
    procedure *WhichWindow*(*x, y*: **integer**): *Window*;

  end *WindowModule*;

NewWindow creates a new window with the given position and size, and returns an internal name for the window for use by later operations on that window. *BringToTop* brings a partially hidden window fully into view; *ChangeWindow* changes the position and size of a window, including a *BringToTop* operation on it. *DeleteWindow* deletes a window. The last operation, *Which-Window*, is interesting. It returns the name of the window to which the point (*x, y*) currently belongs, and is used to determine which window the mouse is currently pointing into. Since there are likely to be only a few windows, efficiency is of little concern here; the problem is to find a simple way to remember which windows are on top of which.

3.4 Define and implement an ADT for polynomials in one variable, with addition, multiplication, and evaluation operations (at least). Include a representation invariant and abstraction function with your implementation, and determine its worst-case complexity.

3.5 *Sparse matrices.* The simplest way to implement matrices is to use a two-dimensional array. However, in many applications the matrices are *sparse*: very large, but with most of the entries equal to 0. In such cases, a linked representation may be more efficient:

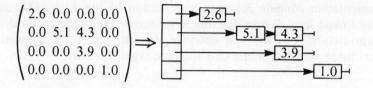

Define an ADT for matrices with addition, transposition, and multiplication operations (at least), and implement it using this linked representation. You may find transposition useful when implementing multiplication. How does your implementation's efficiency compare with the array implementation?

3.6 Consider the following algorithm for adding 1 to a binary number, represented as an array of n bits, assuming that there is no overflow:

```
type Number = array [1..n] of [0..1];

procedure Increment(var A: Number);
var i: integer;
begin
    i := n;
    while A[i] = 1 do
        A[i] := 0;
        i := i - 1;
    end;
    A[i] := 1;
end Increment;
```

This algorithm is clearly $O(n)$ in the worst case. Show that its amortized complexity is $O(1)$.

3.7 One way of finding the convex hull of a set of n points in the plane (see Section 4.3 for a definition of the problem) begins by sorting the points by their x-coordinates. As will be seen in Chapter 8, this step can be implemented to have $O(n \log n)$ complexity in the worst case. Next, the points are added one by one, from left to right, to a growing convex hull:

Show that this step is $O(n)$ using amortized analysis.

Implementation Module 3.1 Implementation of the *List* ADT using doubly linked lists. When deleting x we have taken care to modify p appropriately if x is the first entry of the list. The *CAST* procedure returns its second parameter cast into the type of its first.

```
implementation module List;

    type List = pointer to node;
    type Entry = pointer to node;

    type node = record
        value: EntryVal;
        predecessor, successor: Entry;
    end;

    procedure New(val: EntryVal): Entry;
    var x: Entry;
    begin
        Allocate(x, SIZE (x^));
        x^.value := v;
        return x;
    end New;

    procedure GetEntryVal(x: Entry; var val: EntryVal);
    begin
        val := x^. value;
    end GetEntryVal;

    procedure SetEntryVal(x: Entry; val: EntryVal);
    begin
        x^.value := val;
    end SetEntryVal;

    procedure Initialize(var L: List);
    begin
        L := nil;
    end Initialize;

    procedure Empty(L: List): boolean;
    begin
        return L = nil;
    end Empty;

    procedure FirstEntry(L: List): Entry;
    begin
        return CAST(Entry, L);
    end FirstEntry;
```

```
    procedure NextEntry(x: Entry; L: List): Entry;
    begin
      if x^.successor = CAST(Entry, L) then
        return NilEntry;
      else
        return x^.successor;
      end;
    end NextEntry;

    procedure MakeList(x: Entry): List;
    begin
      x^.successor := x;
      x^.predecessor := x;
      return CAST(List, x);
    end MakeList;

    procedure Append (L1, L2: List): List;
    var Back1, Back2: Entry;
    begin
      if L1 = nil then return L2;
      elsif L2 = nil then return L1;
      else
        Back1 := L1^.predecessor;
        Back2 := L2^.predecessor;
        L1^.predecessor := Back2;
        L2^.predecessor := Back1;
        Back1^.successor := CAST(Entry, L2);
        Back2^.successor := CAST(Entry, L1);
        return L1;
      end;
    end Append;

    procedure Delete(x: Entry; var L: List);
    begin
      if x = FirstEntry(L) then
        if CAST(List, L^.successor) = L then
          L := nil;
        else
          L := CAST(List, L^.successor);
        end;
      end;
      x^.successor^.predecessor := x^.predecessor;
      x^.predecessor^.successor := x^.successor;
    end Delete;

begin
    NilEntry := nil;
end List.
```

Implementation Module 3.2 Implementation of the *FifoQueue* ADT using a circularly linked list accessed by a pointer to the last entry.

```
implementation module FifoQueue;

    from Standard import Error;
    from System import Allocate;
    from SYSTEM import CAST;

    type Entry = pointer to node;
    type FifoQueue = Entry;

    type node = record
        value: EntryVal;
        successor: Entry;
    end;

    procedure New(val: EntryVal): Entry;
    var p: Entry;
    begin
        Allocate(p, SIZE(p^));
        p^.value := val;
        return p;
    end New;

    procedure GetEntryVal(x: Entry; var val: EntryVal);
    begin
        val := x^.value;
    end GetEntryVal;

    procedure SetEntryVal(x: Entry; val: EntryVal);
    begin
        x^.value := val;
    end SetEntryVal;

    procedure Initialize(var Q: FifoQueue);
    begin
        Q := nil;
    end Initialize;

    procedure Empty(Q: FifoQueue): boolean;
    begin
        return Q = nil;
    end Empty;
```

```
procedure FirstEntry(Q: FifoQueue): Entry;
begin
  if Q = nil then
    Error("FifoQueue.FirstEntry: queue is empty");
  else
    return Q^.successor;
  end;
end FirstEntry;

procedure Enqueue(x: Entry; var Q: FifoQueue);
begin
  if Q = nil then
    x^.successor := x;
  else
    x^.successor := Q^.successor;
    Q^.successor := x;
  end;
  Q := CAST(FifoQueue, x);
end Enqueue;

procedure Dequeue(var Q: FifoQueue): Entry;
var result: Entry;
begin
  if Q = nil then
    Error("FifoQueue.Dequeue: queue is empty"),
  end;
  result := Q^.successor;
  if Q^.successor = CAST(Entry, Q) then Q := nil;
  else Q^.successor := Q^.successor^.successor;
  end;
  return result;
end Dequeue;

procedure Append(Q, R: FifoQueue): FifoQueue;
var temp: Entry;
begin
  if R = nil then return Q;
  elsif Q = nil then return R;
  else
    temp := Q^.successor;
    Q^.successor := R^.successor;
    R^.successor := temp;
    return R;
  end;
end Append;

end FifoQueue.
```

Chapter 4

Algorithm Design

Algorithm design is a creative activity, and there is no simple recipe for success. Indeed, there are many important problems for which no efficient algorithms are known. Nevertheless, by classifying algorithms according to similarities in their structure, it is possible to identify certain strategies which often lead to correct, efficient algorithms. These strategies are the subject of this chapter.

4.1 The Design Process

The first step in design is to produce a clear specification of the problem. Petty details, such as the format of the input data, should be ignored, and attention focussed on what seems to be the essential part of the problem. When the problem is expressed in this abstract form, it will often resemble a standard one, and no innovation will be needed. Thus, the first rule of algorithm design is to be familiar with the repertoire of standard problems.

For example, consider the following problem. An architect produces a house plan like the one shown in Figure 4.1. The question is, what is the most economical way to install the plumbing? The places where water is needed, and the place where it enters the house, are marked with an x; pipes may be installed only in the walls.

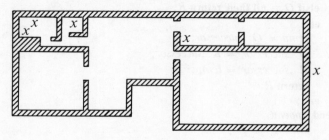

Figure 4.1

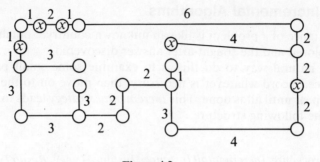

Figure 4.2

Is this a standard problem? To begin with, all the relevant information can be represented in a graph whose edges are walls, and whose vertices are the places where walls intersect with other walls or with places where water is needed, as in Figure 4.2. The numbers indicate the lengths of walls.

Having abstracted the problem in this way it may be expressed as follows: given a graph G whose edges have costs, find a way to connect a specified subset of its vertices together so as to minimize the total cost of the edges used. Expressed in this form, the problem is recognizable as a standard one: finding a Steiner tree of a graph.

This is a particularly instructive example, because the Steiner tree problem is known to be NP-hard, which informally means that it is one of a large class of problems for which no efficient algorithms are known (Garey and Johnson, 1979). Someone unaware of this could waste a lot of time in a frustrating search for an efficient algorithm, without knowing that many experienced computer scientists have tried and failed.

Even when the problem seems to be new, all is not lost, because experience has shown that there are a small number of general strategies which often lead quickly to an algorithm. These strategies are described in the following sections.

When a new algorithm is discovered, it must be examined to determine what operations are performed on its data. These operations constitute an abstract data type, whose implementation can be tackled separately. Often the ADT will resemble a standard one, in which case an efficient implementation of it will lie to hand.

Finally, the new algorithm is analysed, evaluated in other ways (such as for its memory consumption, or simplicity), and the design process repeated if necessary.

4.2 Incremental Algorithms

An instance of a problem is like an unknown country. Somehow it must be explored and the sought-after answer discovered.

A natural way to do this is to examine some small piece of the instance, record whatever is necessary, then move on to the next piece and repeat until all is done. This *incremental strategy* leads to algorithms with the following structure:

```
procedure Incremental(Instance: InstanceType): ResultType;
var Result: ResultType;
begin
    Result := some trivial initial value;
    while Instance ≠ empty do
        x := an element of Instance;
        Delete x from Instance;
        Update Result to reflect the discovery of x;
    end;
    return Result;
end Incremental;
```

Notice how *Instance*, the unknown country, gradually shrinks until it becomes empty.

Having decided to try this approach, the algorithm designer must next consider the choice of x at each stage. There seem to be two broad strategies for choosing x, leading to two distinctive kinds of incremental algorithm.

The first kind of incremental algorithm does not invest any time in choosing x carefully; it simply selects the most accessible of the remaining elements of *Instance*. The advantage of this is that the selection is very simple and efficient; the disadvantage is that the algorithm is blind to the problem instance as a whole, knowing nothing but the values of x it has selected. Accordingly, the algorithm is characterized by a loop invariant of the form

'*Result* is a complete solution to the subproblem represented by the part of the instance that has been deleted'

in which no mention is made of the instance as a whole.

The correctness of an incremental algorithm of this first kind is always obvious. As a very simple example, consider the following algorithm for summing the elements of array $A[a..b]$:

```
sum := 0;
for i := a to b do
    sum := sum + A[i];
end;
```

The loop invariant, '*sum* holds the total of all the elements examined so far', confirms that this is indeed an incremental algorithm of the first kind. In this book, whenever the correctness of an incremental algorithm is passed over without comment, the reader may infer that it is of this kind.

Now consider applying this design method to the problem of sorting a sct of numbers into increasing order. The algorithm required is one whose loop invariant is

'*Result* is a sorted sequence containing the elements of *Instance* that have been deleted.'

So for example, if the instance is {5, 1, 12, 9, 6}, then after deleting 5, 1, and 12, *Result* = ⟨1, 5, 12⟩. Then, after deleting 9, *Result* = ⟨1, 5, 9, 12⟩. Clearly the updating step requires *x* to be inserted into its appropriate place in the result sequence, and this is quite easy to do.

The next step in the design process is to examine the operations on *Instance* and *Result*, to determine what abstract data type these define and so what data structures are appropriate for their representation. This is left to Section 8.1, where the algorithm appears under the name of *insertion sort*.

Incremental algorithms of the second kind.   The danger faced by algorithms that do not look ahead is that a value of *x* could appear which completely upsets what has been done so far. That is, it may not be possible to update *Result* in some simple way to take account of the discovery of *x*.

For example, imagine a group of people packing their knapsacks for a camping trip. They have a number of items to carry, of varying weights, and they want to equalize their loads. Suppose half the load has been stowed, and the knapsacks are of roughly equal weight. There is no simple way to add one item, keeping the loads balanced: if the new item is heavy, a great deal of repacking is inevitable.

Most people would choose to begin the packing with the heaviest items, in the hope that the lighter ones could be fitted around them without any need for repacking. That is, they would invest more effort in choosing *x* carefully at each stage, so avoiding any need to modify what they have already done.

There are a number of algorithms which employ this strategy, so in this book they are given a name: *incremental algorithms of the second kind*. They are characterized by a loop invariant of the form

'*Result* is a part of the solution to the instance as a whole; it will need to be added to, but not modified'

in which the final solution plays a prominent part. This kind of algorithm is invariably more subtle than the other, and this book contains several whose correctness is far from obvious.

The sorting problem again provides a good illustration of this strategy. A sorting algorithm produces a sequence like $\langle 1, 5, 6, 9, 12 \rangle$, which suggests that *Result*, if it is to conform to the given loop invariant, should take successively the values $\langle \rangle$, $\langle 1 \rangle$, $\langle 1, 5 \rangle$, $\langle 1, 5, 6 \rangle$ etc., all of which can be added to without modification to obtain the overall solution. Clearly, x is chosen to be the smallest remaining element of *Instance* at each stage, and it is added to the end of the result sequence. This algorithm is *selection sort*, and it will be studied in Section 8.2.

4.3   Divide-and-Conquer

Divide-and-conquer is a design strategy which is well known for breaking down efficiency barriers. When the method applies, it often leads to a large improvement in time complexity, from $O(n^2)$ to $O(n\log n)$, for example.

One notable algorithm employing this strategy is the *fast Fourier transform*, which is used in the physical sciences for transforming a function of time into a function of frequency, both functions being defined by their values at a large number of points (Aho *et al.*, 1974). A nuclear magnetic resonance spectrometer, for example, regularly produces 2^{16} or more numbers which must be transformed in this way. Without the fast $O(n\log n)$ method made possible by divide-and-conquer, this whole technique would be infeasible.

The divide-and-conquer strategy is as follows: divide the problem instance into two or more smaller instances of the same problem, solve the smaller instances recursively, and assemble the solutions to form a solution of the original instance. The recursion stops when an instance is reached which is too small to divide: the solution to this instance can be produced directly, and it forms the basis for a proof of correctness by induction on the size of the instance (see Section 1.2).

When dividing the instance, one may either use whatever division comes most easily to hand, or invest time in making the division carefully so that the assembly is simplified. This design issue is graphically illustrated in the following example.

Finding the convex hull.   Consider the problem of finding the *convex hull* of a set of points in the plane. The convex hull is a sequence of points from the set which defines a convex figure enclosing all of them:

(A convex figure is a closed figure with no indentations: every line intersects a convex figure at no more than two points.) If the points are not given in any particular order, the simplest way to apply divide-and-conquer is to partition them into two subsets of approximately equal size:

The smaller instances are then solved recursively, and an attempt is made to assemble the two resulting convex hulls into one:

Unfortunately, this assembly operation seems difficult.

In general, it will not always be possible to reassemble the smaller solutions; but before abandoning divide-and-conquer a more careful partitioning method should be sought. For this problem, the point A with maximum y coordinate must be in the convex hull, as must the point B with minimum y coordinate. This suggests the following partitioning:

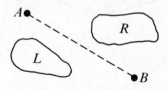

A simple algorithm which finds the maximum and minimum of a set of numbers can be used to determine A and B in linear time, and it turns out that it takes constant time to decide which side of line AB a point lies on. Thus, the partitioning is $O(n)$. Solving subproblems L and R recursively gives

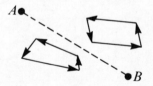

and this is fairly easy to merge into an overall solution. A has to be connected to one of the vertices of the convex hull of L. Just which vertex is appropriate is not quite clear, but it turns out that there is a simple geometrical test which can be applied to each vertex to determine if it is the right one. Similarly, A can be connected to R, and B to L and R, giving the desired hull:

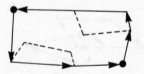

The analysis of this algorithm is similar to that of Quicksort (Section 8.4); it turns out to be $O(n\log n)$ on the average, degenerating to $O(n^2)$ if L or R is empty at each stage. For other algorithms for this problem, see Sedgewick (1988).

Strassen's algorithm.   It was stated earlier that divide-and-conquer has broken efficiency barriers. The matrix multiplication algorithm due to Strassen (1969) is perhaps the most dramatic example of this.

The usual way to multiply two $n \times n$ matrices A and B, yielding result matrix C, is as follows:

```
for i := 1 to n do
  for j := 1 to n do
    C[i, j] := 0;
    for k := 1 to n do
      C[i, j] := C[i, j] + A[i, k] *B[k, j];
    end;
  end;
end;
```

This algorithm requires n^3 scalar multiplications (that is, multiplications of single numbers) and n^3 scalar additions. It very simply reflects the definition of matrix multiplication, and we naturally expect that it cannot be improved upon.

Now apply divide-and-conquer to this problem. It is a fact that, if the three matrices are divided into quarters like this:

$$\begin{pmatrix} A_{11} & A_{12} \\ A_{21} & A_{22} \end{pmatrix} \begin{pmatrix} B_{11} & B_{12} \\ B_{21} & B_{22} \end{pmatrix} = \begin{pmatrix} C_{11} & C_{12} \\ C_{21} & C_{22} \end{pmatrix}$$

then the C_{ij} can be found by the usual matrix multiplication algorithm, substituting matrix operations for scalar ones. That is,

$$C_{11} = A_{11}B_{11} + A_{12}B_{21}$$
$$C_{12} = A_{11}B_{12} + A_{12}B_{22}$$
$$C_{21} = A_{21}B_{11} + A_{22}B_{21}$$
$$C_{22} = A_{21}B_{12} + A_{22}B_{22}$$

This leads to a divide-and-conquer algorithm, which performs an $n \times n$ matrix multiplication by partitioning the matrices into quarters and performing eight $(n/2) \times (n/2)$ matrix multiplications and four $(n/2) \times (n/2)$ matrix additions. The recurrence equation for the number of scalar multiplications performed is

$$T(1) = 1$$
$$T(n) = 8T(n/2)$$

which leads to $T(n) = n^3$ when n is a power of 2, as the reader can easily show.

Strassen's insight was to find an alternative method for calculating the C_{ij}, requiring seven $(n/2) \times (n/2)$ matrix multiplications and eighteen $(n/2) \times (n/2)$ matrix additions and subtractions:

$$M_1 = (A_{12} - A_{22})(B_{21} + B_{22})$$
$$M_2 = (A_{11} + A_{22})(B_{11} + B_{22})$$
$$M_3 = (A_{11} - A_{21})(B_{11} + B_{12})$$
$$M_4 = (A_{11} + A_{12})B_{22}$$
$$M_5 = A_{11}(B_{12} - B_{22})$$
$$M_6 = A_{22}(B_{21} - B_{11})$$
$$M_7 = (A_{21} + A_{22})B_{11}$$

$$C_{11} = M_1 + M_2 - M_4 + M_6$$
$$C_{12} = M_4 + M_5$$
$$C_{21} = M_6 + M_7$$
$$C_{22} = M_2 - M_3 + M_5 - M_7$$

The reader can easily verify that these formulas for the C_{ij} agree with the ones given above.

If this method is used recursively to perform the seven $(n/2) \times (n/2)$ matrix multiplications, then the recurrence equation for the number of scalar multiplications performed is

$$T(1) = 1$$
$$T(n) = 7T(n/2)$$

Solving this for the case $n = 2^k$ is easy:

$$T(2^k) = 7T(2^{k-1})$$
$$= 7^2 T(2^{k-2})$$
$$= \ldots$$
$$= 7^i T(2^{k-i})$$
$$= \ldots$$
$$= 7^k T(1)$$
$$= 7^k$$

That is, $T(n) = 7^{\log_2 n}$. Applying the identity $a^{\log_b c} = c^{\log_b a}$, which is easily proven by taking logarithms to base b,

$$T(n) = n^{\log_2 7} \simeq n^{2.81}$$

The reader is left the task of showing that the number of scalar additions performed is also $O(n^{\log_2 7})$, so concluding that Strassen's algorithm is asymptotically more efficient than the standard algorithm.

In practice, the overhead of managing the many small matrices does not pay off until n reaches the hundreds. Nevertheless, Strassen's algorithm clearly demonstrates the power of divide-and-conquer.

4.4   Dynamic Programming

Consider the problem of finding the nth Fibonacci number, as defined by the recurrence equation

$$F(0) = 0$$
$$F(1) = 1$$
$$F(n) = F(n - 1) + F(n - 2)$$

The obvious solution is to convert the recurrence into a divide-and-conquer algorithm:

```
procedure Fib(n: integer): integer;
begin
   if n ≤ 1 then
      return n;
   else
      return Fib(n − 1) + Fib(n − 2);
   end;
end Fib;
```

This is simple, elegant, and obviously correct. Unfortunately, it has exponential time complexity (Exercise 2.7). By drawing a tree showing all the recursive calls the algorithm makes, it can clearly be seen what is slowing it down:

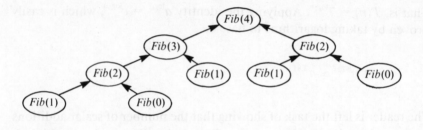

The algorithm solves small instances many times over, and this effect becomes worse as *n* increases. (Arrows are drawn pointing upwards to indicate that the solutions to children are required when solving the parent.)

Whenever a divide-and-conquer algorithm solves small instances repeatedly in this way, the technique of *dynamic programming* may be used to eliminate the redundant work. The solutions are stored in a table, and an instance solved from scratch only when it is encounted for the first time. Thereafter, whenever that solution is needed, it is simply retrieved from the table. For the Fibonacci problem, this approach yields

```
procedure Fib(n: integer): integer;
var i: integer;
begin
   if table[n] = empty then
      if n ≤ 1 then
         table[n] := n;
      else
         table[n] := Fib(n − 1) + Fib(n − 2);
      end;
   end;
   return table[n];
end Fib;
```

where all the values of *table*[0..*n*] are initialized to the value *empty*, for example −1.

Even the test for *empty* can be eliminated if the instances are solved in an order that guarantees that, when a given instance's turn arrives, all the instances whose solution it needs have already been solved. A systematic way to determine this ordering is to let the instances be vertices in a directed graph, and join *x* to *y* by an arrow if the solution to instance *x* is used when solving *y*. For the Fibonacci numbers problem, this graph is:

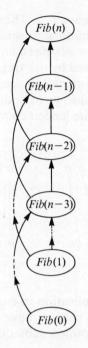

The appropriate ordering is then a *topological ordering* of the vertices (Section 10.4); in this case, either $Fib(0)$, $Fib(1)$, $Fib(2)$, . . . , $Fib(n)$ or $Fib(1)$, $Fib(0)$, $Fib(2)$, . . . , $Fib(n)$ would do.

It often happens that the ordering can be determined in advance and embedded into the algorithm. This can be done for the Fibonacci problem:

```
procedure Fib(n: integer): integer;
var i: integer;
begin
    table[0] := 0;
    table[1] := 1;
    for i := 2 to n do
        table[i] := table[i − 1] + table[i − 2];
    end;
    return table[n];
end Fib;
```

It is now clear that this dynamic programming solution has $O(n)$ complexity. The elimination of recursion is a further practical benefit: dynamic programming is a useful code optimization technique even when it does not reduce the asymptotic complexity (Exercise 8.5).

The longest common subsequence. The following problem is typical of the way dynamic programming arises. Consider two sequences of characters, for example, $x = abdebcbb$ and $y = adacbcb$. A *subsequence* of such a sequence is obtained by deleting any number of elements from any positions. A *longest common subsequence* of two sequences x and y, written $\mathrm{lcs}(x, y)$, is a subsequence of both whose length is maximal. For example, *adcbb* and *adbcb* are longest common subsequences of *abdebcbb* and *adacbcb*:

$$
\begin{array}{cc}
a\ b\ d\ e\ b\ c\ b\ b & a\ b\ d\ e\ b\ c\ b\ b \\
a\ d\ a\ c\ b\ c\ b & a\ d\ a\ c\ b\ c\ b
\end{array}
$$

This problem finds application in comparing new and old versions of files to determine where changes have been made. The parts that do not belong to a longest common subsequence of the two files are presumably the changes.

To begin with the easy cases, if either sequence is empty, the longest common subsequence is also empty. Denoting the empty sequence by the symbol ε, we have

$$\mathrm{lcs}(x, \varepsilon) = \varepsilon$$
$$\mathrm{lcs}(\varepsilon, y) = \varepsilon$$

for any sequences x and y.

Next, assuming now that both sequences are non-empty, their first elements are compared. If they are equal, clearly that first element may be included in the longest common subsequence, which gives

$$\mathrm{lcs}(ax, ay) = a\,\mathrm{lcs}(x, y)$$

This notation means that a longest common subsequence of two sequences beginning with a is a followed by a longest common subsequence of the two remainders.

Now the hard case is left: two sequences ax and by whose first elements differ. If $\mathrm{lcs}(ax, by)$ does not begin with a, it must be equal to $\mathrm{lcs}(x, by)$; otherwise, it does not begin with b, so it must equal $\mathrm{lcs}(ax, y)$. Therefore

$$\mathrm{lcs}(ax, by) = \mathrm{lcs}(x, by) \quad \text{or} \quad \mathrm{lcs}(ax, y)$$

whichever is the longer; both must be evaluated and their lengths compared.

This is a recursive method of evaluating lcs(x, y), but it is not efficient. In the worst case, the two sequences have no common elements, and the last case always applies. Let the length of x be n, and of y be m. Then the worst-case complexity of evaluating lcs(x, y) by this method is

$$W(n, m) = W(n, m - 1) + W(n - 1, m)$$
$$\geq 2W(n - 1, m - 1)$$

and the complexity is exponential in the smaller of n and m. In fact, $W(n, m)$ is closely related to the binomial coefficient (Exercise 2.10).

When evaluating lcs(x, y), eventually lcs(x', y') may be called for any suffixes x' of x and y' of y. (A *suffix* of a sequence is a subsequence consisting of any number of rightmost elements; for example, the suffixes of *bac* are ε, c, ac, and *bac*.) Applying dynamic programming, a two-dimensional table indexed by suffix lengths is therefore needed:

x:	**array**[$1..n$] **of char**;
y:	**array**[$1..m$] **of char**;
table:	**array**[$0..n$], [$0..m$] **of integer**;

The algorithm now presented finds only the length of lcs(x, y). For convenience in indexing x and y, it begins at the right and works leftwards. Thus, *table*[i, j] holds the length of a longest common subsequence of $x[1..i]$ and $y[1..j]$:

```
procedure Lcs(i, j: integer): integer;
begin
  if table[i, j] = empty then
    if (i = 0) or (j = 0) then
      table[i, j] := 0;
    elsif x[i] = y[j] then
      table[i, j] := 1 + Lcs(i - 1, j - 1);
    else
      table[i, j] := max(Lcs(i - 1, j), Lcs(i, j - 1));
    end;
  end;
  return table[i, j];
end Lcs;
```

To achieve the next optimization – embedding a topological ordering of the subinstances into the algorithm, so eliminating the recursion – the directed graph is needed. Observing that $Lcs(i, j)$ depends on $Lcs(i - 1, j - 1)$, $Lcs(i - 1, j)$, and $Lcs(i, j - 1)$, the graph is:

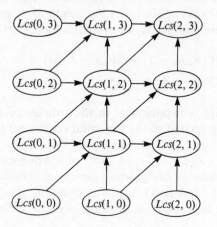

and so on. It is quite easy to find a suitable topological ordering, beginning with the two boundaries:

```
procedure Lcs(n, m: integer): integer;
var i, j: integer;
begin
  for i := 0 to n do table[i, 0] := 0; end;
  for j := 1 to m do table[j, 0] := 0; end;
  for i := 1 to n do
    for j := 1 to m do
      if x[i] = y[j] then
        table[i, j] := 1 + table[i - 1, j - 1];
      else
        table[i, j] := max(table[i - 1, j], table[i, j - 1]);
      end;
    end;
  end;
  return table[n, m];
end Lcs;
```

The time complexity of this dynamic programming algorithm is clearly $O(nm)$. The problem of using the values in the table to reconstruct an actual longest common subsequence is left as an exercise.

There is an interesting alternative algorithm for this problem, due to Hunt and Szymanski (1977). For instances typically encountered in the file comparison application mentioned earlier, their algorithm is significantly faster.

EXERCISES

4.1 Let $f(x)$ be a monotone decreasing function of x, and let n be the largest integer for which $f(n) \geq 0$. Assuming that n exists, one algorithm for finding it is

```
i := 0;
while f(i) ≥ 0 do
    i := i + 1;
end;
n := i − 1;
```

but this has $O(n)$ complexity. Find an algorithm with better asymptotic complexity.

4.2 Find an algorithm for calculating x^n, where n is a non-negative integer, using only multiplication operations (that is, no exponentiation). Your algorithm should be substantially faster than the obvious $O(n)$ one.

4.3 The following matrix recurrence equation may be used to define the Fibonacci numbers:

$$\binom{F(1)}{F(0)} = \binom{1}{0}$$

$$\binom{F(n+1)}{F(n)} = \begin{pmatrix} 1 & 1 \\ 1 & 0 \end{pmatrix} \binom{F(n)}{F(n-1)}$$

Verify this statement, solve the recurrence, and use your result, together with the solution to the previous question, to find an algorithm for calculating $F(n)$ which is substantially faster than the $O(n)$ dynamic programming algorithm given in Section 4.4.

4.4 Develop an incremental algorithm for the convex hull problem of Section 4.3.

4.5 A *celebrity* is someone that everyone knows, but who knows no-one. Find an efficient algorithm for determining whether or not a group of *n* people contains a celebrity, based on asking questions of the form "Excuse me *x*, do you know *y*?" (*Hint*: what can you conclude if the answer is yes? if the answer is no?)

4.6   A computer installation contains a single line printer. At a certain instant, *n* people each send a file to the printer, then wait beside it for their output. The printer must *schedule* the files (that is decide on the order) so as to minimize the total waiting time of the *n* people. The size of each file is known, and from this the printer can determine $t(x)$, the time it will take to print file *x*. The following algorithm is proposed:

> $X := \{ \text{ all the files } \}$;
> **while** $X \neq \{ \}$ **do**
>   *Remove from X a file x of minimum t(x)*;
>   *Print(x)*;
> **end**;

That is, the files are printed in order of size. Prove that this algorithm produces an optimal schedule. (*Hint*: it is an incremental algorithm of the second kind.)

4.7   A *local minimum* of an array $A[a..b]$ is an element $A[k]$ satisfying $A[k] \leq A[k-1]$ and $A[k] \leq A[k+1]$. We assume that $a \leq b$, $A[a] \leq A[a-1]$, and $A[b] \leq A[b+1]$; these conditions guarantee that a local minimum must exist. Design an algorithm for finding a local minimum of the array $A[a..b]$ which is substantially faster than the obvious $O(n)$ one, in the worst case.

4.8   One idea for simplifying the algorithm given in Section 4.3 for finding the convex hull of a set of points is as follows. After partitioning into

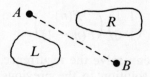

include *A* and *B* in the two subproblems; that is, solve

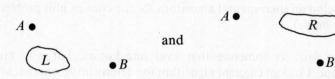

and

giving result

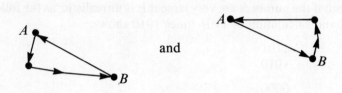

and

which can be trivially combined. Unfortunately, this has a fatal flaw. What is it?

4.9 Design an algorithm for printing out all the subsets of a given finite set. For example, the subsets of $\{a, b, c\}$ are

    $\{\}$ $\{a\}$
    $\{c\}$ $\{a, c\}$
    $\{b\}$ $\{a, b\}$
    $\{b, c\}$ $\{a, b, c\}$

4.10 When a divide-and-conquer algorithm divides a problem of size n into a subproblems, each of size n/b, its complexity is typically given by the recurrence equation

$$T(1) = d$$
$$T(n) = aT(n/b) + f(n)$$

where $f(n)$ is the cost of dividing a subproblem of size n, and subsequently recombining the solutions, and d is a constant. Let $n = b^k$ and show that

$$T(b^k) = da^k + \sum_{i=1}^{k} a^{k-i} f(b^i).$$

4.11 The recurrence equation given in the previous question often occurs with $f(n) = cn^r$ for some positive constants c and r. Show that in this case the solution is

$$T(n) = O(n^r) \qquad \text{if } a < b^r$$
$$= O(n^r \log n) \qquad \text{if } a = b^r$$
$$= O(n^{\log_b a}) \qquad \text{if } a > b^r$$

for $n = b^k$. Thus, divide-and-conquer algorithms become asymptotically less efficient as a increases relative to b^r.

4.12 (Karatsuba and Ofman, 1962) We generally assume that the multiplication of two integers can be performed in constant time, but if the numbers are very large this is unrealistic, as the following hand calculation of 1101 times 1010 shows:

```
        1101
        1010
        ----
        0000
        1101
       0000
      1101
      ----------
      10000010
```

So consider the problem of multiplying two n-bit numbers together, and let the characteristic operation be the multiplication of two 1-bit numbers (addition is of course much cheaper, so we ignore its cost).

(a) Show that the complexity of the hand calculation method is $T(n) = n^2$.

(b) Now consider the following divide-and-conquer approach. Let u and v be the two n-bit binary integers, and assume that n is even. Let u_1 be the $n/2$ most significant bits of u, and let u_0 be the remaining bits, so that $u = 2^{n/2}u_1 + u_0$. Similarly, let $v = 2^{n/2}v_1 + v_0$. The identity

$$uv = (2^n + 2^{n/2})u_1v_1 + 2^{n/2}(u_1 - u_0)(v_0 - v_1) + (2^{n/2} + 1)u_0v_0$$

which may be easily verified by multiplying out the right-hand side, shows that the n-bit multiplication uv may be accomplished with three $n/2$-bit multiplications: u_1v_1, $(u_1 - u_0)(v_0 - v_1)$, and u_0v_0, plus some inexpensive additions and shifts. Derive and solve a recurrence equation for the time complexity of this method, assuming n is a power of 2, and show that it is asymptotically more efficient than the traditional method.

4.13 You are given an $n \times m$ matrix $A[a..b, c..d]$ in which it is known that $A[i, j] \le A[i, j + 1]$ and $A[i, j] \le A[i + 1, j]$ for all i and j. That is, the entries are sorted along the rows and columns. Design an efficient algorithm for determining whether the value x is present in A.

4.14 *The subset sum problem.* The following is a simple example of the problems that arise in making efficient use of a limited storage space, such as a computer's memory. You are given a set of items $A = \{a_1, a_2, \ldots, a_n\}$. Each item a_i has a size, $s(a_i)$, which is a positive integer. The problem is to find a subset of A whose total size (that is, the sum of the sizes of its elements) is as large as possible, but not larger than a given integer C, the capacity of your storage space.

This problem may be solved by generating the 2^n subsets of A, eliminating all those whose total size exceeds C, and returning a remaining subset of maximum size. Unfortunately, this has exponential complexity. Find an algorithm which is substantially faster if C is not too large, and determine the complexity of your algorithm. (*Hint*: a_1 is either in or out. Divide the problem into these two cases, and solve the resulting smaller instances. Then apply dynamic programming.)

4.15 *Bin packing*. You are given K bins, each of capacity C, and a set of items $A = \{a_1, a_2, \ldots, a_n\}$, each with an associated size. The problem is to place all n items into the K bins without exceeding the capacity of any bin, or else to report failure if this is impossible. Using the general approach suggested in the preceding question, design an efficient algorithm for this problem and determine its complexity.

Chapter 5

Properties of Binary Trees

Binary trees are the visible manifestation of the yes-or-no decision making within computers, and this is why they arise so frequently and naturally in data structures and algorithms. This chapter collects together some basic mathematical properties of binary trees, for use later in the analysis of several data structures and algorithms (including binary search trees, Quicksort, and Heapsort), and in developing lower bounds on the complexity of problems (Chapter 11).

5.1 Definitions

A *binary tree* is either empty or it consists of a *root node* and a pair of binary trees, called the *left subtree* and the *right subtree*. For example,

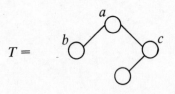

is a binary tree with root node a; the left subtree has root b and its subtrees are empty; the right subtree has root c. The lines connecting nodes to their non-empty subtrees are called *edges*. A non-empty binary tree with n nodes has $n - 1$ edges (Exercise 5.1). The *size* of a tree is the number of nodes it contains.

When drawing binary trees, it is often convenient to represent the empty subtrees explicitly, so that they can be seen. For example, an alternative representation for the tree given above is in which the empty

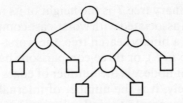

subtrees appear as square nodes. The square nodes are also called *external nodes*, and the set of all external nodes of a binary tree T will be denoted $E(T)$. The square node version is sometimes called an *extended* binary tree. The round nodes are called *internal nodes*, and $I(T)$ will denote the set of internal nodes of T. A binary tree with n internal nodes has $n + 1$ external nodes (Exercise 5.2). For example, the empty tree and its extended version look like this:

$$\Rightarrow \quad \Box$$

The word 'internal' is often dropped; one speaks, for example, of a tree with n nodes, meaning n internal nodes.

Every node has a unique *parent* (the node just above it in the tree), except the root which has no parent. The set of *ancestors* of a node x is recursively defined as x together with the ancestors of its parent, if x has a parent. These nodes form a *path* from x up to the root of the tree. A *proper ancestor* of x is an ancestor of x other than x itself.

Every node has at most two *children* (just below it). Two nodes are *siblings* if they share the same parent. The set of *descendants* of a node x is x together with all the descendants of its children. These nodes, together with the edges that join them, form a subtree rooted at x, often denoted T_x. A *proper descendant* of x is a descendant of x other than x itself. We use the notation $s(x)$ for the number of descendants of x; that is, the size of the subtree rooted at x.

5.2   Height and Path Length

The *height* $h(x)$ of node x is the number of edges on the longest path leading down from x in the extended tree. Alternatively, it is the number of internal nodes on this path, including x if x is internal. For example, the following tree has heights written inside its nodes:

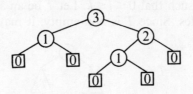

The height $h(T)$ of binary tree T is the height of its root. This measure of the shape of T is often associated with worst-case complexity. For example, if the tree above was a binary search tree, the worst-case complexity of a search in it would be $h(T)$, or three comparisons between keys.

The *depth* $d(x)$ of node x is the number of edges on the path from the root to x. Alternatively, it is the number of internal nodes on this path, excluding x itself. For example, the following tree has depths written inside its nodes:

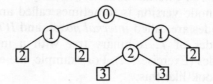

The *internal path length* $i(T)$ is the sum of the depths of the internal nodes of T:

$$i(T) = \sum_{x \in I(T)} d(x)$$

The *external path length* $e(T)$ is the sum of the depths of the external nodes:

$$e(T) = \sum_{x \in E(T)} d(x)$$

For example, the tree above has $i(T) = 4$ and $e(T) = 12$. Internal and external path length are often connected with average complexity. They are closely related, as the following theorem shows.

Theorem 5.1:   Let T be any binary tree with n internal nodes. Then $e(T) = i(T) + 2n$.

Proof: by induction on n.

Basis step: $n = 0$. Then T is empty, $e(T) = i(T) = 0$, and the theorem holds.

Inductive step: Assume the theorem holds for all binary trees with j nodes, for all j such that $0 \le j \le k$. Let T be an arbitrary binary tree with $k + 1$ nodes. Since T is non-empty, it may be drawn as

$$T = \quad$$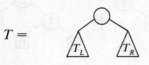

where T_L has i nodes (say), and so T_R has $k - i$ nodes. Since $0 \le i \le k$ and $0 \le k - i \le k$, by the inductive hypothesis

$$e(T_L) = i(T_L) + 2i \qquad\qquad\qquad (1)$$

and

$$e(T_R) = i(T_R) + 2(k - i) \qquad\qquad\qquad (2)$$

Now observe that every external node is one level deeper in T than it is in T_L or T_R. Since there are $k + 2$ external nodes in T, this must give

$$e(T) = e(T_L) + e(T_R) + k + 2 \qquad\qquad\qquad (3)$$

Similarly, the k internal nodes of T_L and T_R are each one level deeper in T, and the root of T has depth 0, so

$$i(T) = i(T_L) + i(T_R) + k \qquad\qquad\qquad (4)$$

Putting these four identities together gives

$$
\begin{aligned}
e(T) &= e(T_L) + e(T_R) + k + 2 &\text{by (3)}\\
&= i(T_L) + 2i + i(T_R) + 2(k - i) + k + 2 &\text{by (1) and (2)}\\
&= i(T_L) + i(T_R) + 3k + 2\\
&= i(T) + 2(k + 1) &\text{by (4)}
\end{aligned}
$$

so the theorem holds for all binary trees with $k + 1$ nodes. ∎

5.3 Skew Trees and Complete Trees

Among all binary trees with n nodes, there will be some whose internal path length is maximum. These are called *skew trees*. By Theorem 5.1, these trees will also have maximum external path length. This definition is made more concrete as follows.

Theorem 5.2: A binary tree is a skew tree if and only if every node in it has at most one internal node among its children.

Proof: First, it must be proved that if T is a skew tree, then every node x in it has at most one internal node among its children. An equivalent statement is the contrapositive: if node x of tree T has more than one internal node among its children, then T cannot be a skew tree. Let x be such a node, and let y be any external node lying in the right subtree of x:

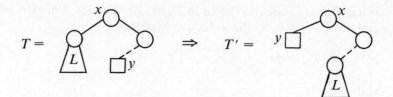

Exchanging y and L, the left subtree of x, produces a new tree T' as shown. In T', the internal nodes of L are deeper than they were in T; all other internal nodes are at the same depth in both trees. Therefore $i(T) < i(T')$, so T is not a skew tree.

Conversely, it must be proved that if every node of T has at most one internal node among its children, then T is skew. Consider the set S of all trees T with the property that every node of T has at most one internal node among its children. For example,

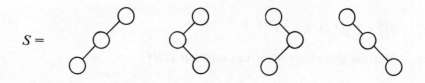

when $n = 3$. By the first part of this proof, the skew trees must lie in S. But the trees in S all have the same internal path length, namely $i(T) = 0 + 1 + \cdots + n - 1 = n(n - 1)/2$, so they all have maximum internal path length, and they are all skew.   ∎

Skew trees also have maximum height, namely $h(T) = n$ (Exercise 5.4).

At the other extreme, among all binary trees with n nodes there will be some whose internal path length (and hence external path length) is minimum. These are called *complete trees*, and they can be characterized as follows.

Theorem 5.3:   A binary tree is a complete tree if and only if there exists a number q such that every external node in the tree has depth q or $q + 1$.

Proof: First, it must be shown that if T is a complete tree, then the number q exists. The contrapositive is proved: if no q exists, then T is not complete.

If q does not exist, then there must be at least two external nodes x and y whose depths differ by at least two. Assuming without loss of generality that $d(x) < d(y)$, we exchange x with y's parent, yielding a new tree T':

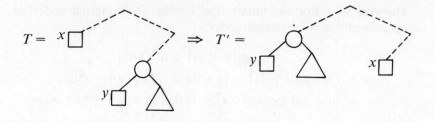

The only internal nodes affected are the descendants of y's parent. These nodes all rise at least one level, so $i(T) > i(T')$, which proves that T is not a complete tree.

Conversely, we must prove that, if a number q exists such that every external node of T has depth q or $q + 1$, then T is complete. This follows as in Theorem 5.2 from the fact that the external path lengths of all such trees are equal. ■

For example, here are two complete trees ($n = 10$):

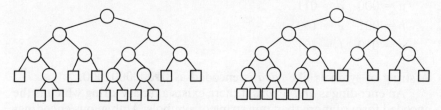

It is clear that all complete trees T with n nodes have equal height. Examination of examples reveals that when $n = 2^k - 1$, $h(T) = k$; while when $n = 2^k$, $h(T)$ jumps to $k + 1$. The appropriate formula is therefore $h(T) = \lceil \log_2(n + 1) \rceil$, which holds for $n \geq 0$. It can be shown that all binary trees T with n nodes have height $h(T) \geq \lceil \log_2(n + 1) \rceil$ (Exercise 5.5), so complete trees have minimum height as well as minimum path length.

The exact formula for the external path length of a complete tree is rather messy (Exercise 5.6), but the following approximation is good enough here. For all external nodes x,

$$h(T) - 1 \leq d(x) \leq h(T),$$

and summing this over the $n + 1$ external nodes of T yields

$$(n + 1)(\lceil \log_2(n + 1) \rceil - 1) \leq e(T) \leq (n + 1)\lceil \log_2(n + 1) \rceil.$$

This ends our investigation of complete trees. The following theorem summarizes the results of this section.

Theorem 5.4: For any binary tree T with $n \geq 0$ internal nodes, or equivalently $n + 1$ external nodes.

$$\lceil \log_2(n + 1) \rceil \leq h(T) \leq n$$
$$(n + 1)(\lceil \log_2(n + 1) \rceil - 1) - 2n \leq i(T) \leq n(n - 1)/2$$
$$(n + 1)(\lceil \log_2(n + 1) \rceil - 1) \leq e(T) \leq n(n - 1)/2 + 2n$$

Proof: These inequalities are proved above.   ∎

5.4 Huffman Trees

Consider a finite set S of *symbols*, for example, $S = \{a, b, c, d, e, f\}$. A *binary encoding* of S is an assignment of a binary string (sequence) to each symbol. For example, one encoding of S is

$a = 000$ $d = 011$
$b = 001$ $e = 100$
$c = 010$ $f = 101$

A string of symbols like *caba* is encoded as 010000001000.

An encoding is *ambiguous* if there exists a binary string which is the encoded form of more than one string of symbols. Ambiguous encodings are not of interest because it is necessary to be able to convert from uncoded to coded form and back again at will. This need to avoid ambiguity prevents the assigning of, say, code word 0 to every symbol. Yet the encoded string needs to be short, so as to save storage space or transmission time. This leads to the *optimal encoding problem*: given a finite set S of symbols, and a finite string of symbols from S, find an unambiguous binary encoding for S that minimizes the length of the encoded string. Unfortunately, it is not always easy to tell whether a given encoding is ambiguous or not, and this makes the optimal encoding problem very hard.

One way to be sure that an encoding is unambiguous is to find a decoding algorithm for it. Perhaps the simplest decoding algorithm is based on a binary tree, like this tree for the encoding given above:

$T =$

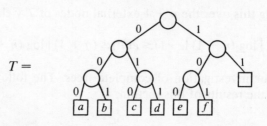

Left branches are labelled 0, right branches are labelled 1, and each external node is labelled with the symbol (if any) whose code word adorns the path to that node. For example, to decode 100010 follow the path marked 1–0–0 to external node e, then start again and follow 0–1–0 to c. If an encoding can be represented by such a tree, it is clearly unambiguous. Such encodings are called *prefix encodings*, because no code word is a prefix of any other. From now on the problem is modestly limited to finding, not an optimal encoding, but an optimal prefix encoding.

Suppose symbol x occurs $w(x)$ times in the string being optimally encoded. The length of x's code word is $d(x)$, the depth of x in the decoding tree T, so the total length of the encoded string is

$$L = \sum_{x \in E(T)} w(x)d(x)$$

and the prefix encoding is needed that minimizes L. For example, if $S = \{a, b, c, d\}$, and the string is *cdabcddccc*, then $w(a) = 1$, $w(b) = 1$, $w(c) = 5$, $w(d) = 3$, and an optimal prefix encoding is

$$T = $$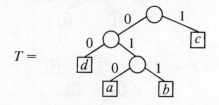

which gives $L = 3 \cdot 2 + 1 \cdot 3 + 1 \cdot 3 + 5 \cdot 1 = 17$. Notice that we do not require any particular left-to-right ordering for the symbols within T, nor that the code words be of equal length.

This problem can be reformulated in a way that is independent of the particular application to optimal encodings. Let T be a binary tree, and attach a *weight* (non-negative real number) $w(x)$ to each external node x. Define $wepl(T)$, the *weighted external path length of T*, by

$$wepl(T) = \sum_{x \in E(T)} w(x)d(x)$$

For a fixed multiset of $n \geq 1$ weights, it can be asked which trees with those weights attached have minimum *wepl*. For example, if the weights are $\{1, 1, 3, 5\}$, then

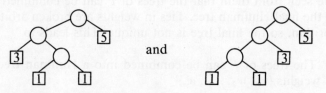

both have minimum *wepl*, namely 17. Trees of minimum *wepl* are called *Huffman trees*, after the discoverer of the algorithm given below. Notice that, if the weights are all 1, then $wepl(T) = e(T)$, and the Huffman trees are exactly the complete trees.

The algorithm due to Huffman (1952) for finding trees of minimum *wepl* is a miracle of simplicity. At the heart of the algorithm is a *forest* (set of trees) F, which is initially composed entirely of external nodes, one for each given weight. Each tree T in F has a weight associated with it, which is just the sum of the weights of the external nodes of T. The weight is conventionally written in the root of T. The algorithm selects two trees of minimum weight from F and combines them into one. This step is repeated until only one tree is left.

For example, given the weights $\{3, 1, 1, 5\}$, at the start of each iteration of the loop,

$$F = \quad \{ \boxed{3}, \quad \boxed{1}, \quad \boxed{1}, \quad \boxed{5} \}$$

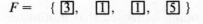

and the algorithm has produced one of the Huffman trees seen earlier. This algorithm uses the priority queue ADT of Chapter 7, so its implementation and analysis will be deferred to Exercise 7.8.

Correctness of Huffman's algorithm. Examples of the algorithm in operation, as given above, are helpful when guessing the loop invariant. It can be seen from them that the trees of F can be combined together to form the final Huffman tree. Ties in weights are broken arbitrarily by the algorithm, so the final tree is not unique. This leads to

$I = $ 'The trees of F can be combined into a Huffman tree for the weights $\{w_1, w_2, \ldots, w_n\}$'

for the loop invariant. I is clearly true initially, and when the loop terminates, I implies that the sole remaining tree is a Huffman tree. So this is a promising choice, and further encouragement is gained by the realization that, if correct, this loop invariant would show that Huffman's algorithm is an incremental algorithm of the second kind (Section 4.2).

Call F a *fringing forest* for T whenever, by a sequence of zero or more combinings of the kind done by Huffman's algorithm, the trees of F may be converted into T. Here is a proof that the proposed loop invariant is correct. The correctness of Huffman's algorithm follows immediately.

Theorem 5.5:   At the beginning of the kth iteration of the loop in Huffman's algorithm, F is a fringing forest for some Huffman tree for the weights $w_1, w_2, \ldots, w_n$.

Proof: by induction on k.

Basis step: At the beginning of the first iteration, the algorithm has set F to $\{\boxed{w_1}, \boxed{w_2}, \ldots, \boxed{w_n}\}$, which is certainly a fringing forest for some (in fact any) Huffman tree for the weights $w_1, w_2, \ldots, w_n$.

Induction step: The inductive hypothesis is that, at the beginning of the kth iteration of the loop of Huffman's algorithm, F is a fringing forest for some Huffman tree T for the weights $w_1, w_2, \ldots, w_n$. It must be shown that this is true of the forest (call it F') at the beginning of the next iteration of the loop.

Let z be any internal node of T, excluding the nodes of F, such that z has maximum depth. Then the two children of z must be roots of trees in F, and

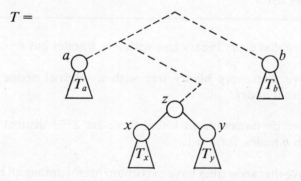

$$T =$$

where T_a, T_b, T_x, and T_y are all in F, and T_a and T_b are the trees selected from F by Huffman's algorithm.

Since z is of maximum depth outside F, $d(a) \leq d(x)$; since T_a was chosen by Huffman's algorithm, $w(T_a) \leq w(T_x)$. These two conditions imply that T_a and T_x may be exchanged without increasing $wepl(T)$ (nor decreasing it, since $wepl(T)$ is minimum by assumption). Similarly, T_b may be exchanged with T_y, and so the tree

$$T' = $$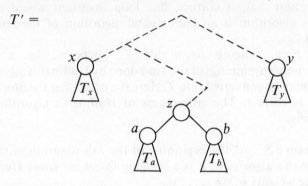

has $wepl(T') = wepl(T)$, so that T' is also a Huffman tree for the weights $w_1, w_2, \ldots, w_n$. But

$$F' = $$

is a fringing forest for T', so the theorem is true for F'.   ∎

EXERCISES

5.1 Prove that every binary tree with $n \geq 1$ nodes has $n - 1$ edges.

5.2 Prove that every binary tree with n internal nodes has $n + 1$ external nodes.

5.3 Prove by induction on n that there are 2^{n-1} distinct skew trees with n nodes, for $n \geq 1$.

5.4 Prove that skew trees have maximum height among all binary trees with n nodes.

5.5 Prove that, for any binary tree T with $n \geq 0$ nodes, $h(T) \geq \lceil \log_2(n + 1) \rceil$.

5.6   Develop an exact formula for the external path length of a complete binary tree with n nodes.

5.7   Define the *size balance* of a node x in a binary tree to be the size of its right subtree minus the size of its left subtree. For example, the following tree has size balances written inside its nodes:

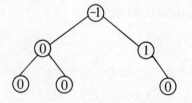

A binary tree is said to be *size-balanced* if the size balance of every node is either -1, 0, or 1. Show that every size-balanced binary tree is complete (the converse does not hold).

5.8   There is a strong connection between the binary search of an array of n elements, such as

| 2.5 | 3.7 | 5.9 | 6.1 | 6.3 | 9.8 |

and a certain binary tree T_n, which in this example is

$T_n =$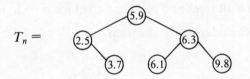

Investigate this connection, show that T_n is size-balanced (see the previous question), and conclude that the worst-case complexity of binary search is $W(n) = \lceil \log_2(n + 1) \rceil$.

5.9   Prove that $i(T) = \displaystyle\sum_{x \in I(T)} s(x)$

5.10   There are algorithms, for example, those used with AVL trees (Adel'son-Vel'skii and Landis, 1962) and splay trees (Section 6.6), that attempt to keep binary trees balanced by performing *rotations* on them. A *Type I rotation* does this:

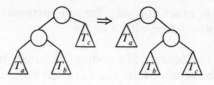

A *Type II* rotation does this:

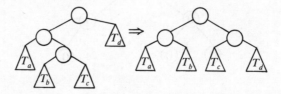

Both forms have mirror images that need not be considered further. In these diagrams, the subtrees may be empty, but the nodes shown must exist. When will a Type I rotation reduce the internal path length? When will a Type II rotation reduce it? Give the simplest conditions that you can.

5.11 This question aims to find out how many distinct binary trees there are with n nodes. Let this number be $C(n)$. If $n = 0$, there is only the empty tree, so $C(0) = 1$. If $n = 1$, there is only the one-node tree, so $C(1) = 1$.

(a) Draw all trees and calculate $C(n)$ for $n = 2, 3$, and 4.

(b) By considering the diagram

$$T =$$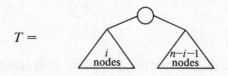

find a recurrence equation for $C(n)$. It cannot be solved by repeated substitution, and so its solution is beyond the scope of this book.

(c) Use your recurrence equation to calculate $C(n)$ for $n = 1, 2, 3,$ 4, and 5. The first four values should agree with the values above.

5.12 Let $t \geq 2$ be a fixed integer. A t-ary tree is either empty or it consists of a root node and t t-ary trees, called the first, second,

..., and tth subtrees. For example, binary trees are 2-ary trees, and

$T =$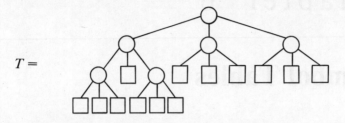

is a 3-ary tree. Develop a theorem analogous to Theorem 5.4 for t-ary trees.

5.13 At each stage of the Huffman algorithm a tree is constructed by combining two previously constructed trees. Let the tree constructed during the ith loop iteration be T_i, for $1 \le i \le n - 1$. Prove that

$$w(T_i) \le w(T_{i+1})$$

($1 \le i < n - 1$); in other words, prove that the trees have monotone increasing weight.

5.14 Using the result of the previous question, find an $O(n)$ implementation of Huffman's algorithm, assuming that the initial weights are given in sorted order.

Chapter 6

Symbol Tables

The *symbol table* ADT, which is the subject of this chapter, takes its name from program compilation, where it is used to record the variables of a program, together with their type, address, etc. Symbol table operations are also fundamental to database systems, and the hash table and B-tree data structures discussed here are among the most popular for implementing databases on external storage devices.

6.1 Specification

A *symbol table* is a set of *entries*, each containing a *key* and a *value*. Each key uniquely identifies its entry (that is, the keys alone form a set). Here is its Modula-2 specification:

> **definition module** *SymTab*;
>
>   **type** *Entry*;
>
>   **var** *NilEntry*: *Entry*;
>   **procedure** *New*(*key*: *KeyType*; *value*: *ValueType*): *Entry*;
>   **procedure** *KeyOf*(*x*: *Entry*): *KeyType*;
>   **procedure** *ValueOf*(*x*: *Entry*): *ValueType*;
>   **procedure** *Update*(*x*: *Entry*; *value*: *ValueType*);
>
>   **type** *SymbolTable*;
>
>   **procedure** *Initialize*(**var** *S*: *SymbolTable*);
>   **procedure** *Insert*(*x*: *Entry*; **var** *S*: *SymbolTable*);
>   **procedure** *Delete*(*x*: *Entry*; **var** *S*: *SymbolTable*);
>   **procedure** *Retrieve*(*key*: *KeyType*; **var** *S*: *SymbolTable*): *Entry*;
>
> **end** *SymTab*.

The first group of operations is for handling isolated entries. Entries may be created, their keys and values accessed, and their values (but not their keys) changed. The *Initialize* operation initializes a symbol table to empty. The other three symbol table operations allow an entry to be inserted into a symbol table, to be deleted (but not destroyed), and to be retrieved by key (but not deleted). If an entry with the given key cannot be found, *Retrieve* returns *NilEntry*.

Abstractly, a symbol table defines a mapping (function) from keys to values. The mapping is modified by insertions and deletions, and accessed by retrievals.

Occasionally additional operations are needed, based on an ordering of the keys. There are a variety of possible operations of this type, but the following are typical:

procedure *RetrieveMin*(**var** *S*: *SymbolTable*): *Entry*;
procedure *RetrieveFrom*(*key*: *KeyType*; **var** *S*: *SymbolTable*): *Entry*;
procedure *RetrieveNext*(*x*: *Entry*; **var** *S*: *SymbolTable*): *Entry*;

RetrieveMin retrieves the entry with minimum key; *RetrieveFrom* retrieves the entry with minimum key not less than the given key; and *RetrieveNext* retrieves the entry whose key is next in order to the key of the given entry. All these operations return *NilEntry* if no suitable entry can be found. The last two make it possible to retrieve all entries whose keys lie in the range [*a, b*]:

x := *RetrieveFrom*(*a, S*);
while (*x* ≠ *NilEntry*) **and** (*KeyOf*(*x*) ≤ *b*) **do**
    Visit(*x*);
    x := *RetrieveNext*(*x, S*);
end;

A symbol table with extra operations of this type is called an *ordered symbol table*.

6.2   Linked Lists

When it is known that the symbol table will always be small (say, containing no more than about 20 entries), it is not worth while to use the elaborate implementations that will shortly be studied. A simple list of the entries is sufficient:

The entries could be kept in sorted order, but since this complicates the code slightly, and has no significant effect on efficiency, sorting is not recommended unless ordered symbol table operations are required.

The operations are easily implemented using the *List* ADT from Section 3.2, so they will not be repeated here in any detail. For the record, however, here is *Insert*:

```
procedure Insert(x: Entry; var S: SymbolTable);
var y: Entry;
begin
   y := FirstEntry(S);
   while y ≠ NilEntry do
      if KeyOf(y) = KeyOf(x) then
         Error("SymbolTable.Insert: key already present");
      end;
      y := NextEntry(y, S);
   end;
   S := Append(MakeList(x), S);
end Insert;
```

Care has been taken to check for duplicate keys before inserting *x*.

The reader may easily verify that most of the operations have $O(n)$ complexity, making this implementation unsuitable for all but small tables. The next section describes an interesting variant of the method.

6.3 Locality of Reference and Self-adjusting Lists

In the context of symbol tables, *locality of reference* is the name given to the tendency for retrievals of a given symbol to cluster together in the operation sequence.

Locality of reference is hard to quantify, but it is very common. For example, when a compiler encounters the statement $n := n + 1$, two retrievals of the symbol *n* will be generated, one immediately following the other. Customers of a bank may request two or three transactions on their accounts within a minute or two, then not visit the bank again for a week.

If significant locality of reference is expected, it may be worthwhile to adapt the implementation to take advantage of it. One simple way to do this, which applies to any data structure, is to remember the most recently accessed entry (an *access* is an insertion or retrieval). The first step in a retrieval is to compare the key being looked for with the key of the remembered entry. If they are equal, a search of the data structure is avoided. Several entries could be remembered and checked before the data structure is searched. A computer's memory is generally organized in this way; the set of remembered entries is called a *cache memory* by computer architects, and it is very effective in reducing the average cost of accessing memory.

Operation sequences are not obliged to exhibit locality of reference, so in the worst case no advantage is gained from this scheme, and in fact one is slightly worse off. Interest in it arises from the conviction that, if a probability model of operation sequences which incorporated the locality of reference that occurs in real sequences could be constructed, then the average complexity analysis would show that the method has value. Of course, the usual problems of finding credible probability models may prevent this analysis from being done; but there might be empirical evidence to support this conviction. Methods like 'remember the most recently accessed entry', whose advantages seem real but not readily quantifiable, are called *heuristics*.

In the remainder of this section, these ideas are applied to the unsorted linked list:

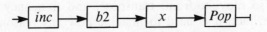

To insert an entry, the entire list is scanned to make sure that the new key is not already present, then the new entry is added to the back (in the example above, after *Pop*). It will be convenient to take the cost of this to be $n + 1$, although only n comparisons between keys are made. To retrieve an entry, the list is searched sequentially. The cost of retrieving the ith entry is i comparisons between keys.

It is not hard to think of a variety of plausible heuristics for improving the performance of this data structure; research has concentrated on three:

(1) *Move-to-front* (*MF*): After accessing an entry, move it to the front of the list.
(2) *Transpose* (*T*): After accessing an entry, if it is not the first entry then exchange it with its predecessor in the list.
(3) *Frequency count* (*FC*): Record in each entry the number of times it has been accessed, and keep the list sorted in non-increasing order of this number.

The rationale for each of these heuristics should be clear. Move-to-front expects the accessed entry to be accessed again very soon; if this happens immediately, the second access will cost only 1. Transpose has similar ideas, but is more timid about disturbing the status quo. Frequency count expects that some entries will be accessed more often than others, but bases its decisions on the entire history of the operation sequence, rather than on the hope of exploiting locality of reference. A linked list equipped with a heuristic like these is called a *self-adjusting* (or *self-organizing*) *list*.

All self-adjusting lists have a worst-case complexity of $O(n)$ per operation, for the simple reason that, no matter how cleverly the list is reordered, there is always an entry at the back, and it could be the one that is accessed next. (This type of observation is called an *adversary argument*, and is studied in Section 11.2.) Self-adjusting lists are therefore unsuitable as symbol table implementations in their own right, but they can be used to improve the performance of the lists in a chained hash table (Section 6.8).

Analysis of self-adjusting lists.   An interesting way to compare the performance of these heuristics has been found by Sleator and Tarjan (1985a). A self-adjusting list heuristic is said to be *admissible* if it takes the form, 'after accessing an entry, move it zero or more places forward in the list'. No restriction is placed on how the amount of movement is determined, so move-to-front, transpose, and frequency count are all admissible; in fact, it is hard to imagine how any reasonable heuristic could fail to be admissible. The movement of an entry one step forward in the list is called an *exchange*.

For any heuristic H and sequence of symbol table operations p, $C_H(p)$ is defined to be the total cost of the sequence when applied to a self-adjusting list with heuristic H. Similarly, $E_H(p)$ is the total number of exchanges made.

Theorem 6.1:   For any admissible heuristic H, and any sequence p of m insertions and successful retrievals, starting with the empty list,

$$C_{MF}(p) \le 2C_H(p) - E_H(p) - m$$

That is, the total cost under the move-to-front heuristic is never more than twice the cost under any other admissible heuristic.

Proof: The idea behind this proof is to run MF and H side by side on p, comparing the costs incurred on each operation. At each intermediate moment, the two lists will contain the same entries, but in different orders. For example, if H is transpose, then Table 6.1 applies.

The total costs are $C_{MF}(p) = 1 + 2 + 3 + 4 + 1 + 4 + 1 = 16$, and $C_T(p) = 1 + 2 + 3 + 4 + 3 + 4 + 3 = 20$. Transpose makes $E_T(p) = 0 + 1 + 1 + 1 + 1 + 1 + 1 = 6$ exchanges, and there are 7 operations, so the theorem states that $16 \le 2 \cdot 20 - 6 - 7$.

Table 6.1

	MF	T
$Insert(a, S)$	a	a
$Insert(b, S)$	$b \to a$	$b \to a$
$Insert(c, S)$	$c \to b \to a$	$b \to c \to a$
$Insert(d, S)$	$d \to c \to b \to a$	$b \to c \to d \to a$
$Retrieve(d, S)$	$d \to c \to b \to a$	$b \to d \to c \to a$
$Retrieve(a, S)$	$a \to d \to c \to b$	$b \to d \to a \to c$
$Retrieve(a, S)$	$a \to d \to c \to b$	$b \to a \to d \to c$

If the entries happen to be in the same order in both lists, the cost of the next operation will be the same for both heuristics. The situation becomes unbalanced when the orders become very different. An *inversion* is a pair of distinct entries $\{x, y\}$ such that x precedes y in one list and y precedes x in the other. For example, the two final lists above yield the inversions $\{a, b\}$, $\{d, b\}$, and $\{c, b\}$. The total number of inversions, which in this example is 3, is a measure of how differently the entries are ordered in the two lists.

The total amortized complexity of p under the move-to-front heuristic will now be determined. This will be an upper bound on $C_{MF}(p)$. For our potential function we will use the total number of inversions between MF's list and H's list.

Suppose the ith operation is $Retrieve(x, S)$, and that x is the jth element of MF's list and the kth element of H's list. For convenience, the two lists are shown as arrays:

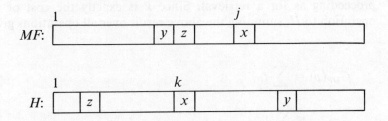

The actual complexity of the retrieval is j. Following it, x is moved to the front of MF's list, and moved forward e_i places (say) on H's list. The change in potential that these movements cause must be calculated.

First consider the effect on Φ of moving x to the front of MF's list; x passes over $j - 1$ entries during this move. An entry like y in the example above, which formed an inversion with x before the move, no longer does so afterwards; while an entry like z, which did not form an inversion with x before the move, does form one afterwards. If c is the number of entries preceding x in MF's list that form an inversion with x before the move, c inversions are destroyed by the move, and $j - 1 - c$ inversions are created.

With x now at the front of MF's list, every entry that precedes x in H's list forms an inversion with x. So when x moves forward e_i places on H's list, exactly e_i inversions are destroyed. Therefore the amortized complexity of the retrieval is

$$
\begin{aligned}
a_i &= t_i + \Phi(S_i) - \Phi(S_{i-1}) \\
&= j - c + (j - 1 - c) - e_i \\
&= 2(j - 1 - c) - e_i + 1
\end{aligned}
$$

A clever observation can now be made: $j - 1 - c$ was the number of entries preceding x on MF's list which did not form an inversion with x. Therefore, these $j - 1 - c$ entries must also have preceded x on H's list, so $j - 1 - c \le k - 1$, and

$$
\begin{aligned}
a_i &\le 2(k - 1) - e_i + 1 \\
&= 2k - e_i - 1
\end{aligned}
$$

The analysis of insertions is very similar, beginning by adding x to the back of both lists, which does not change the potential, and then proceeding as for a retrieval. Since k is exactly the cost of the operation to H, summing the above result over all operations gives

$$
\begin{aligned}
C_{MF}(p) &= \sum_{i=1}^{m} t_i \\
&\le \sum_{i=1}^{m} a_i \\
&\le 2C_H(p) - E_H(p) - m
\end{aligned}
$$

and the theorem is proved.   ■

6.4 The Binary Search Tree

In this well-known implementation of the ordered symbol table ADT, the entries are stored, one per node, in a binary tree. Their keys obey the *binary search tree invariant*: the key of any node is greater than the keys of all the nodes in its left subtree, and less than the keys of all the nodes in its right subtree. For example,

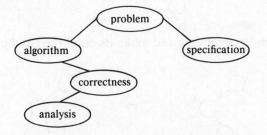

is a binary search tree. The keys are in alphabetical order, and values are not shown. An inorder traversal will visit the nodes in increasing key order, which makes the order-dependent operations easy to implement.

Type *Entry* is identified with a pointer to a node, *SymbolTable* with a pointer to the root of the tree, and *NilEntry* with a nil pointer (see Implementation Module 6.1).

Operations on the binary search tree are naturally expressed recursively. For example, to insert a new entry, its key is compared with the root. If it is smaller, it must be inserted in the left subtree; if larger, it goes into the right subtree. If the tree is empty, the new entry replaces it:

```
procedure Insert(x: Entry; var S: SymbolTable);
begin
  if S = nil then
    S := CAST(SymbolTable, x);
    x^.leftchild := nil;
    x^.rightchild := nil;
  elsif x^.key = S^.key then
    Error("SymbolTable.Insert: key already present");
  elsif x^.key < S^.key then
    Insert(x, S^.leftchild);
  else
    Insert(x, S^.rightchild);
  end;
end Insert;
```

This works correctly even when given an empty tree. In Implementation

Module 6.1 non-recursive implementations of the operations are given, since recursion has some cost.

Deletion of a node x is a little more complicated. If x has no children, it can simply be removed:

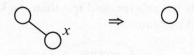

If x has one child, remove x and make its child the child of x's parent:

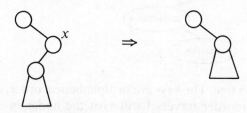

If x has two children, find its inorder predecessor y, which is the rightmost node of x's left subtree, and delete it. Since $y^\wedge.rightchild = $ **nil**, this involves applying one of the first two cases above. Then substitute y for x and remove x. For example, this is what happens when the root of this tree is deleted:

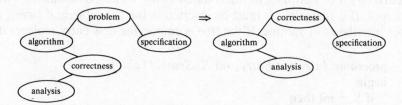

The implementation of this algorithm is rather messy. Notice that the parent of x must be known. This requires either that parent pointers be added to the implementation, or that the deletion begin with a search downwards from the root to x.

Taking one comparison between keys (with a three-way outcome) as the characteristic operation, and letting n be the number of entries in the tree, the worst-case complexity of each operation is easily seen to be $O(n)$. For example, the worst-case complexity of an insertion into a binary search tree T is equal to $h(T)$, the height of the tree. This is maximized when T is skew, when its value is n. This worst case would occur, for example, if entries were inserted in increasing order; in effect, the tree has degenerated into a list.

The binary search tree can be expected to do much better than this on the average. In the next section, it will be shown that, loosely speaking, the average complexity is $O(\log n)$ per operation.

6.5   Analysis of Binary Search Tree Insertions

Intuitively, the binary search tree should perform much better than indicated by the worst-case analysis just seen. This suggests that an average complexity analysis should be performed. Unfortunately, a true average complexity analysis of the binary search tree implementation of the symbol table as a whole cannot be done, because no meaningful probabilities for the instances can be found.

Instead, the average complexity of a sequence of n insertions into an initially empty tree can be analysed:

type *Entries* = **array** [1..n] **of** *Entry*;

procedure *Build*(*A*: *Entries*);
  S: *SymbolTable*;
begin
  Initialize(*S*);
  for i := 1 **to** n **do**
    Insert(*A*[i], *S*);
  end;
end *Build*;

The average complexity of *Build* will provide some insight into the average behaviour of the binary search tree, while avoiding the intractable problems of the full analysis.

A sequence of keys like ⟨problem, specification, correctness, analysis⟩ might just as well be ⟨3, 4, 2, 1⟩, since *Build* treats the two identically. So the instances of *Build* are just the $n!$ permutations of the numbers 1, 2, . . . , n. For example, if n = 3 there are six permutations; and denoting by $B(a)$ the tree produced by *Build*(*a*):

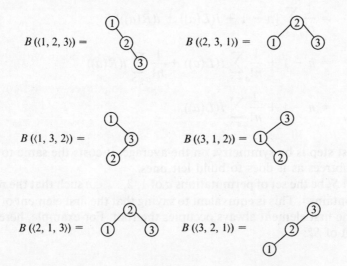

The cost of inserting a node x is equal to its depth in $B(a)$, since x is compared once with each of its proper ancestors during its insertion. Summing over all nodes, the total cost of $Build(a)$ is the internal path length $i(B(a))$. For example, the cost of building $B(\langle 2, 1, 3 \rangle)$ is $0 + 1 + 1 = 2$. Since skew trees have maximal internal path length, namely $n(n - 1)/2$, this shows that the worst-case complexity of $Build(a)$ is $W(n) = n(n - 1)/2$.

For the average complexity analysis, it may as well be assumed that a is equally likely to be any element of the set S_n of permutations of 1, 2, ..., n. Averaging over these $n!$ instances gives

$$A(n) = \sum_{a \in S_n} \frac{1}{n!} i(B(a))$$

For example, $A(3) = [3 + 3 + 2 + 2 + 3 + 3]/6 = 8/3$.

This difficult sum for $A(n)$ can be converted into a recurrence equation. Clearly $A(0) = 0$. For $n > 0$, let

$$B(a) = \quad$$

Now $i(B(a)) = n - 1 + i(L(a)) + i(R(a))$, as is known from the proof of Theorem 5.1. Therefore

$$A(n) = \frac{1}{n!} \sum_{a \in S_n} i(B(a))$$

$$= \frac{1}{n!} \sum_{a \in S_n} [n - 1 + i(L(a)) + i(R(a))]$$

$$= n - 1 + \frac{1}{n!} \sum_{a \in S_n} i(L(a)) + \frac{1}{n!} \sum_{a \in S_n} i(R(a))$$

$$= n - 1 + \frac{2}{n!} \sum_{a \in S_n} i(L(a))$$

This last step is by symmetry: on the average, it costs the same to build right subtrees as it does to build left ones.

Let S_n^j be the set of permutations a of 1, 2, ..., n such that the root of $B(a)$ contains j. This is equivalent to saying that the first element of a is j, since the first element always occupies the root. For example, here is an element of S_8^6:

$$B(a) =$$

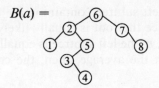

The example shows that, if $a \in S_n^j$, $L(a)$ is determined by the order in which the numbers $1, 2, \ldots, j - 1$ appear within a. Since there are $(j - 1)!$ possible orderings (permutations) of $1, 2, \ldots, j - 1$, all equally likely to occur within S_n^j, and since S_n^j has $(n - 1)!$ elements, each permutation of $1, 2, \ldots, j - 1$ must occur exactly $(n - 1)!/(j - 1)!$ times within S_n^j. As far as its effect on left subtrees is concerned, S_n^j is just $(n - 1)!/(j - 1)!$ copies of S_{j-1}. Therefore,

$$\sum_{a \in S_n^j} i(L(a)) = \frac{(n - 1)!}{(j - 1)!} \sum_{a \in S_{j-1}} i(B(a)) = (n - 1)! A(j - 1)$$

by the definition of $A(n)$. Immediately then

$$A(n) = n - 1 + \frac{2}{n!} \sum_{a \in S_n} i(L(a))$$

$$= n - 1 + \frac{2}{n!} \sum_{j=1}^{n} \sum_{a \in S_n^j} i(L(a))$$

$$= n - 1 + \frac{2}{n!} \sum_{j=1}^{n} (n - 1)! A(j - 1)$$

and so, as promised, a recurrence equation has been found for $A(n)$:

$$A(0) = 0$$

$$A(n) = n - 1 + \frac{2}{n} \sum_{j=1}^{n} A(j - 1)$$

There is a less formal derivation of this formula, which runs as follows. To build an 'average' tree, the root must be inserted, and then $n - 1$ comparisons made between it and the other keys as they pass through the root on the way to the left and right subtrees:

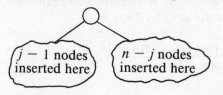

To build an average left subtree containing $j - 1$ nodes costs $A(j - 1)$ comparisons, and, since the root is equally likely to contain any one of the numbers $1, 2, \ldots, n$, the left subtree is equally likely to contain $0, 1, \ldots, n - 1$ nodes. On the average, then, the cost of building the left subtree must be

$$\frac{1}{n} \sum_{j=1}^{n} A(j - 1)$$

and, by symmetry, the average right subtree has the same cost, giving

$$A(n) = n - 1 + \frac{2}{n} \sum_{j=1}^{n} A(j - 1)$$

for the average complexity of *Build*, as before. This derivation should be treated with caution: it does gloss over some points that are more carefully handled in the first derivation.

The first step in solving the recurrence equation is to eliminate the summation, which is done by a clever trick. Multiplying by n,

$$nA(n) = n(n - 1) + 2 \sum_{j=1}^{n} A(j - 1)$$

and substituting $n - 1$ for n gives

$$(n - 1) A(n - 1) = (n - 1)(n - 2) + 2 \sum_{j=1}^{n-1} A(j - 1)$$

Now subtracting the second equation from the first, the summation disappears:

$$nA(n) - (n - 1) A(n - 1) = n(n - 1) - (n - 1)(n - 2) + 2A(n - 1)$$

and so

$$nA(n) = 2(n - 1) + (n + 1) A(n - 1)$$

It is possible to divide by n and apply repeated substitution, but the algebra is simpler dividing by $2n(n + 1)$:

$$\frac{A(n)}{2(n + 1)} = \frac{(n - 1)}{n(n + 1)} + \frac{A(n - 1)}{2n}$$

By partial fractions, $(n - 1)/n(n + 1) = 2/(n + 1) - 1/n$, so

$$\frac{A(n)}{2(n + 1)} = \frac{2}{n + 1} - \frac{1}{n} + \frac{A(n - 1)}{2n}$$

$$= \frac{2}{n + 1} - \frac{1}{n} + \left[\frac{2}{n} - \frac{1}{n - 1} + \frac{A(n - 2)}{2(n - 1)}\right]$$

$$= \frac{2}{n + 1} - \frac{1}{n} + \left[\frac{2}{n} - \frac{1}{n - 1} + \left[\frac{2}{n - 1} - \frac{1}{n - 2}\right.\right.$$
$$\left.\left. + \frac{A(n - 3)}{2(n - 2)}\right]\right]$$

$$= \frac{2}{n + 1} + \frac{2}{n} + \frac{2}{n - 1} - \frac{1}{n} - \frac{1}{n - 1} - \frac{1}{n - 2}$$
$$+ \frac{A(n - 3)}{2(n - 2)}$$

$$= \ldots$$

$$= \frac{2}{n + 1} + \frac{2}{n} + \ldots + \frac{2}{n - (i - 2)} - \frac{1}{n} - \frac{1}{n - 1} - \ldots$$
$$- \frac{1}{n - (i - 1)} + \frac{A(n - i)}{2(n - (i - 1))}$$

and letting $i = n$,

$$\frac{A(n)}{2(n + 1)} = \frac{2}{(n + 1)} + \frac{2}{n} + \ldots + \frac{2}{2} - \frac{1}{n} - \frac{1}{n - 1} - \ldots - \frac{1}{1} + 0$$

$$= \frac{2}{(n + 1)} + 2\left[\frac{1}{n} + \frac{1}{n - 1} + \ldots + \frac{1}{2}\right] - \left[\frac{1}{n} + \frac{1}{n - 1}\right.$$
$$\left. + \ldots + \frac{1}{2}\right] - \frac{1}{1}$$

$$= \frac{2}{(n + 1)} + \left[\frac{1}{n} + \frac{1}{n - 1} + \ldots + \frac{1}{2}\right] + \frac{1}{1} - 2$$

$$= \sum_{i=1}^{n} 1/i - \frac{2n}{n + 1}$$

and finally, multiplying through by $2(n + 1)$, proves

> **Theorem 6.2:**   The average complexity of a sequence of n insertions into an initially empty binary search tree, assuming that each of the $n!$ distinct permutations of $1, 2, \ldots, n$ is equally likely to be an instance, is
>
> $$A(n) = 2(n + 1)H_n - 4n$$
>
> where $H_n = \sum_{i=1}^{n} 1/i$ is the nth *Harmonic number*.   ■

The formula $\sum_{i=1}^{n} 1/i$ cannot be simplified any further, as far as anyone knows, but there is an approximation $H_n \approx \ln n + \gamma$, where $\gamma \approx 0.5572$ is Euler's constant. So $A(n)$ is about $1.38n\log_2 n$ for the n insertions, which, loosely speaking, is $O(\log n)$ per insertion — considerably less than the worst case.

This analysis can be extended to include retrievals (Exercise 6.6) and updates (which are $O(1)$, since a pointer to the entry is given). But it tells us nothing about the binary search tree when deletions occur, and in fact almost nothing is known (Knuth, 1973b).

6.6   Splay Trees

In Section 6.3 several heuristics for adjusting a linked list to take advantage of locality of reference in the operation sequence were studied. The most successful one was move-to-front: after accessing entry x, move it to the front of the list. This suggests that the analogous heuristic for binary search trees should be tried: after accessing node x, move it to the root of the tree, where it will be found quickly by subsequent accesses.

A binary search tree is not as simple to adjust as a linked list, because the condition that the key in a node be greater than all the keys in its left subtree and smaller than all the keys in its right subtree must be preserved. (This condition was called the *binary search tree invariant* in Section 6.4.) Nevertheless, there is a way.

Consider any internal node y that has a left child x which is also internal. A *right rotation at y* adjusts the tree so that y becomes the right child of x:

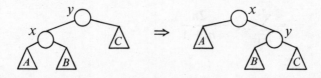

A, *B*, and *C* are arbitrary subtrees, possibly empty. The adjusted tree has the same nodes as the original, and, most important, the binary search tree invariant is preserved. This is easily verified by traversing the two trees in inorder: both give the ordering *A*, *x*, *B*, *y*, *C*, so if the invariant holds in the first tree, it holds in the second.

A *left rotation* is similar, going the other way:

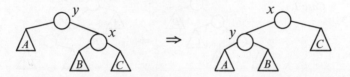

Again, the binary search tree invariant is preserved. These rotations provide a general way to adjust binary trees; they were first used by Adel'son-Vel'skii and Landis (1962).

Rotations are useful here because in each case the depth of node *x* decreases by 1. Thus, a sequence of rotations at the parent of *x* will move *x* to the root. For example,

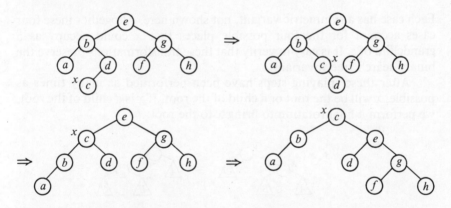

This gives a first heuristic for binary search trees: after accessing (that is, inserting or retrieving) a node *x*, move it to the root by a sequence of left and right rotations. This heuristic, which is called *move-to-root*, has been studied by Allen and Munro (1978) and by Bitner (1979).

Move-to-root should improve the performance of the binary search tree when there is locality of reference in the operation sequence, but it is not ideal. The final tree in the example above is marginally less balanced than the starting tree, and the example

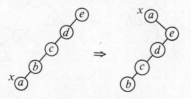

makes it clear that move-to-root will not turn an unbalanced tree into a balanced one.

Sleator and Tarjan (1985b) have found a way to move x to the root and simultaneously clean up an unbalanced tree. They perform the equivalent of two rotations at each *splaying step*:

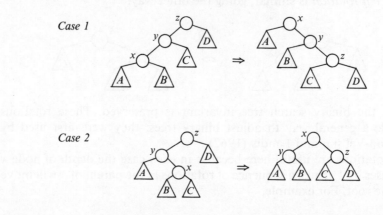

Each case has a symmetric variant, not shown here. Altogether these four cases account for the four possible places that x could occupy as a grandchild of z. It is easy to verify that these transformations preserve the binary search tree invariant.

After these splaying steps have been performed as many times as possible, x will be the root or a child of the root. If x is a child of the root, we perform a final rotation to bring x to the root:

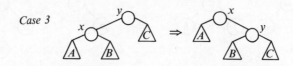

The whole process is called a *splay at x*, and a binary search tree with splaying is called a *splay tree*.

It happens that Cases 2 and 3 do exactly what move-to-root would do in the same situation. However, applying move-to-root to Case 1 would yield

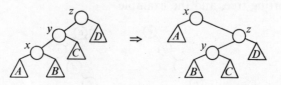

which is not the same. The crucial difference is that, while move-to-root leaves B at its original depth, the splaying step moves both subtrees of x up at least one level. Although subtrees C and D appear to lose out in splaying's Case 1 transformation, they become descendants of x and so move upwards in later splaying steps. Here is a larger example which shows clearly how splaying balances an unbalanced tree:

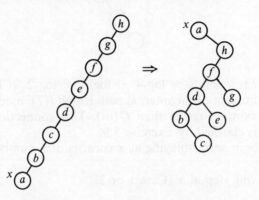

When implemented carefully, splay trees are very fast in practice (Jones, 1986).

Amortized analysis of splay trees.   An insertion or retrieval has two stages: the search down some path, followed by splaying back up the path. The search can be ignored, since its cost is of the same order as the splay, and the number of rotations performed while splaying (or equivalently, the depth of the accessed node) can be taken as the measure of complexity.

The potential function used in this analysis is quite remarkable. Let $s(x)$ be the number of nodes in the subtree rooted at x, and let $r(x)$, the *rank* of x, be defined by $r(x) = \log_2 s(x)$. For any splay tree T, define

$$\Phi(T) = \sum_{x \in T} r(x) = \sum_{x \in T} \log_2 s(x)$$

If T is complete, Φ is small. For example,

$$T = \quad$$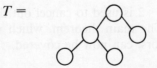

yields $\Phi(T) = \log_2 5 + \log_2 3 + 3\log_2 1 \approx 3.9$. If T is skew, $\Phi(T)$ is large:

$$T =$$

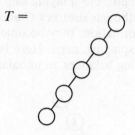

yielding $\Phi(T) = \log_2 5 + \log_2 4 + \log_2 3 + \log_2 2 + \log_2 1 \approx 5.9$. So $\Phi(T)$ is reminiscent of the internal path length $i(T)$, modified to have an $O(n\log n)$ maximum rather than $O(n^2)$. This connection with internal path length is clarified by Exercise 5.9.

As has been seen, splaying at x consists of a number of steps:

1   splaying step at x (Case 1 or 2)

⋮   ⋮

i splaying step at x (Case 1 or 2)

⋮   ⋮

m splaying step at x (Case 1, 2 or 3)

The amortized complexity $a_i = t_i + \Phi(T_i) - \Phi(T_{i-1})$ will be calculated for each step. Then the total amortized complexity of all the steps will equal the amortized complexity of splaying at x, which is taken to be the cost of the insertion or retrieval.

Before starting the main analysis, the following technical lemma is required.

Lemma: For all α and β such that $\alpha > 0$, $\beta > 0$, and $\alpha + \beta \le 1$, $\log_2\alpha + \log_2\beta \le -2$.

Proof: Since $\log_2\alpha + \log_2\beta = \log_2\alpha\beta$, and the logarithm is a monotone increasing function, its value will be maximum when $\alpha\beta$ is maximum. In the given region, it is clear that this occurs when $\alpha = \beta = 1/2$, when $\log_2\alpha + \log_2\beta = -2$. ∎

As will be seen, this -2 is used to cancel out the actual complexity of 2 per splaying step. The main theorem, which was named the 'Access Lemma' by its inventors, can now be covered.

Theorem 6.3 (Access Lemma for Splay Trees):   Suppose that node x has size $s_{i-1}(x)$ and rank $r_{i-1}(x)$ just before the ith splaying step, and that after the step its size and rank are $s_i(x)$ and $r_i(x)$. Then the amortized complexity of the ith splaying step is at most $3r_i(x) - 3r_{i-1}(x)$, unless it is the final step, in which case the amortized complexity is at most $1 + 3r_i(x) - 3r_{i-1}(x)$.

Proof: Consider first the amortized complexity of a Case 1 splaying step:

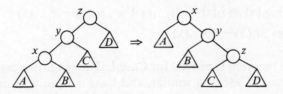

The actual complexity is two rotations, and only x, y, and z change in size and rank. So

$$a_i = t_i + \Phi(T_i) - \Phi(T_{i-1})$$
$$= 2 + r_i(x) + r_i(y) + r_i(z) - r_{i-1}(x) - r_{i-1}(y) - r_{i-1}(z)$$
$$= 2 + r_i(y) + r_i(z) - r_{i-1}(x) - r_{i-1}(y)$$

This last line follows because $s_{i-1}(z)$, the size of the subtree rooted at z before the step, equals $s_i(x)$, the size of the subtree rooted at x after the step.

Now before the step, y is an ancestor of x, so $r_{i-1}(y) \geq r_{i-1}(x)$. Similarly, after the step, y is a descendant of x, so $r_i(y) \leq r_i(x)$. Substituting these values gives

$$a_i \leq 2 + r_i(x) + r_i(z) - 2r_{i-1}(x)$$

The lemma is now used to cancel out the actual complexity of 2. Let $\alpha = s_{i-1}(x)/s_i(x)$, and let $\beta = s_i(z)/s_i(x)$. Clearly, $\alpha > 0$ and $\beta > 0$, but we also have

$$\alpha + \beta = (s_{i-1}(x) + s_i(z))/s_i(x) \leq 1$$

This follows because, as the diagram above shows, $s_{i-1}(x)$ encompasses A, x, and B; $s_i(z)$ encompasses C, z, and D; and together these contain exactly one node less than $s_i(x)$. Therefore, by the lemma,

$$\log_2(s_{i-1}(x)/s_i(x)) + \log_2(s_i(z)/s_i(x)) \leq -2$$

so that

$$r_{i-1}(x) + r_i(z) - 2r_i(x) \leq -2$$

and then

$$2r_i(x) - r_{i-1}(x) - r_i(z) - 2 \geq 0.$$

This non-negative quantity can now be added to the expression for a_i above, giving

$$a_i \leq [2 + r_i(x) + r_i(z) - 2r_{i-1}(x)] + [2r_i(x) - r_{i-1}(x) - r_i(z) - 2]$$
$$= 3r_i(x) - 3r_{i-1}(x)$$

and the theorem is proved for Case 1. The other two cases are left as an exercise; Case 2 is similar, and Case 3 is quite simple.   ∎

Now the total amortized complexity of an insertion or retrieval is

$$\sum_{i=1}^{m} a_i = \sum_{i=1}^{m-1} a_i + a_m$$
$$\leq \sum_{i=1}^{m-1} (3r_i(x) - 3r_{i-1}(x)) + 1 - 3r_m(x) - 3r_{m-1}(x)$$
$$= 1 + 3r_m(x) - 3r_0(x)$$
$$\leq 1 + 3r_m(x)$$
$$= 1 + 3\log_2 n$$

since x is the root after the final rotation, so that $s_m(x) = n$. Thus the amortized complexity of an insertion or retrieval is $O(\log n)$. Any sequence of m of these splay tree operations will have $O(m\log n)$ worst-case complexity, which is much better than the $O(mn)$ worst-case complexity of the binary search tree.

6.7 B-trees

Having studied the binary search treee, which has $O(\log n)$ average complexity per operation, and the splay tree, which has $O(\log n)$ amortized complexity, a data structure of $O(\log n)$ complexity in the worst case, the *B-tree* of Bayer and McCreight (1972), will now be considered.

The B-tree is only one of a large class of tree structures which achieve this performance; the first was the AVL tree of Adel'son-Vel'skii and Landis (1962). The B-tree has been chosen because it is a popular method of implementing ordered symbol tables on disk units – that is, databases – and so is the most widely used of all the methods.

First, the binary search tree is generalized. A *multiway search tree* may have more than one entry in each node. For example,

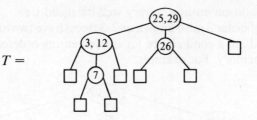

$T =$

is a multiway search tree. The entries within each node are stored in sorted order. For each gap between two entries, there is a subtree containing all the entries whose keys lie between those two entries. To the left of the entry with the smallest key in the node is a subtree whose entries are all smaller than that entry; similarly there is a subtree containing large entries at the right end. Thus, the number of subtrees of any internal node is one greater than the number of keys in the node.

Searching and traversal in a multiway search tree are simple generalizations of the corresponding algorithms for binary search trees. For example, consider searching for a key x in the tree shown above. If $x < 25$ the search goes left; if $25 < x < 29$ the search goes down; and if $29 < x$ the search goes right. Linear search within the node may be used if there are only a few entries in it, or binary search if there are many. The process is repeated recursively. Traversal in inorder is also quite simple: to traverse a tree T, traverse its first subtree, then visit the first entry of its root, then traverse the second subtree, etc., finishing with a traverse of the last subtree.

A *B-tree of order m* is a multiway search tree that obeys the following invariant:

(1) The root is either an external node, or it has between 2 and m children inclusive;
(2) Every internal node (except possibly the root) has between $\lceil m/2 \rceil$ and m children inclusive;
(3) The external nodes all have equal depth.

For example, here are some B-trees of order $m = 4$:

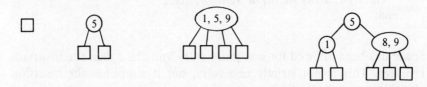

The first two conditions make it possible to allocate a fixed amount of memory to each node (space for m links, $m - 1$ entries, and a count field), yet be sure of wasting less than half of it, except possibly in the root.

The third condition ensures a very well-balanced tree.

B-trees of order 3 (also known as 2-3 trees) have two or three children per node, and are a good choice for implementing ordered symbol tables in internal memory. For example,

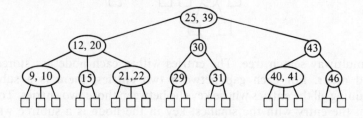

is a 2-3 tree. B-trees on disk units typically have $m = 256$ or more, chosen so that one node fits neatly into one disk block. This makes for a very shallow tree, which reduces the number of nodes examined (and hence the number of disk accesses) during searching. In such applications it is common to store only the keys in the internal nodes, keeping the values in the external nodes. This is done to make m as large as possible.

The type declarations might look like this:

```
type Entry = pointer to
record
    key: KeyType;
    value: ValueType;
end;

type EntryArray = array [1..m] of Entry;

type SymbolTable = pointer to treenode;

type treenode =
record
    count: [1..m];
    entries: EntryArray;
    children: array [0..m] of SymbolTable;
end;
```

Space has been allowed for one more entry and child than the invariant requires. This is not strictly necessary, but it simplifies the insertion algorithm, as will shortly be seen.

The B-tree invariant is rather stringent, and it is not obvious that efficient insertion and deletion algorithms which preserve it exist. Let us begin by inserting 44 into the 2-3 tree given above:

Insertions are always made in the first instance into internal nodes of maximum depth. If there is room there, any entries with larger keys are shuffled up and the insertion is made. If the node is full (for example, now insert 45), it is first inserted there anyway, creating a 'problem node' with m keys:

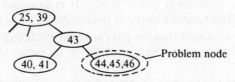

and then the problem node is split into three pieces: a node containing the first $\lceil m/2 \rceil - 1$ entries; a single entry, the $\lceil m/2 \rceil$ th; and a node containing the remaining $m - \lceil m/2 \rceil$ entries:

Then the isolated entry is inserted into the parent node:

Notice that one pointer in the parent is replaced by two pointers and one entry. These insertions into parents may propagate upwards if the parent is full. For example, if 42 is now inserted:

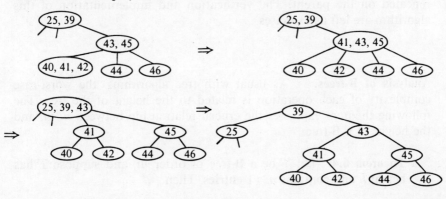

The height of the B-tree increases by one in this example, because the root was split.

It is easy to see that the B-tree invariant is preserved by this insertion algorithm. All nodes end up with at most m children, since otherwise they are split in two. All nodes except possibly the root end up with at least $\lceil m/2 \rceil - 1$ entries, since the two new nodes have $\lceil m/2 \rceil - 1$ and $m - \lceil m/2 \rceil$ entries respectively, and $m - \lceil m/2 \rceil \geq \lceil m/2 \rceil - 1$. Finally, external nodes change their depth only when the root is split, and this increases all depths by 1, so condition 3 is maintained. The algorithm is presented in Figure 6.1.

As usual, deletion is rather tricky. It is assumed that a pointer to a node and the index of the entry in that node which is to be deleted are given. It is also assumed that the parent of the node can be found. The simplest way to obtain this information is to begin the deletion with a retrieval.

First, if the entry x to be deleted does not lie at the bottom level, its inorder predecessor y (which must exist) must be found and x overwritten with y. This reduces the problem to the deletion of an entry from the bottom level.

The entry is removed by shuffling its right neighbours to the left. If the node still contains at least $\lceil m/2 \rceil - 1$ entries (as it usually will), then one can stop. Otherwise the node will contain $\lceil m/2 \rceil - 2$ entries, unless it is the root.

Next, the left or right sibling of this node is examined (if there is no sibling, the node must be the root and the process can stop). If the sibling contains more than $\lceil m/2 \rceil - 1$ entries, the entries can be distributed between the two nodes so that both nodes have at least $\lceil m/2 \rceil - 1$ entries.

Otherwise there are two sibling nodes containing $\lceil m/2 \rceil - 2$ and $\lceil m/2 \rceil - 1$ entries respectively. Together with the entry in the parent that separates these two nodes, this is $2\lceil m/2 \rceil - 2 \leq m - 1$ entries. These entries can be squeezed into one node, in a manner exactly inverse to the node splitting used by insertions.

Since the parent now has one less entry, the process may need to be repeated on the parent. The verification and implementation of this algorithm are left as exercises.

Analysis of B-trees.   As usual with tree algorithms, the worst-case complexity of each operation is related to the height of the tree. The following theorem expresses the crucial relationship between n, m, and the height of a B-tree.

Theorem 6.4: Let T be a B-tree of order m, and suppose T has height h and contains $n \geq 1$ entries. Then

$$n \geq 2\lceil m/2\rceil^{h-1} - 1$$

Proof: We construct the B-tree of order m and height h that contains the minimum possible number of entries, by assigning the minimum possible number to each node. The root has at least one entry, and all the other nodes have at least $\lceil m/2\rceil - 1$ entries, so this tree is

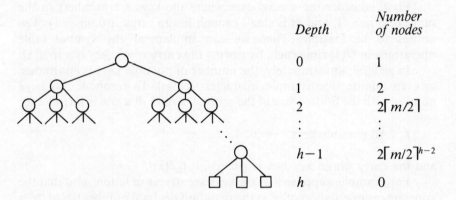

	Depth	Number of nodes
	0	1
	1	2
	2	$2\lceil m/2\rceil$
	⋮	⋮
	$h-1$	$2\lceil m/2\rceil^{h-2}$
	h	0

Excluding the root, the number of nodes is

$$2 + 2\lceil m/2\rceil + \ldots + 2\lceil m/2\rceil^{h-2} = 2\frac{\lceil m/2\rceil^{h-1} - 1}{\lceil m/2\rceil - 1}$$

by the standard formula for the sum of a geometric progression. Each of these nodes contains $\lceil m/2\rceil - 1$ entries, making $2(\lceil m/2\rceil^{h-1} - 1)$ entries altogether in these nodes. Plus one entry in the root gives a total of $2\lceil m/2\rceil^{h-1} - 1$ entries. Since this was the minimum possible, the result follows. ∎

Turning this result around, it can be seen immediately that any B-tree T of order m, containing $n \geq 1$ entries, has height

$$h(T) \leq \log_{\lceil m/2\rceil}\left(\frac{n+1}{2}\right) + 1$$

The cost of searching a node is $O(\log m)$, and the cost of shuffling entries is $O(m)$. However, m is a constant and so it is fair to consider both of these as $O(1)$. It follows that insertions and retrievals are $O(\log n)$ in the worst case.

6.8   Hashing

A radically different implementation of the symbol table ADT will now be considered: *hashing*. Hashing exploits the nature of random access memory to achieve $O(1)$ average complexity per operation, which is faster than any of the methods based on trees. Its worst case, however, is a poor $O(n)$, and it does not implement the ordered symbol table operations efficiently. It is widely used in compilers and databases.

First, consider the special case where the keys are numbers in the range 0 to $m - 1$, and m is small enough for an array $A[0..m - 1]$ of m entries to be feasible. Then we can implement the symbol table operations in $O(1)$ time each, by storing the entry whose key is x in $A[x]$.

In general, unfortunately, the number of possible keys is enormous, or even infinite (for example, character strings). To reconcile this huge number with the limited size of the array A, a *hash function* is introduced:

$$f: \{ \text{All possible keys} \} \rightarrow \{0, 1, \ldots, m - 1\}$$

and the entry whose key is x is stored in $A[f(x)]$.

For example, suppose that the keys are strings of letters, and that the concrete representation of 'a' is the two-digit decimal number 01, of 'b' is 02, etc. Then "fred" has concrete representation 06180509. Taking $m = 10$ and $f(x) = x \bmod m$ for the hash function,

$$f(\text{"fred"}) = 06180504 \bmod 10 = 4$$
$$f(\text{"inc"})\ = 091403 \bmod 10\ \ \ = 3$$
$$f(\text{"put"})\ = 162120 \bmod 10\ \ \ = 0$$

since the '**mod** 10' function simply returns the last decimal digit of its argument. Entries with these keys can be inserted into $A[0..9]$:

0	1	2	3	4	5	6	7	8	9
put			inc	fred					

A

Retrieval is easy. For example, to retrieve the entry whose key is "inc", $f(\text{"inc"}) = 3$ is calculated, and $A[3]$ examined.

Since f maps from a large set to a small one, it is inevitable that *collisions*, in which two keys hash to the same position, will occur. For example, $f(\text{"hd"}) = 4$, but $A[4]$ is already occupied. Strategies for resolving these collisions will be studied shortly.

Although collisions are inevitable, their frequency can be reduced by choosing a hash function which spreads the entries uniformly through the table. The value of a good hash function will be affected by all parts of the key, in an unpredictable way. For example, $x \bmod 256$ would not be used on a binary machine, because it depends only on the last 8 bits of x.

Choosing the middle k bits of x^2 is also poor, since it will yield 0 whenever x is small.

How then can one tell whether a hash function is good? In practice, it is checked to see that it does not have problems like those just considered, and then it is tested empirically. One simple function that has been found to work very well is

$$f(x) = x \bmod m$$

provided m is a prime number not close a power of 2. Knuth (1973b) discusses this hash function and several others. Unless the function is being implemented on hardware where division is unusually slow, there is no need to look further.

If the key is larger than a single machine word (for example, if it is a string of characters), it must first be compressed. This is most easily done by treating each element as an integer and adding them together. Of course, permutations like *abc* and *cba* will collide.

Resolving collisions   No matter how carefully the hash function is chosen, there will always be collisions, and the technical literature abounds with ingenious strategies for resolving them. A strategy called *chaining* is nearly always preferred; but before discussing chaining, two other strategies that are occasionally useful will be discussed.

Linear probing should be considered when memory is scarce. The entries are stored directly in the array. When a collision occurs, the array is searched to the right for a free slot to accommodate the new entry:

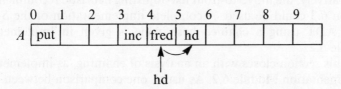

The search is circular: $A[0]$ follows $A[m-1]$. If the table is full, it is searched right through for a free slot, and fails when the search returns to the starting point. A retrieval must follow the same path, stopping either at the desired entry, or at the first free slot (in which case the entry is not present.

The worst-case complexity is clearly $O(n)$ per operation; its average complexity analysis is beyond the scope of this book (however, see Exercise 6.18). Although linear probing makes efficient use of memory, requiring no overhead at all, this advantage is bought at some cost. Its operations are tricky to implement, especially deletion (Exercise 6.16);

and if the table fills up, a tedious 'rehashing' is required: the entries must be moved to a new and larger table.

Buckets are used by hash tables stored on disk units when fast retrieval is more important than efficient use of space. The idea is to allow space for several entries at each position:

0	1	2	3	4	5	6	7	8	9
put			inc	fred					
				hd					

Typically, one bucket occupies one disk block, and since the entry with key x is almost always in bucket $A[f(x)]$, a retrieval is expected to require only about one disk block read on average. Bucket overflows may be handled by chaining or linear probing; a formal analysis is again beyond our scope.

Chaining is the simplest collision resolution strategy, and usually the best. Each element of the hash table is a pointer to a linked list of entries:

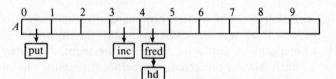

To retrieve an entry, its key is hashed and the appropriate list searched. If the entries are well spread through the table, this list can be expected to contain only a few entries, so they may be kept in no particular order. Alternatively, the move-to-front list-adjusting heuristic recommended in Section 6.3 could be used. A complete implementation of the *Symbol-Table* ADT using a chained hash table is given in Implementation Module 6.2.

This section closes with an analysis of chaining, as implemented in Implementation Module 6.2. As usual, one comparison between keys is taken as the characteristic operation, except for *Delete*, where one test of the form '$p \neq x$' is used.

In the worst case, the n entries all hash to the same position, and the analysis reduces to that of an unsorted linear list. Insertions, retrievals, and deletions are all obliged to search this list, so are $O(n)$.

There is a remarkable average complexity analysis of chaining – remarkable, because, for once, meaningful probabilities can be assigned to the instances, and the ADT analysed as a whole. Assume that the hash table is of size m, and that n entries are present. Nothing is assumed about where those n entries are.

Consider first the operation *Insert*(x, S). Assuming that x is equally likely to hash to any of the m table positions, this gives then Table 6.2.

Table 6.2

i	Instance	p_i	$T_i(n)$
1	$f(x) = 0$	$1/m$	Length of list 0
2	$f(x) = 1$	$1/m$	Length of list 1
	$\ldots$		
m	$f(x) = m - 1$	$1/m$	Length of list $m - 1$

So the average complexity of the insertion is

$$
\begin{aligned}
A(n) &= \sum_{i=0}^{m-1} p_i T_i(n) \\
&= \frac{1}{m} \sum_{i=0}^{m-1} [\text{Length of list } i] \\
&= n/m
\end{aligned}
$$

since the total length of all lists is just the total number of entries in the table, n. This analysis shows that, if $m \simeq n$, $A(n) = O(1)$.

Consider next an unsuccessful retrieval – that is, one which fails to find an entry with the desired key. Again it may be assumed that each table position is equally likely. The list must be scanned to the end, since the retrieval fails. But this situation is identical to an insertion, so the average complexity is again n/m.

When analysing successful retrievals, it cannot be assumed that each table position is equally likely to be the outcome of the hash. If the corresponding list is empty, for example, then clearly no successful retrieval will ever search it. A better assumption is that each of the n entries is equally likely to be the outcome of the retrieval, and an analysis will now be given based on this assumption. The analysis is not very rigorous, but it is simple and it gives the right answer (Knuth, 1973b).

Observe that the cost of retrieving an entry is one greater than the cost of inserting it (assuming that the insertion was at the back of the list). Consider the jth entry inserted into the table. The average cost of inserting it was shown above to be $(j - 1)/m$ comparisons, so the average cost of retrieving it is $(j - 1)/m + 1$. Averaging over the n entries, the average complexity of a successful retrieval is:

$$
\begin{aligned}
A(n) &= \frac{1}{n} \sum_{j=1}^{n} [(j - 1)/m + 1] \\
&= \frac{1}{nm} \sum_{j=1}^{n} (j - 1) + 1 \\
&= \frac{n - 1}{2m} + 1
\end{aligned}
$$

which is again $O(1)$ if $m \simeq n$. The reader is encouraged to check this formula for the cases $n = 1$ and $n = 2$.

Finally, deletion as implemented in Implementation Module 6.2 has the same cost as a successful retrieval, so if the deletion is equally likely to be applied to any entry, its average complexity is also $(n - 1)/2m + 1$.

6.9   Choosing a Symbol Table Implementation

This chapter concludes with some advice on how to choose the appropriate symbol table implementation for a given application.

The basic linked list should be used when n is known to be small (say, $n \le 20$); however, it is inefficient for larger n.

The $O(1)$ average complexity of hashing makes it very attractive, and it is widely used in compilers and databases. There are three circumstances when hashing is not appropriate: when efficiency in the worst case is desired (for example, in life-critical applications); when ordered symbol table operations are required; and when no reasonable choice for the table size can be made, since nothing is known about how many entries are expected (however, Exercise 6.19 overcomes this problem).

If hashing is chosen, the simplicity and efficiency of chaining generally make it the method of choice. Only if the entries are very small, on the order of the size of one pointer, would the space overhead of the links suggest a change to linear probing. In a chained hash table, the move-to-front heuristic is very cheap to implement, and will be worthwhile whenever there is locality of reference in the operation sequence. Hash tables on disk generally employ a number of hardware-dependent optimizations: the use of buckets, for example.

If hashing is rejected, some kind of search tree must be used. On disk, one would always choose some balanced multiway search tree like the B-tree, and optimize it to minimize the number of disk block reads, as described in Section 6.7. In memory, the binary search tree is often used: it provides good average complexity for the ordered symbol table operations, and is very simple. For greater efficiency, the more complex splay tree provides $O(\log n)$ amortized complexity per operation and in practice seems to run very fast. For $O(\log n)$ worst-case performance, a variety of balanced tree methods are available; 2-3 trees are as simple as any, although some of the others, for example red-black trees (Sedgewick, 1988), are also recommended.

The reader interested in further study of symbol table implementations will find many in Knuth (1973b). Knuth's treatment of hashing is particularly interesting, containing descriptions and analyses of a large number of ingenious variants.

EXERCISES

6.1 How does the move-to-front list-adjusting heuristic compare with making no adjustment at all?

6.2 Using the potential function given in the text, find the amortized complexity of a deletion in a linked list employing the move-to-front heuristic. Assume that the list must be scanned to find the deletion point.

6.3 Suppose you are given, for each entry x_i in a symbol table, a fixed probability p_i that x_i will be retrieved next. If the entries are kept in an unsorted linked list, in what order should they appear so as to minimize the average complexity of the next retrieval? Prove your result.

6.4 Let T be a fixed binary search tree containing n nodes. Show that, under reasonable assumptions, the average complexity of a successful retrieval in T is $i(T)/n$, and of an unsuccessful retrieval is $e(T)/(n + 1)$, where $i(T)$ and $e(T)$ are the internal and external path lengths of T.

6.5 What is the average complexity of the last insertion of a sequence of n insertions into an initially empty binary search tree?

6.6 Consider a sequence of n insertions into an initially empty binary search tree, followed by a single retrieval. What is the average complexity of the retrieval, if (a) it is successful (that is, an entry with the given key is present)? and (b) it is unsuccessful?

6.7 *Right-threaded binary search trees* (Perlis and Thornton, 1960). This question is devoted to a method of implementing the ordered symbol table ADT using binary search trees, which avoids most of the space overhead of parent pointers. Each node contains an additional, boolean field called *rightthread*. In nodes x that have a non-nil right subtree, $x^\wedge.rightthread = $ **false** and $x^\wedge.rightchild$ points to the right child in the usual way. However, in nodes where $x^\wedge.rightchild$ would normally be nil, $x^\wedge.rightthread = $ **true** and $x^\wedge.rightchild$ points to the inorder successor of x, or is nil if x has no successor. These extra pointers are called *right threads*, and they are conventionally shown as dashed arrows. For example, here is a typical right-threaded binary search tree:

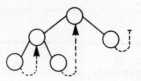

It is surprisingly easy to insert a new node while maintaining the threads correctly. If the new node is a left child, the insertion is like this:

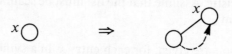

If the new node is right child, it is like this:

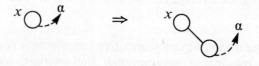

with one thread copied into the new node. Implement the ordered symbol table ADT using right-threaded binary search trees.

6.8 Complete the proof of the Access Lemma for Splay Trees (Theorem 6.3) by verifying the statements made about the amortized complexity of a Case 2 and Case 3 splaying step.

6.9 Adopt the following more general potential function for splay trees. Assign to each node x an arbitrary positive number $w(x)$. Let $W = \Sigma\, w(x)$ be the total weight. Let

$$s(x) = \sum_{y \in T_x} w(y)$$

where T_x is the subtree rooted at x; and let $r(x) = \log_2 s(x)$ as usual.

(a) Verify that the original potential function is a special case of this one.

(b) Modify the Access Lemma and its proof appropriately.

(c) Consider a splay tree with some fixed number of nodes. Initially the tree could have any shape. Show that, for any sequence of retrievals whatsoever, the change in potential cannot exceed

$$\sum_{x \in T} \log_2(W/w(x))$$

Hence show that, if s is any sequence of m retrievals, and $q(x)$ is the number of times x is retrieved in s, then the total cost of the sequence is of the order of

$$m + \sum_{x \in T} q(x) \log_2(m/q(x))$$

You may assume $q(x) \geq 1$. The result says that splay trees are within a constant factor of the entropy bound (Section 11.4), and so are asymptotically optimal.

6.10 What is the maximum number of entries that will fit into a B-tree of order m and height h?

6.11 If you had a file of 500 000 entries stored as a B-tree of order m, and only the root could be fitted into main memory, how large would m have to be to guarantee that every entry could be found in at most 2 disk accesses? Assume that it takes one access per node regardless of m.

6.12 The cost of splitting a B-tree node into two is $O(m)$. This question aims to show that splittings happen so rarely that their overall cost is negligible.

(a) Show that a B-tree of order m, containing n keys, has at most $(n - 1)/(\lceil m/2 \rceil - 1) + 1$ nodes.

(b) Use (a) to show that, over the course of n insertions into an initially empty B-tree, the number of node splittings per insertion is at most $1/(\lceil m/2 \rceil - 1)$. The creation of a new root is not a node splitting.

6.13 Write a program to implement an ordered symbol table using a B-tree. Each key is a string of letters, and its value is an integer. The program is to process input lines of the form

> *i* <string> <integer>   Insert this entry into the table. If the key is already present, respond with an error message and leave the table unchanged.

r <string>	Retrieve an entry with this key from the table. If it is present, print its key and value, otherwise print a 'not found' message.
m	If the table is non-empty, print out the entry whose key is minimum. Else given an error message.
l <string> <string>	Print a list of all the entries whose keys lie between the two given ones (inclusive). The entries are to appear in increasing order.
p	Print out all the entries in the table, with keys in increasing order.
q	Quit.

This problem presents an excellent opportunity for organizing your solution into a well-structured, modular program.

6.14 2-3 trees were introduced in order to get $O(\log n)$ worst-case performance per operation. There are several other data structures that achieve this; one well-known one is the *AVL tree*, named after its originators, Adel'son-Vel'skii and Landis (1962). An AVL tree is a binary tree which is *height-balanced*: that is, for any internal node x of T, the heights of x's left and right subtrees may differ by at most 1. For example, T_1 below is height-balanced but T_2 is not, because the node marked with a * violates the requirement:

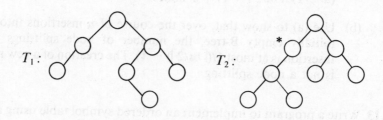

Let $N(h)$ be the minimum possible number of external nodes in a height-balanced tree of height h. Show that

$$N(0) = 1$$
$$N(1) = 2$$
$$N(h) = N(h - 1) + N(h - 2)$$

From this, it follows that $N(h) = F(h + 2) \geq \Phi^h$, where $\Phi \approx 1.6180339$ (see Exercise 2.6). For any height-balanced tree T with n internal nodes, therefore, $h(T) \leq \log_\Phi(n + 1)$.

6.15 Using the two-digit decimal character set 'a' = 01, ... , 'z' = 26, find three identifiers that hash to the same location when the hash function is

(a) $f(X) = X \bmod 53$

(b) $f(X) = X(1)* \, X(2) \bmod 100$

(c) $f(X) = (X^2 \bmod 10000) \bmod 100$

6.16 The problem with deletions in linear probing hash tables can be seen from the following example, in which it is assumed that $f(a) = f(b) = f(c) = 3$:

0	1	2	3	4	5	6	7	8	9
			a	b	c				

After *Delete* (b), if location 4 is simply left blank, later retrievals will fail to find c. Devise a deletion algorithm that overcomes this problem.

6.17 Implement the *SymbolTable* ADT using a hash table with linear probing. Be careful with deletions (see the preceding question), and also with correct termination of the insertion and retrieval algorithms.

6.18 Let $p_1, p_2, \ldots, p_m$ be any sequence of symbol table operations beginning with *Initialize*, and containing no deletions. Consider two hash tables, one employing linear probing and the other employing chaining, but both using the same hash function. Show that, for all i, the cost of p_i in the linear probing table is at least as great as its cost in the chained hash table.

6.19 One way to overcome the problem of choosing an appropriate hash table size m, when the maximum number of entries n is unknown, is to begin with a small table, and if n comes to exceed cm, where c is some fixed constant (for example, 0.9), to switch to a new table of size $2m$, with a new hash function. This is, of course, quite expensive, since every entry must be 'rehashed'. Show that the total complexity of all rehashes is $O(n)$, where n is the maximum number of entries in the table, and hence conclude that rehashing does not dominate the overall cost.

6.20 The following ADT is used by text editors to maintain the sequence of lines that make up the file being edited:

definition module *LineSeq*;

    type *LineSeq*; (* *a sequence of lines* *)

    procedure *Initialize*(**var** *S*: *LineSeq*);
    procedure *FirstLine*(*S*: *LineSeq*): *Line*;
    procedure *LastLine*(*S*: *LineSeq*): *Line*;
    procedure *PrevLine*(*L*: *Line*; *S*: *LineSeq*): *Line*;
    procedure *NextLine*(*L*: *Line*; *S*: *LineSeq*): *Line*;
    procedure *IndexLine*(*i*: **integer**; *S*: *LineSeq*): *Line*;
    procedure *InsertLine*(*NewL, L*: *Line*; **var** *S*: *LineSeq*);
    procedure *AppendLine*(*NewL, L*: *Line*; **var** *S*: *LineSeq*);
    procedure *DeleteLine*(*L*: *Line*; **var** *S*: *LineSeq*);

end *LineSeq*.

The lines are numbered from 1 to n, where n is the current number of lines in the sequence. *FirstLine* and *LastLine* return the first and last lines; *PrevLine* and *NextLine* return the line just before or just after a given line; and *IndexLine* returns the ith line. If the specified line does not exist, a special value called *NilLine* is returned.

    InsertLine and *AppendLine* add a new line to the sequence, just before or just after a specified line. *DeleteLine* deletes a line. The awkward part of this problem is that the numbers of all the following lines are changed by these operations.

    Find an efficient implementation of this ADT. The number of lines is expected to be very large, so operations of $O(n)$ complexity are not acceptable.

6.21 *Best-fit memory allocation.* A computer's internal memory is a valuable resource, and one of the tasks of an operating system is to keep track of which parts of the memory are in use, and which are available. Processes wishing to acquire a slice of memory do so via the following ADT:

definition module *MemoryAllocator*;

   type *Slice*; (* *a slice of memory* *)

   procedure *StartAddress*(*s*: *Slice*): *Address*;
   procedure *SliceSize*(*s*: *Slice*): **integer**;
   procedure *Allocate*(*size*: **integer**): *Slice*;
   procedure *Deallocate*(*s*: *Slice*);

end *MemoryAllocator*.

A *Slice s* is a record describing a contiguous block of memory, which begins at *StartAddress*(*s*) and contains *SliceSize*(*s*) units of memory. A process requests a slice of a certain size by calling *s* := *Allocate*(*k*); when this memory is no longer required by the process, it returns it to the operating system by the call *Deallocate*(*s*).

The memory allocator views the entire memory as a sequence of slices, some free and some allocated:

The allocated memory is fragmented in this way because of the unpredictable way in which slices are allocated and deallocated.

A *best-fit memory allocator* responds to *Allocate*(*k*) by finding a smallest free slice whose size is at least as large as *k*. This is split into two slices; the first is of size *k* and is returned to the caller; the second holds the rest and remains free. When a slice is deallocated, it must be joined with neighbouring free slices to prevent the memory from fragmenting into many small adjacent free slices.

Write abstract implementations of *Allocate* and *Deallocate*, and use them to determine appropriate data structures for representing the sequence of slices. You should be able to achieve $O(\log n)$ complexity per operation, where *n* is the number of *free* slices.

6.22 *The block cache.* Most of the information stored inside a computer is held on disk, where it is organized into *blocks*, each typically holding 1024 bytes. Two operations, *ReadBlock*(*i*: **integer**; *p*: *Address*) and *WriteBlock*(*i*: **integer**; *p*: *Address*) are provided for copying the block whose number is *i* into or out of the main memory of the computer, starting at address *p*. These operations are slow, and so it is worthwhile to keep copies of blocks in main memory. The copies may be accessed much more cheaply than the actual blocks, and even if there is room for only a few block copies in main memory, the method will be worthwhile whenever block accesses exhibit locality of reference.

In order to take advantage of these ideas, an operating system prevents programs from calling *ReadBlock* and *WriteBlock* directly; instead, it provides the follow ADT:

definition module *BlockHandler*;

  type *BlockCopy*;

  procedure *StartAddress*(*b*: *BlockCopy*): *Address*;
  procedure *OpenBlock*(*i*: **integer**): *BlockCopy*;
  procedure *CloseBlock*(*b*: *BlockCopy*);

  end *BlockHandler*.

A *BlockCopy b* is a pointer to a record containing information private to the ADT, plus one 1024-byte field, whose address is *StartAddress*(*b*), holding the copy of the block. A program gains access to a copy *b* of block number *i* by calling *b* := *OpenBlock*(*i*), and it informs the operating system that it is finished with the block by calling *CloseBlock*(*b*). Several programs may share the same block; a copy must remain in main memory until all are finished with it.

The ADT manages a set of block copies, whose total number cannot exceed some fixed number *M* determined by the amount of main memory available. If *M* block copies exist and a new block must be opened, it is first necessary to make room for it by writing out a closed block, which should be the one least recently closed. If all *M* blocks are open, the correct action is to wait until a block closes; but, since concurrent programming is beyond the scope of this book, an error message will be printed and the program aborted in this case. Find an efficient implementation of this ADT.

6.23 The symbol table in a compiler for a block-structured programming language is defined by the following ADT:

definition module *Block*;

    type *BlockTable*;

    procedure *Initialize*(**var** *S*: *BlockTable*);
    procedure *Insert*(*x*: *Entry*; **var** *S*: *BlockTable*);
    procedure *Retrieve*(*key*: *KeyType*; *S*: *BlockTable*): *Entry*;
    procedure *EnterBlock*(**var** *S*: *BlockTable*);
    procedure *LeaveBlock*(**var** *S*: *BlockTable*);

end *BlockTable*;

EnterBlock is called when the compiler reaches the beginning of a block (for example, the start of a procedure definition), and *LeaveBlock* is called when the compiler reaches the end of the block, at which point all entries inserted since the corresponding *EnterBlock* must be deleted. For example, in the sequence

    EnterBlock(*S*);
    Insert(*p*, *S*);
    EnterBlock(*S*);
    Insert(*q*, *S*);
    Insert(*r*, *S*);
    LeaveBlock(*S*);
    LeaveBlock(*S*);

entries *q* and *r* must be deleted by the first *LeaveBlock*, and *p* by the second.

    Another complication is that it is possible for entries to have the same key, provided that they are inserted in different blocks. In such cases, *Retrieve* is to return the innermost (most recently inserted) of the entries.

    Devise an implementation of this ADT based on hashing.

Implementation Module 6.1   Non-recursive implementation of the symbol table ADT using binary search trees. If ordered symbol table operations are required, parent pointers or their equivalent must be used. The loop invariant of *Insert* is '$p \neq$ **nil and** x belongs in the subtree rooted at p'.

```
implementation module SymTab;

from Standard import Error;
from System import Allocate;
from SYSTEM import CAST;

type Entry = pointer to node;
type SymbolTable = pointer to node;

type node =
record
  key: KeyType;
  value: ValueType;
  leftchild, rightchild: SymbolTable;
end;

procedure New(key: KeyType; value: ValueType): Entry;
var x: Entry;
begin
  Allocate(x, SIZE(x^));
  x^.key := key;
  x^.value := value;
  return x;
end New;

procedure KeyOf(x: Entry): KeyType;
begin
  return x^.key;
end KeyOf;

procedure ValueOf(x: Entry): ValueType;
begin
  return x^.value;
end ValueOf;

procedure Update(x: Entry; value: ValueType);
begin
  x^.value := value;
end Update;

procedure Initialize(var S: SymbolTable);
begin
  S := nil;
end Initialize;
```

```
procedure DeleteRoot(var S: SymbolTable);
var x, y: SymbolTable;
begin
  if S^.leftchild = nil then S := S^.rightchild;
  elsif S^.rightchild = nil then
    S := S^.leftchild;.
  else
    y := S^.leftchild;
    if y^.rightchild ≠ nil then
      repeat
        x := y; y := y^.rightchild;
      until y^.rightchild = nil;
      x^.rightchild := y^.leftchild;
      y^.leftchild := S^.leftchild;
    end;
    y^.rightchild := S^.rightchild; S := y;
  end;
end DeleteRoot;

procedure Delete(x: Entry; var S: SymbolTable);
var p: SymbolTable;
begin
  if x = CAST(Entry, S) then
    DeleteRoot(S);
  else
    p := S;
    loop
      if p = nil then
        Error("Delete: entry not present");
      elsif x^.key < p^.key then
        if p^.leftchild = CAST(SymbolTable, x) then
          DeleteRoot(p^.leftchild);
          exit;
        end;
        p := p^.leftchild;
      else
        if p^.rightchild = CAST (SymbolTable, x) then
          DeleteRoot(p^.rightchild);
          exit;
        end;
        p := p^.rightchild;
      end;
    end;
  end;
end Delete;
```

```
procedure Insert(x: Entry; var S: SymbolTable);
var p: SymbolTable;
begin
    x^.leftchild := nil; x^.rightchild := nil;
    if S = nil then S := CAST (SymbolTable, x);
    else
        p := S;
        loop
            if x^.key = p^.key then
                Error("key already present");
            elsif x^.key < p^.key then
                if p^.leftchild = nil then
                    p^.leftchild := CAST (SymbolTable, x);
                    exit;
                end;
                p := p^.leftchild;
            else
                if p^.rightchild = nil then
                    p^.rightchild := CAST (SymbolTable, x);
                    exit;
                end;
                p := p^.rightchild;
            end;
        end;
    end;
end Insert;

procedure Retrieve(key: KeyType; var S: SymbolTable): Entry;
var p: SymbolTable;
begin
    p := S;
    while (p ≠ nil) and (key ≠ p^.key) do
        if key < p^.key then
            p := p^.leftchild;
        else
            p := p^.rightchild;
        end;
    end;
    return CAST (Entry, p);
end Retrieve;

begin
    NilEntry := nil;
end SymTab.
```

```
procedure BInsert(x: Entry; p: SymbolTable; var y: Entry; var q:
SymbolTable): boolean;
  var i: integer; z: Entry; r: SymbolTable;
  begin
    if p = nil then
      y := x; q := nil;
      return false;
    elsif BinarySearch(p^.entries, 1, p^.count, x^.key, i) then
      Error("SymbolTable.Insert: key already present");
    elsif BInsert(x, p^.children[i], z, r) then
      return true;
    elsif ShuffleUp(p, i + 1, z, r) then
      return true;
    else
      Split(p, y, q);
      return false;
    end;
  end BInsert;

procedure Insert(x: Entry: var S: SymbolTable);
var p, q: SymbolTable;
  y: Entry;
begin
  if not BInsert(x, S, y, q) then
    Allocate(p, SIZE(p^)); p^.count := 1;
    p^.children[0] := S; p^.children[1] := q;
    p^.entries[1] := y; S := p;
  end;
end Insert;
```

Figure 6.1 Top-level implementation of the B-tree insertion algorithm. The type declarations are given in the text. To simplify the algorithm, room is allowed for one more entry and child in each node than is actually necessary. *BInsert(x, p, y, q)* attempts to insert entry *x* into subtree *p*. If it succeeds in doing this without splitting the root of *p*, it returns **true**, and *y* and *q* are not used. If the root of *p* must be split, then the three fragments are returned in *p*, *y*, and *q*.

Procedure *BinarySearch(A, a, b, key, i)* performs a binary search of the array of entries $A[a..b]$, searching for an entry whose key is *key*. If found, it returns **true**, and *i* is the position of the entry; otherwise it returns **false**, and *i* is the position just to the left of the gap that key falls in (see Exercise 1.7 for an implementation).

Procedure *ShuffleUp* inserts *r* into the *children* array of *p*, and *z* into the *entries* array, both at position $i + 1$, and returns **true** if the resulting node is not overfull. Procedure *Split* performs the node splitting.

Implementation Module 6.2   The chained hash table implementation of *SymbolTable*. *New*, *KeyOf*, *ValueOf*, and *Update* are as in Implementation Module 6.1 and are omitted.

```
implementation module SymTab;

    from System import Allocate;

    const m = 1009;

    type Entry = pointer to node;

    type node =
    record
        key: KeyType;
        value: ValueType;
        next: Entry;
    end;

    type SymbolTable = pointer to array [0..m − 1] of Entry;

    procedure Initialize (var S: SymbolTable);
    var i: integer;
        p: SymbolTable;
    begin
        Allocate(p, SIZE(p^));
        S := p;
        for i := 0 to m − 1 do
            S^[i] := NilEntry;
        end;
    end Initialize;

    procedure Retrieve(key: KeyType; var S: SymbolTable) : Entry;
    var p: Entry;
    begin
        p := S^[ f(key) ];
        while (p ≠ NilEntry) and (p^.key ≠ key) do
            p := p^.next;
        end;
        return p;
    end Retrieve;
```

```
procedure Insert(x: Entry; var S: SymbolTable);
var i: integer;
    p: Entry;
begin
    i := f(x^.key);
    p := S^[i];
    while p ≠ NilEntry do
        if p^.key = x^.key then
            Error("SymbolTable.Insert: key already present");
        end;
        p := p^.next;
    end;
    x^.next := S^[i];
    S^[i] := x;
end Insert;

procedure Delete(x: Entry; var S: SymbolTable);
var i: integer;
    p, q: Entry;
begin
    i := f(x^.key);
    q := NilEntry;
    p := S^[i];
    while (p ≠ NilEntry) and (p ≠ x) do
        q := p;
        p := p^.next;
    end;
    if p = NilEntry then
        Error ("SymbolTable.Delete: entry not present");
    elsif q = NilEntry then
        S^[i] := p^.next;
    else
            q^.next := p^.next;
    end;
end Delete;

begin
    NilEntry := nil;
end SymTab.
```

Chapter 7

Priority Queues

The priority queue ADT, whose implementations are studied in this chapter, appears in many algorithms. Its name comes from an application in operating systems: the maintenance of a queue of processes, to be run according to their priorities. And it lies at the heart of one of the most time-consuming of all applications: simulation.

7.1 Specification

A *priority queue*, like a symbol table, is a set of entries, each containing a key and a value. However, a given key may appear in more than one entry, the keys are always ordered and the operations differ:

> **definition module** *PriQueue*;
>
>   **type** *Entry*;
>
>   **procedure** *New(key*: *KeyType*; *value*: *ValueType*): *Entry*;
>   **procedure** *KeyOf(x*: *Entry*): *KeyType*;
>   **procedure** *ValueOf(x*: *Entry*): *ValueType*;
>   **procedure** *Update(x*: *Entry*; *value*: *ValueType*);
>
>   **type** *PriorityQueue*;
>
>   **procedure** *Initialize* (**var** *Q*: *PriorityQueue*);
>   **procedure** *Empty(Q*: *PriorityQueue*): **boolean**;
>   **procedure** *Insert(x*: *Entry*; **var** *Q*: *PriorityQueue*);
>   **procedure** *FindMin(**var** *Q*: *PriorityQueue*): *Entry*;
>   **procedure** *DeleteMin(**var** *Q*: *PriorityQueue*): *Entry*;
>
> **end** *PriQueue*.

As with symbol tables, the first group of operations is for handling isolated entries. Entries may be created, their keys and values accessed, and their values (but not their keys) updated. There seems to be no need for a nil entry. The five priority queue operations allow one to initialize a priority queue to empty, to test whether a priority queue is empty, to insert an entry, to retrieve (but not delete) an entry with minimum key, and to delete (but not dispose) and return an entry with minimum key.

Although the ordered symbol table implementations of Chapter 6 can be used for priority queues (suitably modified to permit non-unique keys), there are simpler ways to achieve $O(\log n)$ worst-case complexity per operation. And occasionally operations like the following will be needed:

procedure *Delete*(*x*: *Entry*; **var** *Q*: *PriorityQueue*);
procedure *Meld*(*P*, *Q*: *PriorityQueue*): *PriorityQueue*;
procedure *DecreaseKey*(*x*: *Entry*; *key*: *KeyType*; **var** *Q*: *PriorityQueue*);

Delete deletes entry *x* from priority queue *Q*; *Meld* takes two priority queues and merges them into one; *DecreaseKey* takes entry *x* of priority queue *Q* and alters the value of its key to *key*, which is guaranteed to be no larger than the old value. This last operation is particularly exotic, but it happens to be required by some of the graph algorithms of Chapter 10, so it is included here.

As an example of the use of priority queues, consider the simulation of a supermarket checkout line. The aim is to determine experimentally the average time that a customer can expect to wait for service, given certain assumptions about the rate at which customers arrive, and the time it takes to serve one customer.

The customer's experience of the supermarket line can be described as a sequence of *events*, which occur over time:

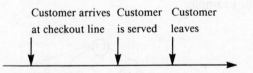

The simulation as a whole must keep track of many customers, arriving at random times, so we can expect hundreds or thousands of events.

Suppose the event 'customer *C* is served' occurs at time *t*. If it is assumed that it takes between 30 and 300 seconds to serve one customer, a random number generator can be used to decide that at time $t + 227$, the customer will leave. Thus, a new event is defined, 'customer *C* leaves,' which we know will happen at time $t + 227$: a *pending event*.

A pending event is represented by an entry whose key equals the time at which the event will occur, and whose value describes the nature of the event. If these entries are stored in a priority queue, the simulation can then proceed as follows. First, *DeleteMin* is used to determine which event will happen next. The event is declared to have happened, and whatever action is needed is performed to simulate its occurrence. For example, the action for the event 'customer *C* is served' is the insertion of a new event 'customer *C* leaves,' with time $t + 227$ or whatever, into the priority queue. The action for 'customer *C* leaves' is the insertion of 'customer *D* is served' with time 5 seconds later, where customer *D* is the customer next in line, as recorded in some auxiliary data structure (which in this case would be a fifo queue).

In outline, then, the simulation algorithm is

> *Insert some initializing event into Q*;
> **while not** *Empty(Q)* **do**
>   *event := DeleteMin(Q)*;
>   Execute the appropriate action for *event*,
>   possibly including one or more
>   *Insert* operations defining new events;
> **end**;

A variety of observations would be recorded as the simulation proceeds, so that statistics such as the average wait can be calculated after the simulation ends.

7.2 Heap-ordered Trees

The data structures of this chapter are all based on the idea of heap-ordered trees. In a *heap-ordered* (or *partially ordered*) tree, each non-root node obeys the *heap invariant*: its key is greater than or equal to the key of its parent. For example,

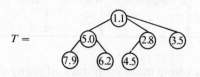

is heap-ordered. The root holds a minimum key, and the keys increase on moving down any path. The second minimum could lie in any child of the root. A node may have any number of children, and $c(x)$ is defined to be the number of (internal) children of node x.

AddLeaf.   There are two ways to build a heap-ordered tree of a given shape. The first way is based on an operation we will call *AddLeaf*: the attachment of a single node to a given node of the tree (or, if the tree is empty, its replacement by a tree consisting of a single node). For example, attach a node containing 5.0 to the node containing 6.2 in this tree:

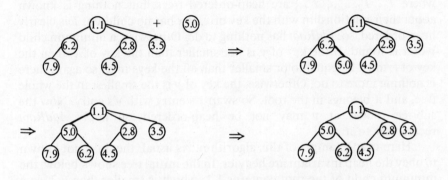

The new node is not known to satisfy the heap invariant, as indicated by a darkened link. *AddLeaf* compares 5.0 with 6.2, discovers that they are out of order, and exchanges the entries. Now 5.0 is not known to obey the heap invariant with its parent 1.1. *AddLeaf* compares them, discovers that the invariant is in fact satisfied, and halts. The new entry moves up the path towards the root, stopping when the heap invariant is satisfied. The new key is only compared with keys on this path: since it is smaller than each key it replaces, it can only be out of order with its parent, not its children.

In the worst case, the new key is compared once with each of its proper ancestors, giving a cost of $d(x)$, where $d(x)$ is the depth of the new node. An entire tree T with n nodes can be built by repeated *AddLeaf* operations; the worst-case complexity of building T in this way is

$$W(n) = \sum_{x \in I(T)} d(x)$$
$$= i(T)$$

the internal path length of T.

AddRoot.   The second way to build a heap-ordered tree of a given shape is based on an operation which can be called *AddRoot*. Suppose there is a non-empty tree

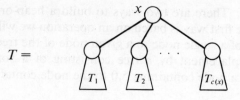

where $T_1, T_2, \ldots, T_{c(x)}$ are heap-ordered trees, but nothing is known about their relationship with the key of x. If x has no children, T is clearly heap-ordered, so *AddRoot* has nothing to do. Otherwise, a minimum child y of x is found. If the key of y is not smaller than the key of x, then the key of x must be equal to or smaller than all the keys in T, so again there is nothing more to do. Otherwise, the key of y is the smallest in the whole tree, and it belongs in the root. So swap x's entry with y's entry. Now the subtree rooted at y may not be heap-ordered, so apply *AddRoot* recursively to it.

Here is an example of this algorithm. As usual, the links not known to obey the heap invariant are heavier. In the initial tree shown below, the minimum child of the root contains 1.1, which is smaller than 6.2, so a swap is performed:

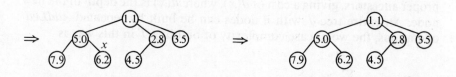

Now *AddRoot* must be applied recursively. The minimum child of the node now containing 6.2 contains 5.0, so again a swap must be made:

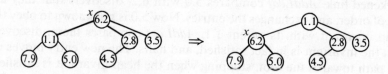

Now the node containing 6.2 has no children, so the procedure stops.

The new root moves down some path until its children all satisfy the heap invariant, or there are no children. Since the entry of x is replaced by the entry of its minimum child y, after the swap all the children of x satisfy the heap invariant. But the key of y is increased by the swap, so the heap invariant may be violated by some of its children — hence the recursive call.

Beginning with the keys of T in no particular order, a heap-ordered tree T can be built using repeated *AddRoot* operations. The nodes with no children already constitute heap-ordered trees, so one may work upwards from them, using the dynamic programming principle of ensuring that all the subtrees of x are heap-ordered before calling $AddRoot(x)$. For example,

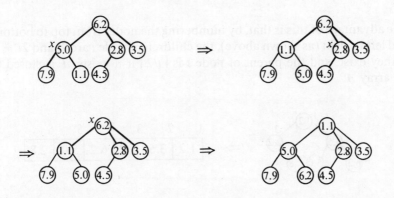

It takes $c(x) - 1$ comparisons between keys to determine the minimum child y of x (a find-the-minimum on the $c(x)$ children of x), plus one comparison of x with y, for a total of $c(x)$ comparisons to move the root down one level. In the worst case, the new entry propagates all the way down. The longest possible such path contains $h(x)$ nodes, by the definition of the height $h(x)$, but the last node has no children, so it contributes nothing to the cost. So the maximum number of nodes on the path may be taken to be $h(x) - 1$. Letting $C = \max_{x \in I(T)} c(x)$, then $C[h(x) - 1]$ is an upper bound for the cost of $AddRoot(x)$, and the worst-case complexity of building an n-node tree by repeated $AddRoot$ operations is

$$W(n) \le C \sum_{x \in I(T)} [h(x) - 1]$$

where $I(T)$, as usual, is the set of internal nodes of T. Such a sum of heights has not been encountered before, so it is not clear how this method of building a heap compares with the method of repeated $AddLeaf$ operations.

7.3   The Heap

Since a heap-ordered tree of any chosen shape can be built, it is natural to consider building a complete binary tree. It can also be stipulated that the nodes at the bottom level be *left-justified*:

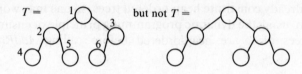

The advantage of this is that, by numbering the nodes from top to bottom and left to right (as shown above), the children of node i are $2i$ and $2i + 1$ if they exist, and the parent of node i is $\lceil i/2 \rceil$ if it exists. T is stored in an array A:

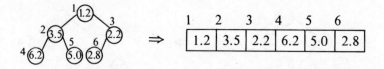

No links are needed: to move about in the tree, simply calculate the indices of parents and children. A heap-ordered left-justified complete binary tree stored in this way is called a *heap*.

The current array size needs to be stored with A, so formally

> **type** *PriorityQueue* = **pointer to**
> **record**
> A: **array** [$1..MaxSize$] **of** *Entry*;
>   *size*: **integer**;
> **end**;

Note that heaps are subject to overflow, since the size of A is fixed.

The insertion of a new entry into a heap of size n can easily be implemented by an *AddLeaf* to position $n + 1$. The code for this appears in Implementation Module 7.1.

The analysis is also quite simple, given a number of results that have been developed previously. Let n be the size of the ADT just before the insertion takes place, or in other words, the number of entries in the heap. In the last section the cost of this *AddLeaf* operation was found to be equal to $d(x)$, the depth of the new node. Since this new node x is an internal node of maximum depth in the $n + 1$-node complete tree T which is the result of this operation, the worst-case complexity of *Insert* is

$$W(n) = h(T) - 1$$
$$= \lceil \log_2(n + 2) \rceil - 1$$

by Theorem 5.4.

The *DeleteMin* operation is a little messier. There is no problem locating a minimum entry, since the root contains one, but when it is extracted what remains has to be re-formed into a heap. This is done by moving the last entry to the root and calling *AddRoot*:

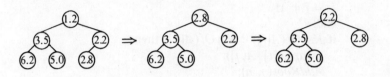

See Implementation Module 7.1 for the code.

Again, let *n* be the number of entries in the heap just before the *DeleteMin* operation. If $n = 1$, no call to *AddRoot* is made and the complexity of *DeleteMin* is $W(1) = 0$. Otherwise, the complexity is equal to the cost of $AddRoot(x)$, where x is the root of the $n - 1$-node complete tree T which is the result of the operation. Therefore, the worst-case complexity of $DeleteMin(Q)$ is

$$W(n) \le 2(h(x) - 1)$$
$$= 2(\lceil \log_2 n \rceil - 1)$$

by the formula for the complexity of *AddRoot* developed in the preceding section, and by Theorem 5.4.

To summarize, the heap is an efficient implementation of the priority queue ADT which provides $O(\log n)$ worst-case complexity for *Insert* and *DeleteMin*, and $O(1)$ worst-case complexity for *Initialize*, *Empty*, and *FindMin*. This is achieved without any overhead in space, and with code of modest length.

7.4   Heapsort

While on the subject of heaps, a short deviation is in order to discuss a sorting algorithm based on them. One could sort *n* entries by performing *n Insert* operations followed by *n DeleteMin* operations, for a cost of about $3n\log_2 n$ comparisons between keys in the worst case; but a more highly tuned, rather clever in-place sorting algorithm can be produced.

Suppose that initially there is an unsorted array $A[1..n]$ of entries. It turns out that maximum elements will need to be extracted, not minimum ones, so here is *AddRoot* again:

```
procedure AddRoot(i, n: integer);
var j: integer;
begin
  j := 2*i;
  if j ≤ n then
    if (j < n) and (KeyOf(A[j]) < KeyOf(A[j + 1])) then
      j := j + 1;
    end:
    if KeyOf(A[i]) < KeyOf(A[j]) then
      Swap(A[i], A[j]);
      AddRoot(j, n);
    end;
  end;
end AddRoot;
```

The first optimization is to use *AddRoot* operations instead of repeated insertions to build the heap. That is, beginning with the *n* entries in arbitrary order, call

```
procedure BuildHeap(n: integer);
var i: integer;
begin
  for i := n div 2 to 1 by − 1 do
    AddRoot(i, n);
  end;
end BuildHeap;
```

to build the heap. The second optimization is to store the extracted maximum entries at the top of *A* as the heap shrinks. Altogether, this is *Heapsort* (Williams, 1964; Floyd, 1964):

```
procedure Heapsort(n: integer);
var i: integer;
begin
  BuildHeap(n);
  for i := n to 2 by − 1 do
    Swap(A[1], A[i]);
    AddRoot(1, i − 1);
  end;
end Heapsort;
```

For example, suppose this heap is built:

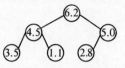

Then the first two iterations of the loop produce

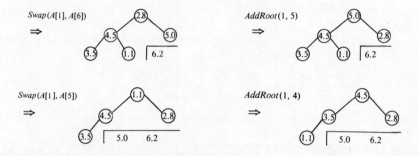

and this continues until the array is sorted.

Analysis of Heapsort.   The case $n = 0$ in *Heapsort* is special, because the formula for the number of times the body of the loop 'for i := a to b . . .' is executed only applies when $a \le b + 1$. Clearly $W(0) = 0$, so the remainder of this analysis will assume that $n \ge 1$. According to Section 7.2, the complexity of *BuildHeap*(n) is

$$W(n) \le 2 \sum_{x \in I(T)} [h(x) - 1]$$

where T is the final tree. Letting $h(T) = h$, the following situation holds:

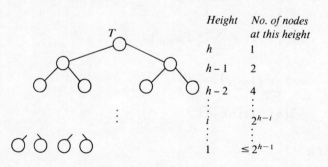

	Height	No. of nodes at this height
	h	1
	$h-1$	2
	$h-2$	4
	$\vdots$	$\vdots$
	i	2^{h-i}
	$\vdots$	$\vdots$
	1	$\le 2^{h-1}$

The bottom level may not be full, so 2^{h-1} is only an upper bound on the number of nodes it contains. Since there are at most 2^{h-i} internal nodes at height i, for all i, then

$$W(n) \le 2 \sum_{x \in I(T)} [h(x) - 1]$$

$$\le 2 \sum_{i=1}^{h} 2^{h-i}(i - 1)$$

$$= 2 \sum_{i=0}^{h-1} i 2^{h-i-1}$$

$$= 2^h \sum_{i=0}^{h-1} i 2^{-i}$$

$$\le 2 \cdot 2^h$$

using the standard result $\Sigma_{i=0}^{\infty} i 2^{-i} = 2$. Since $n \ge 2^{h-1}$, it can be concluded that

$$W(n) \le 4n$$

The startling result is then that a heap may be built in linear time. In fact, a more careful analysis shows that $W(n) \le 2(n - 1)$: a non-empty heap may be built with just twice as many comparisons as it takes to find the minimum element (Exercise 7.5).

The cost of $AddRoot(1, i - 1)$ is at most $2[h(x) - 1]$, where $h(x)$ is the height of the root in a complete tree of $i - 1$ nodes, which by Theorem 5.4 is $\lceil \log_2 i \rceil$. The conclusion is that the worst-case complexity of $Heapsort(n)$ is

$$W(n) = \text{cost of } BuildHeap(n) + \sum_{i=2}^{n} \text{cost of } AddRoot(1, i - 1)$$

$$\le 2(n - 1) + \sum_{i=2}^{n} 2(\lceil \log_2 i \rceil - 1)$$

$$= 2 \sum_{i=2}^{n} \lceil \log_2 i \rceil$$

$$\le 2(n - 1) \lceil \log_2 n \rceil$$

provided $n \ge 1$.

7.5 Binomial Queues

This section covers a data structure, the *binomial queue* of Vuillemin (1978), which efficiently implements melding (that is, merging two priority queues into one). It is also a stepping stone to the Fibonacci heaps of the next section.

Binomial queues are based on an interestingly shaped tree: the *binomial tree* B_r defined inductively by

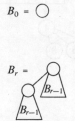

This means that the tree B_r is created by linking together two copies of B_{r-1}. For example,

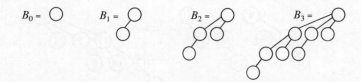

It is easy to prove by induction on r that B_r has 2^r nodes, that $h(B_r) = r + 1$, and that the root of B_r has exactly r children. Other interesting properties include

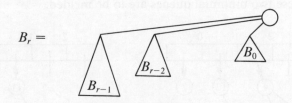

and (for readers familiar with binomial coefficients) the fact that B_r contains exactly $\binom{r}{i}$ nodes of depth i, which explains why these trees bear the name they do. From this it can easily be shown that the internal path length $i(B_r)$ is $r2^{r-1}$.

A *binomial queue* is a forest of heap-ordered binomial trees. For convenience of presentation, pointers to the roots of these trees will be stored in an array, although a linked list would do as well. The tree sizes are determined by the binary representation of n, the number of nodes required in the forest; for example, if $n = 9 = 1001_2$, one B_3 and one B_0 are needed:

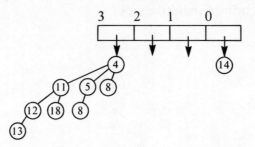

The usefulness of this representation arises from an efficient way to link two heap-ordered binomial trees B_r together, to form a heap-ordered binomial tree B_{r+1}:

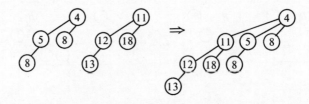

The keys of the two roots are compared, and the larger made the first child of the smaller. This costs just one comparison between keys.

Now two binomial queues can be melded together. For example, suppose these two binomial queues are to be melded:

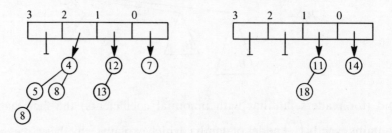

It is done in a manner quite analogous to the binary addition $0111 + 0011 = 1010$. The first step is to link the two B_0 trees together, giving no B_0 trees and a carry of one B_1:

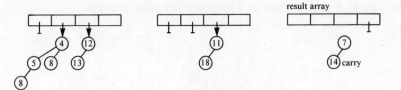

Now there are three B_1 trees. One is inserted into the result array and the other two are linked into a carry of one B_2:

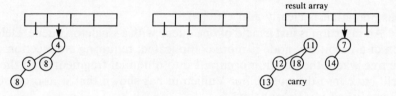

Now the two B_2 trees are linked, giving no B_2 trees in the result, and a carry of one B_3 which can be inserted into the result:

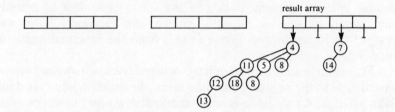

At most one link per array position is performed, giving an $O(\log n)$ worst-case complexity per meld, where n is the number of entries in the result queue. This follows because the largest B_r has at most n nodes, and since B_r has 2^r nodes, $r \le \log_2 n$.

A *DeleteMin* must first find the smallest of the $O(\log n)$ roots of all the trees, then delete it, and meld the binomial queue consisting of the trees rooted at the deleted node's children back into the main queue. For example, *DeleteMin* applied to the result of the above melding operation would proceed as follows. First the smallest root is found and deleted, yielding

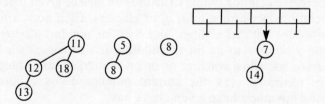

Then these fragments are melded back into the queue:

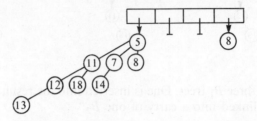

This operation is clearly also $O(\log n)$.

An insertion is just a meld of one queue with a singleton queue. Deletion of an arbitrary node is more complicated, requiring a dissection of the tree where the deletion occurred into binomial fragments and their meld back into the queue, but Vuillemin has shown that it also can be accomplished in $O(\log n)$ time.

7.6 Fibonacci Heaps

The most efficient implementation of the full complement of priority queue operations that is currently known, the *Fibonacci heap*, was developed by Fredman and Tarjan (1987) from the binomial queue of Section 7.5.

A Fibonacci heap is a forest of heap-ordered trees, which need not be any particular shape or size. Some nodes may be *marked*, which is done with an asterisk. A root node is never marked. A pointer to a root node containing a minimum entry is maintained. For example,

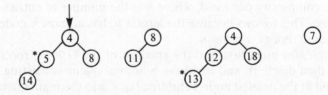

is a Fibonacci heap with two marked nodes, and minimum pointer pointing to the node containing 4.

A concrete realization of this structure will now be given that enables all the operations performed on it to be efficient. Each node x lies on a doubly linked list with its siblings, and contains pointers $x.parent$ to its parent, and $x.children$ to its list of children. It also contains a boolean field $x.marked$ recording whether or not it is marked, and integer field $x.childnum$ recording $c(x)$, the current number of its children. For example, the Fibonacci heap given above has

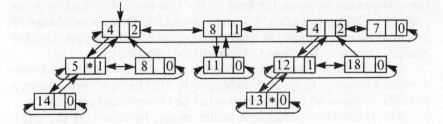

for its implementation. Observe that the roots of the trees are linked together as though they were siblings, and that the Fibonacci heap as a whole is accessed via a pointer to the first root on the list, which always holds a minimum entry.

Whenever the *Meld* operation is used, there must be several priority queues in existence. In such circumstances it is better to regard the ADT as a set of disjoint priority queues; the *Initialize* operation adds a new, empty priority queue to this set, and each priority queue is implemented by one Fibonacci heap. For a reason that will become clear when *DeleteMin* is implemented, an *accumulator A*, which is an array of $M + 1$ pointers to nodes, is added to the set. M is some upper bound on the number of children of any node, and will be determined later. Initially, these pointers are all nil. The picture of a typical state of the ADT is thus

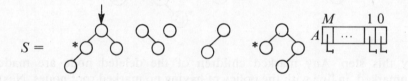

The potential of this state is defined to be

$$\Phi(S) = 3 \times \textit{the number of marked nodes} +$$
$$2 \times \textit{the total number of roots} +$$
$$1 \times \textit{the number of non-nil elements of A}$$

Thus, the structure is poorly balanced when there are many marked nodes, many roots, or A is in use (in fact, A will be used only by the *Delete-Min* operation). For example, the structure shown above has potential $\Phi(S) = 3.2 + 2.5 + 0 = 16$.

The *Initialize* operation returns a nil pointer; the *Empty* operation checks whether its argument is nil. Both have $O(1)$ actual complexity, and since they cause no change in potential, they have $O(1)$ amortized complexity also.

The operation *Meld(P, Q)* appends the two lists of roots together, in such a way as to ensure that the smallest root comes first. This requires one comparison between the keys of the two roots, followed by a list append, so it clearly has $O(1)$ actual complexity. There is no change in potential, since, although the trees are regrouped, their number does not change. Therefore *Meld* has $O(1)$ amortized complexity.

To implement the operation *Insert*(x, Q), x is converted into a one-element Fibonacci heap, and melded with Q. The new node causes a potential increase of 2, so *Insert* also has $O(1)$ amortized complexity.

The *DeleteMin* operation is rather messy. By removing the minimum node, its children are made into the roots of trees. For example, the Fibonacci heap

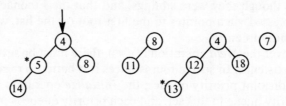

is transformed into

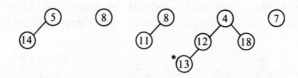

by this step. Any marked children of the deleted node are made unmarked, in line with the policy of having no marked root nodes. Next these trees are fed one by one into the accumulator, which links them together in the same way as was done for binomial queues in Section 7.5. With binomial queues, B_r is always linked with B_r; since the root of B_r has exactly r children, the equivalent here is to link trees whose roots have the same number of children:

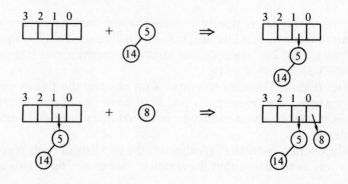

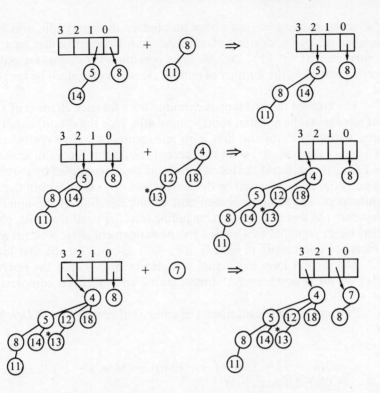

Recall that $c(x)$, the number of children of x, is stored in each node x, so it is available to index the accumulator array. Finally, the accumulator is scanned and the resulting trees collected. As this is done, the minimum key is determined. This example has the Fibonacci heap

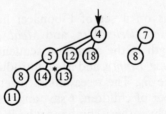

for its final result.

The analysis of *DeleteMin* will follow the implementation given in Implementation Module 7.2. The test $A[i] \neq$ **nil** is chosen for the characteristic operation; this is clearly realistic. Since the number of marked nodes cannot increase during *DeleteMin*, the potential function may be simplified to

$$\Phi(S) = 2 \times \text{ the total number of roots } +$$
$$1 \times \text{ the number of non-nil elements of } A$$

If k is the number of root nodes just before the operation, and k' the number of root nodes just afterwards, then clearly the first part of Φ contributes $2(k' - k)$ to the change in potential. From now on, only the second part of Φ, the number of non-nil elements of A, need be kept track of.

The body of the first loop is executed once for each element of p. The list p contains the k initial roots, minus min, plus the $c(min)$ children of min; so the body of the first loop is executed $k - 1 + c(min)$ times. Whenever the test $A[i] \neq$ **nil** is executed inside this loop, an actual cost of 1 is incurred. But if the test succeeds, its cost is cancelled by the change in potential of -1 caused by the assignment $A[i] :=$ **nil** within the inner **while** loop. The total amortized cost of one iteration of the outer loop therefore reduces to 1 for the concluding test $A[i] \neq$ **nil** that fails, plus an increase in potential of 1 caused by the assignment $A[i] := x$, for a total amortized complexity of exactly $2(k - 1 + c(min))$ for the first loop.

The second loop has actual complexity $M + 1$, but the operation $A[i] :=$ **nil** is performed k' times, giving an amortized complexity of $M + 1 - k'$.

Putting the pieces together, the amortized complexity of *DeleteMin* is

$$
\begin{aligned}
a_i &= 2(k' - k) + 2(k - 1 + c(min)) + (M + 1 - k') \\
&= k' + 2c(min) + M - 1 \\
&\leq 4M
\end{aligned}
$$

since $k' \leq M + 1$ (there cannot be more final trees than positions in A), and $c(min) \leq M$ (by definition, M is an upper bound on the number of children of any node).

If the operations on a set of Fibonacci heaps are restricted to *Initialize*, *Empty*, *Insert*, *DeleteMin*, and *Meld*, it is easy to prove by induction on the length of the operation sequence that every tree is a binomial tree. *Initialize*, *Empty*, and *Meld* introduce no new trees. *Insert* introduces a new tree B_0. The trees linked together during *DeleteMin* have the same number of children, r say, and since both are binomial trees by the inductive hypothesis, both must be B_r, and hence the result is a binomial tree.

Since a binomial tree whose root has r children has exactly 2^r nodes, every node of a binomial tree can have at most $\lfloor \log_2 n \rfloor$ children. For the restricted set of operations *Initialize*, *Empty*, *Insert*, *DeleteMin*, and *Meld*, then, $M = \lfloor \log_2 n \rfloor$, and it has been shown that *DeleteMin* has $O(\log n)$ amortized complexity, and the other operations all have $O(1)$ amortized complexity.

Up to this point, a Fibonacci heap is just a binomial queue with the linking operations postponed until the next *DeleteMin*. Fibonacci heaps are sometimes called *lazy* for this reason. It is in the implementation of the two remaining operations, *DecreaseKey* and *Delete*, that new ideas emerge.

The problem with *DecreaseKey* and *Delete* is that they move away from the realm of binomial trees, with the result that the formula $M = \lfloor \log_2 n \rfloor$ no longer applies, and there is a danger of losing, not the analysis of *DeleteMin*, which applies for all M, but the quality of the bound it gives. Specifically, if many grandchildren of a node x are deleted, $c(x)$ is unaffected, but $s(x)$, the number of nodes in the subtree rooted at x, may drop as low as $c(x) + 1$, which would require that $M = n - 1$. Fibonacci heaps solve this problem by insisting that, if a node loses more than a few grandchildren, it must lose a child as well.

This strategy is based on an operation called *CascadeCut*(x, Q), which is defined for any non-root node x of Q. The link between x and its parent is broken (this is called a *cut*), and T_x becomes an independent tree of Q. If the parent is marked when the cut occurs, the parent is itself cut from its parent, and so on. Otherwise the cut places a mark in the parent.

In the following example of *CascadeCut*(x, Q), the first two proper ancestors of x are marked, and this leads to a cascade of three cuts:

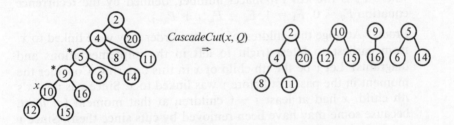

A cut has actual complexity 1 (say), but adds a new root to the Fibonacci heap, which increases the potential by 2. If the cut is not the last one in the cascade, the new root goes from marked to unmarked, which decreases the potential by 3. So all but the final cut is free, and the amortized complexity of *CascadeCut*(x, Q) is at most 6: that is, 1 for the final cut, 2 for the last new root, and possibly 3 for the new mark created by the final cut. This is essentially the same trick as the one used to control the cost of carry propagation in *DeleteMin*'s accumulator, and explains why the components of the potential function were weighted as they were.

The *DecreaseKey* operation is now trivial to implement. To decrease the key of a node x, the value is modified and a cascade cut applied at x:

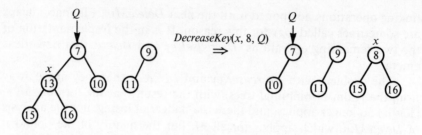

The amortized complexity is at most 6. Note that, since the key of x is known to decrease, x cannot become out of order with any of its children. Deletion is similar (Exercise 7.10); its amortized complexity turns out to be $O(M)$.

This analysis is drawing to a close. It remains to find an upper bound M on the number of children of any node.

Theorem 7.1:   Let x be any node in a Fibonacci heap. Then the size of the subtree rooted at x obeys

$$s(x) \geq F_{c(x) + 2}$$

where F_k is the kth Fibonacci number, defined by the recurrence equation $F_0 = 0$, $F_1 = 1$, $F_k = F_{k-1} + F_{k-2}$.

Proof: Arrange the children of x in the order they were linked to x, from earliest to latest (right to left in the implementations and diagrams). Let y be the ith child of x in this ordering. Consider the moment in the past just before y was linked to x. Since y is now x's ith child, x had at least $i - 1$ children at that moment (*at least*, because some may have been removed by cuts since then). Since y was linked to x, at that moment $c(y) = c(x)$, and hence $c(y) \geq i - 1$.

Now back in the present, y is still a child of x. If y had lost more than one child through cuts, it would itself have been cut from x. It hasn't been cut from x, so at most one child has been lost, and $c(y) \geq i - 2$.

The ith child of x has at least $i - 2$ children, so the general picture is

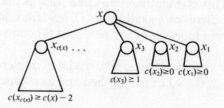

The next question is, what is the minimum possible value of $s(x)$, given that $c(x) = k$? Let this minimum be S_k. Trivially, $S_0 = 1$ and $S_1 = 2$. From the figure above, a node x with $k \geq 2$ children has children with at least $k - 2, k - 3, \ldots, 1, 0, 0$ children, giving the recurrence

$$S_k = 2 + \sum_{i=0}^{k-2} S_j$$

($k \geq 2$). The 2 counts the root and its rightmost child; the sum counts the minimum possible number of nodes in the subtrees rooted at the remaining children. But now substituting $k + 1$ for k, gives $S_{k+1} = 2 + \sum_{j=0}^{k-1} S_j$, and subtracting the two equations gives $S_{k+1} - S_k = S_{k-1}$, or $S_{k+1} = S_k + S_{k-1}$, so that the S_k are just the Fibonacci numbers, with $S_0 = F_2 = 1$. Since $s(x) \geq S_k$, where $k = c(x)$, the result follows immediately. ∎

The properties of the Fibonacci numbers are well known; according to Exercise 2.6, $F_k \geq \phi^{k-2}$, where $\phi = (1 + \sqrt{5})/2 \simeq 1.6180$. Therefore

$$n \geq s(x) \geq F_{c(x)+2} \geq \phi^{c(x)}$$

and so $c(x) \leq \log_\phi n \simeq 1.44 \log_2 n$. M can therefore be taken as $\lfloor \log_\phi n \rfloor$ in the analyses; the conclusion is that the amortized complexity of *Initialize*, *Empty*, *Insert*, *DecreaseKey*, and *Meld* is $O(1)$, and the amortized complexity of *DeleteMin* and *Delete* is $O(\log n)$.

7.7   Choosing a Priority Queue Implementation

This chapter closes with a comparison of the priority queue implementations studied so far, and some suggestions about when each should be used. First, Table 7.1 gives their complexities. Note that the times for Fibonacci heaps are amortized; an individual operation may be more expensive. The other complexities are all worst-case.

For completeness, the unsorted doubly linked list is included. In operation sequences featuring *Meld* and *DecreaseKey*, it has something to offer; and it would be preferred for small n.

Also included are 2-3 trees to represent the ordered symbol table implementations. These are preferred when operations like *RetrieveNext* are needed (Section 6.1).

The heap is the simplest efficient structure, and for the core operations *Initialize*, *Empty*, *Insert*, *FindMin*, and *DeleteMin*, which are all that are required in the majority of applications, it is generally the

Table 7.1

	Unsorted doubly linked list	2-3 tree	Heap	Binomial queue	Fibonacci heap (amortized)
Initialize	$O(1)$	$O(1)$	$O(1)$	$O(1)$	$O(1)$
Empty	$O(1)$	$O(1)$	$O(1)$	$O(1)$	$O(1)$
Insert	$O(1)$	$O(\log n)$	$O(\log n)$	$O(\log n)$	$O(1)$
DeleteMin	$O(n)$	$O(\log n)$	$O(\log n)$	$O(\log n)$	$O(\log n)$
FindMin	$O(n)$	$O(\log n)$	$O(1)$	$O(\log n)$	$O(1)$
Delete	$O(1)$	$O(\log n)$	$O(\log n)$	$O(\log n)$	$O(\log n)$
Meld	$O(1)$	$O(n)$	$O(n)$	$O(\log n)$	$O(1)$
DecreaseKey	$O(1)$	$O(\log n)$	$O(\log n)$	$O(\log n)$	$O(1)$

method of choice. If *DecreaseKey* and *Delete* are needed, back indexes in the entries are required as in Implementation Module 7.1.

Vuillemin's binomial queue provides efficient melds. It also runs fast in practice, and the code for the five core operations is quite simple.

The complexity bounds shown above for the Fibonacci heap lead to asymptotically efficient implementations of several important graph algorithms, as will be seen in Chapter 10. Unfortunately, the space overhead per entry is quite high, and the operations are somewhat cumbersome to implement. It is anticipated that future research will improve on the Fibonacci heap in this respect; several alternative data structures already exist (Fredman *et al.*, 1986; Peterson, 1987; Driscoll *et al.*, 1988).

The paper by Jones (1986) is a good starting point for further study of priority queues. It contains descriptions and empirical comparisons of a number of implementations, including several not covered here. There is also an interesting alternative approach, in which the key is used to index an array in a manner roughly analogous to hashing (Brown, 1988).

EXERCISES

7.1 Give a formal specification of the priority queue ADT which accords with the informal one given in Section 7.1. Describe the priority queue as a multiset of pairs $\{\langle k_1, v_1 \rangle, \ldots, \langle k_n, v_n \rangle\}$.

7.2 Write a program to simulate a checkout queue. Make reasonable assumptions about service times, and determine experimentally the effect of customer arrival rate on waiting time.

7.3   In many operating systems, the priority of a process is an integer in some small, fixed range, say between 1 and 20. Show how to implement the priority queue ADT in $O(1)$ time per operation, when the keys are restricted to such a range.

7.4   A priority queue implementation is *stable* if entries with equal keys are returned by *DeleteMin* in the order they were inserted. Stability has been a traditional requirement of simulations. What advice would you give to someone who is looking for an efficient, stable priority queue implementation?

7.5   In Section 7.4, it is shown that for a heap T with n nodes,

$$\sum_{x \in I(T)} [h(x) - 1] \le 2n$$

Show that, in fact,

$$\sum_{x \in I(T)} [h(x) - 1] \le n - 1$$

7.6   The following variant of *AddRoot* has been attributed by Knuth (1973b) to R. W. Floyd. In the first phase, the roots of the two trees are compared and the smaller becomes the new root:

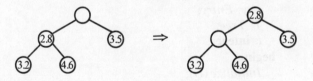

Then this process is repeated on the appropriate subtree; the effect is to move the 'hole' from the root to a leaf. In the second phase, *AddLeaf* is used to insert an entry into this hole:

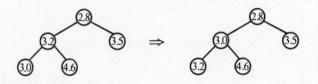

Compare the efficiency of this version of *AddRoot* with the one given in the text.

7.7 Eliminate tail recursion from procedure *AddRoot* of Section 7.4, and hence produce a tuned version of *Heapsort* that contains no procedure calls. Can you find any other ways to tune the algorithm?

7.8 Here is an implementation of Huffman's algorithm, as presented informally in Section 5.4. The n weights ($n \geq 1$) are initially stored in the array $w[1..n]$.

```
type Weights = array [1..n] of
record
  sym: char;
  weight: integer;
end;

type Tree = pointer to node;

type node =
record
  sym: char;
  leftchild, rightchild: Tree;
end;

procedure Huffman(w: Weights): Tree;
var Q: PriorityQueue;
  x, y: Entry;
  T: Tree;
  i: integer;
begin
  Initialize (Q);
  for i := 1 to n do
    Allocate(T, SIZE(T^));
    T^.sym := w[i].sym;
    T^.leftchild := nil;
    T^.rightchild := nil;
    Insert(New(w[i].weight, T), Q);
  end;
```

```
    x := DeleteMin(Q);
    while not Empty(Q) do
        y := DeleteMin(Q);
        Allocate(T, SIZE(T^));
        T^.leftchild := ValueOf(x);
        T^.rightchild := ValueOf(y);
        Insert(New(KeyOf(x) + KeyOf(y), T), Q);
        x := DeleteMin(Q);
    end;

    return ValueOf(x);
end Huffman;
```

Analyse this algorithm.

7.9 Invent a simple potential function for binomial queues and use it to find amortized bounds of $O(1)$ for *Insert* and $O(\log n)$ for *DeleteMin*.

7.10 Find a deletion algorithm for Fibonacci heaps of $O(\log n)$ amortized complexity. Deletion of the distinguished minimum element must be treated as a special case.

7.11 The implementation of Fibonacci heaps given in Section 7.6 requires four pointers per node. Can this large memory overhead be reduced without affecting the asymptotic amortized complexity of any operation?

Implementation Module 7.1:   Implementation of the priority queue ADT, using the heap data structure. *Meld* has been omitted, since it cannot be efficiently implemented. For *New*, *KeyOf*, *ValueOf*, and *Update*, see Implementation Module 6.1.

```
implementation module PriQueue;

const MaxSize = 256;     (* maximum number of entries *)

type Entry = pointer to
record
  key: KeyType;
  value: ValueType;
  back: integer;
end;

type PriorityQueue = pointer to
record
  A: array [1..MaxSize] of Entry;
  size: integer;
end;

procedure Swap(var x, y: Entry);
var z: Entry;
begin
  z := x; x := y; y := z;
end Swap;

procedure AddLeaf (i: integer; Q: PriorityQueue);
var j: integer; x: Entry;
begin
  with Q^ do
    x := A[i];
    j := i div 2;
    while (j > 0) and (A[j]^.key > x^.key) do
      A[i] := A[j];
      A[i]^.back := i;
      i := j;
      j := i div 2;
    end;
    A[i] := x;
    A[i]^.back := i;
  end;
end AddLeaf;
```

```
procedure AddRoot(i: integer; var Q: PriorityQueue);
var j: integer;
begin
  with Q^ do
    j := 2*i;
    if j ≤ size then
      if (j < size) and (A[j]^.key > A[j + 1]^.key) then
        j := j + 1;
      end;
      if A[i]^.key > A[j]^.key then
        Swap(A[i], A[j]);
        A[i]^.back := i;
        A[j]^.back := j;
        AddRoot(j, Q);
      end;
    end;
  end;
end AddRoot;

procedure Initialize(var Q: PriorityQueue);
var p: PriorityQueue;
begin
  Allocate(p, SIZE(p^));
  Q := p;
  Q^.size := 0;
end Initialize;

procedure Empty(var Q: PriorityQueue): boolean;
begin
  return Q^.size = 0;
end Empty;

procedure Insert(x: Entry; var Q: PriorityQueue);
var i, j: integer;
begin
  with Q^ do
    if size = MaxSize then
      Error("PriQueue.Insert: priority queue is full");
    end;
    size := size + 1;
    A[size] := x;
    A[size]^.back := size;
    AddLeaf(size, Q);
  end;
end Insert;
```

```
      procedure FindMin(var Q: PriorityQueue): Entry;
      begin
         if Q^.size = 0 then
            Error("PriQueue.FindMin: priority queue is empty");
         end;
         return Q^.A[1];
      end FindMin;

      procedure DeleteMin(var Q: PriorityQueue): Entry;
      var x: Entry;
      begin
         if Q^.size = 0 then
            Error ("PriQueue.DeleteMin: priority queue is empty");
         end;
         with Q^ do
            x := A[1]; size := size - 1;
            if size > 0 then
               A[1] := A[size + 1]; A[1]^.back := 1;
               AddRoot(1, Q);
            end;
            return x;
         end;
      end DeleteMin;

      procedure Delete (x: Entry; var Q: PriorityQueue);
      var i: integer;
      begin
         with Q^ do
            size := size - 1;
            if x^.back ≤ size then
               i := x^.back;
               A[i] := A[size + 1]; A[i]^.back := i;
               AddRoot(i, Q); AddLeaf(i, Q);
            end;
         end;
      end Delete;

      procedure DecreaseKey(x: Entry; key: KeyType;
                            var Q: PriorityQueue);
      begin
         if x^.key < key then
            Error("PriQueue.DecreaseKey: new key is larger than old");
         end;
         x^.key := key;
         AddLeaf(x^.back, Q);
      end DecreaseKey;

   end PriQueue.
```

Implementation Module 7.2:   Implementation of the priority queue ADT, including *FindMin*, *Meld*, and *DecreaseKey*, using Fibonacci heaps. *New*, *KeyOf*, *ValueOf*, and *Update* have been omitted (see Implementation Module 6.1); *Delete* has been left as an exercise. It is possible to use the *List* ADT of Section 3.2 to implement the doubly linked lists, but unfortunately a large number of type coercions are needed, and as they seriously obscure the code this has not been done.

```
implementation module PriQueue;

    from System import Allocate;
    from SYSTEM import CAST;

    type Entry = pointer to node;
    type PriorityQueue = pointer to node;

    type node =
    record
        predecessor, successor, parent: Entry;
        children: PriorityQueue;
        key: KeyType;
        value: ValueType;
        marked: boolean;
        childnum: integer;
    end;

    const M = 50;
    var A: array [0..M] of Entry;
    var i: integer;

    procedure Append(P, Q: PriorityQueue): PriorityQueue;
    var Backp, Backq: Entry;
    begin
        if P = nil then
            return Q;
        elsif Q = nil then
            return P;
        else
            Backp := P^.predecessor;
            Backq := Q^.predecessor;
            P^.predecessor := Backq;
            Q^.predecessor := Backp;
            Backp^.successor := CAST (Entry, Q);
            Backq^.successor := CAST (Entry, P);
            return P;
        end;
    end Append;
```

```
procedure MakeList(x: Entry): PriorityQueue;
begin
    x^.predecessor := x;
    x^.successor := x;
    return CAST (PriorityQueue, x);
end MakeList;

procedure DeleteEntry(x: Entry; var Q: PriorityQueue);
begin
    if x = CAST (Entry, Q) then
        if CAST (PriorityQueue, Q^.successor) = Q then
            Q := nil;
        else
            Q := CAST (PriorityQueue, Q^.successor);
        end;
    end;
    x^.successor^.predecessor := x^.predecessor;
    x^.predecessor^.successor := x^.successor;
end DeleteEntry;

procedure Initialize(var Q: PriorityQueue);
begin
    Q := nil;
end Initialize;

procedure Empty (Q: PriorityQueue): boolean;
begin
    return Q = nil;
end Empty;

procedure Meld(P, Q: PriorityQueue): PriorityQueue;
begin
    if not Empty(P) and not Empty(Q) and (P^.key ≤ Q^.key) then
        return Append(P, Q);
    else
        return Append(Q, P);
    end;
end Meld;

procedure Insert(x: Entry; var Q: PriorityQueue);
begin
    x^.marked   := false;
    x^.childnum := 0;
    x^.children  := nil;
    x^.parent    := nil;
    Q := Meld(MakeList(x), Q);
end Insert;
```

```
procedure FindMin(var Q: PriorityQueue): Entry;
begin
   return CAST (Entry, Q);
end FindMin;

procedure CascadeCut(x: Entry; var Q: PriorityQueue);
var y: Entry;
begin
   y := x^.parent;
   x^.parent := nil;
   x^.marked := false;
   y^.childnum := y^.childnum − 1;
   DeleteEntry(x, y^.children);
   Q := Meld(MakeList(x), Q);
   if y^.marked then
      y^.marked := false;
      CascadeCut(y, Q);
   elsif y^.parent ≠ nil then
      y^.marked := true;
   end;
end CascadeCut;

procedure DecreaseKey (x: Entry; key: KeyType;
                             var Q: PriorityQueue);
begin
   x^.key := key;
   if x^.parent ≠ nil then
      CascadeCut(x, Q);
   end;
end DecreaseKey;

procedure Link(x, y: Entry): Entry;
begin
   if x^.key ≥ y^.key then
      x^.parent := y;
      y^.childnum := y^.childnum + 1;
      y^.children := Append(MakeList(x), y^.children);
      return y;
   else
      y^.parent := x;
      x^.childnum := x^.childnum + 1;
      x^.children := Append(MakeList(y), x^.children);
      return x;
   end;
end Link;
```

```
procedure DeleteMin(var Q: PriorityQueue): Entry;
var i: integer;
  x, min: Entry;
  p: PriorityQueue;
begin

  (* detach the minimum entry; p := all remaining trees *)
  min := CAST (Entry, Q);
  DeleteEntry(min, Q);
  p := Append(min^.children, Q);

  (* insert each tree in p into A, linking as we go *)
  while p ≠ nil do
    x := CAST(Entry, p);
    DeleteEntry(x, p);
    x^.parent := nil;
    x^.marked := false;
    i := x^.childnum;
    while A[i] ≠ nil do
      x := Link(x, A[i]);
      A[i] := nil;
      i := i + 1;
    end;
    A[i] := x;
  end;

  (* reassemble the trees of A into Q *)
  Initialize(Q);
  for i := 0 to M do
    if A[i] ≠ nil then
      Q := Meld(MakeList(A[i]), Q);
      A[i] := nil;
    end;
  end;

  return min;
end DeleteMin;

begin
  NilEntry := nil;
  for i := 0 to M do
    A[i] := nil;
  end;

end PriQueue.
```

Chapter 8

Sorting

A sorted sequence (one whose entries are arranged in non-decreasing order by key) has several advantages over an unsorted one: for example, it may be searched efficiently, and entries with equal keys are found together. Sorting is also the classical example of a problem where careful design produces algorithms of low complexity, whereas naive approaches are only marginally feasible. For these reasons it is not surprising that sorting is the most-studied and most-solved problem in the theory of algorithms.

In abstract terms, the result of sorting is a sequence of entries, each containing a key and a value, with the keys in non-decreasing order. The entries may initially appear in an array. (Only the keys are shown in these diagrams.)

| 3.5 | 6.2 | 2.8 | 5.0 | 1.1 | 4.5 |

To sort such an array it is necessary to move the entries around in it. If this causes a problem – for example, because the value fields are very large and moving them is expensive – an array of pointers to entries may be used instead:

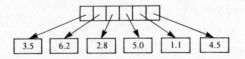

During the sort, only the pointers move, yet the resulting structure is just as convenient, except for the space overhead of one pointer per entry.

Alternatively, a linked list of entries may be used:

Again there is a space overhead of one pointer per entry, and the advantage that only pointers are moved. The choice of representation is mainly determined by the use we intend to make of the sorted sequence. For example, binary search might need to be applied to it, in which case an array must be used.

Most sorting algorithms are based on comparisons between keys, and the number of these comparisons will be taken as the measure of complexity. Although equalities among the keys are allowed, the algorithms to be studied do not exploit this, so it may be assumed for the purposes of analysis that the keys are distinct. A sequence of keys like ⟨problem, specification, correctness, analysis⟩ might just as well be ⟨3, 4, 2, 1⟩, since any comparison-based sorting algorithm will treat the two sequences identically. This means that the instances of the sorting problem are the n! permutations of the numbers 1, 2, ..., n, and the average complexity analyses will assume that each of these instances is equally likely to occur.

8.1 Insertion Sorting

The first sorting strategy is a very simple one. The sorted sequence is built up incrementally, by inserting one entry into it, in the appropriate place, at each stage, as shown in Table 8.1. In this example it is always the first entry of the instance which is chosen for insertion into the result, but any entry would do.

In abstract terms, then, the algorithm is

Table 8.1

Instance	Result
{3.5, 6.2, 2.8, 5.0, 1.1, 4.5}	⟨ ⟩
{6.2, 2.8, 5.0, 1.1, 4.5}	⟨3.5⟩
{2.8, 5.0, 1.1, 4.5}	⟨3.5, 6.2⟩
{5.0, 1.1, 4.5}	⟨2.8, 3.5, 6.2⟩
{1.1, 4.5}	⟨2.8, 3.5, 5.0, 6.2⟩
{4.5}	⟨1.1, 2.8, 3.5, 5.0, 6.2⟩
{ }	⟨1.1, 2.8, 3.5, 4.5, 5.0, 6.2⟩

```
procedure InsertionSort(Instance: multiset): sequence;
var Result: sequence;
    x: Entry;
begin
    Initialize(Result);
    while not Empty(Instance) do
        x := DeleteAny(Instance);
        Insert(x, Result);
    end;
    return Result;
end InsertionSort;
```

The loop invariant, 'Result is a sorted permutation of the elements deleted from Instance', shows that InsertionSort is an incremental algorithm of the first kind, in the classification introduced in Section 4.2.

The operations on Instance are easily implemented by the SimpleSet ADT of Section 3.1, but the insertion of x into its appropriate place in Result is more expensive, and suggests that Result should be implemented using an ordered symbol table, modified to accept equal keys. For example, suppose a binary search tree is used to implement Result. The analysis of Section 6.5 shows that the n insertions require $n(n - 1)/2$ comparisons between keys in the worst case, and $2(n + 1)H_n - 4n$ comparisons on average. Once the insertions are complete, an inorder traversal of the tree will visit the entries in non-decreasing order. This takes $O(n)$ time, which is negligible compared with the insertions. Therefore the binary search tree sort has $O(n^2)$ worst-case complexity, and $O(n\log n)$ average complexity.

Alternatively, 2–3 trees could be used to implement the ordered symbol table, giving $O(n\log n)$ complexity in the worst case.

The remainder of this section is devoted to a very simple implementation of insertion sort, known as *straight insertion*. Although straight insertion is not efficient, its simplicity makes it the method of choice for small instances (say, $n \le 10$), and it is also a good choice when the input is known to be almost sorted.

The entries appear in an array $A[a..b]$, and are sorted in place. The sorted sequence grows through the array from left to right, by engulfing the entry x just to its right at each stage:

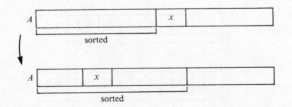

This is achieved by moving entries at the right of the sorted sequence one step to the right, until a gap opens up at the place where x belongs. It is assumed that a sentinel entry $A[a - 1]$ exists and is no larger than the minimum element of $A[a..b]$. Here is the code:

```
procedure StraightInsertionSort(a, b: integer);
var i, j: integer;
    x: Entry;
begin
  for i := a to b do
    j := i;
    x := A[j];
    while KeyOf(A[j - 1]) > KeyOf(x) do
      A[j] := A[j - 1];
      j := j - 1;
    end;
    A[j] := x;
  end;
end StraightInsertionSort;
```

The outer loop's invariant is '$A[a..i - 1]$ contains a sorted permutation of the original contents of $A[a..i - 1]$'. Here is an example of the algorithm in operation, with $A[a..i - 1]$ bracketed at each stage:

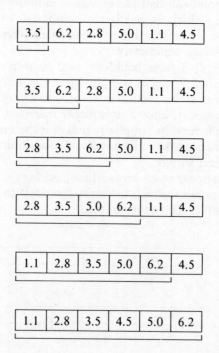

Table 8.2

a	Inversions	$I(a)$
3 5 2 1 4	(3, 2), (3, 1), (5, 2), (5, 1), (5, 4), (2, 1)	6
1 2 3 4 5		0
5 4 3 2 1	(5, 4), (5, 3), (5, 2), (5, 1), (4, 3), (4, 2), (4, 1), (3, 2), (3, 1), (2, 1)	10

Analysis of straight insertion sort.   It is not hard to see that the worst-case complexity of straight insertion sort is $O(n^2)$. Consider an initial array whose keys are in decreasing order. At each stage, the entry x to be inserted is smaller than all the entries in the sorted sequence to its left, and so it must be compared with all of them and with the sentinel. If x is the ith entry, this makes i comparisons to insert x, and so the total cost is

$$\sum_{i=1}^{n} i = n(n + 1)/2$$

comparisons between keys. This is clearly the worst case.

To go further into the analysis of straight insertion sort, and other simple sorting algorithms containing two nested loops, *inversions* must be studied. Let $a = a_1, a_2, \ldots, a_n$ be a permutation of $1, 2, \ldots, n$. An inversion of a is a pair (a_i, a_j) such that $i < j$ and $a_i > a_j$, which means that a_i and a_j are out of order. The number of inversions of a, denoted $I(a)$, is a measure of how disordered a is. For example, Table 8.2 gives three permutations and their inversions.

The permutation $n, n - 1, \ldots, 1$ has $(n - 1) + (n - 2) + \ldots + 0 = n(n - 1)/2$ inversions. This is the maximum number of inversions that any permutation of $1, 2, \ldots, n$ can have, since a_1 can be the first element of at most $n - 1$ inversions, namely $(a_1, a_2), \ldots, (a_1, a_n)$; then a_2 can be the first element of at most $n - 2$ inversions; and so on.

There is a clever trick for finding the average number of inversions, assuming that each of the $n!$ permutations of $1, 2, \ldots, n$ is equally likely. Each permutation a has a *reflection* $\hat{a}$, which is a written backwards. For all a, every inversion of $n, n - 1, \ldots, 1$ appears either in a or in $\hat{a}$, as Table 8.3 illustrates.

Table 8.3

	Inversions
$a = 3\ 5\ 2\ 1\ 4$	(3, 2), (3, 1), (5, 2), (5, 1), (5, 4), (2, 1)
$\hat{a} = 4\ 1\ 2\ 5\ 3$	(4, 1), (4, 2), (4, 3), (5, 3)

To see why this is so, consider any inversion, say $(5, 2)$. If $(5, 2)$ is an inversion of a, then 5 appears before 2 in a; but then 5 appears after 2 in $\hat{a}$, and so $(5, 2)$ is not an inversion of $\hat{a}$. Conversely, if $(5, 2)$ is not an inversion of a, then 5 appears after 2 in a, and $(5, 2)$ is an inversion of $\hat{a}$.

It may be concluded that $I(a) + I(\hat{a}) = n(n - 1)/2$, for all a. Now by definition, the average number of inversions, $A(n)$, is

$$A(n) = \frac{1}{n!} \sum_{a \in S_n} I(a)$$

where S_n is the set of all permutations of $1, 2, \ldots, n$. But as a runs through S_n, so does $\hat{a}$. Therefore,

$$A(n) = \frac{1}{n!} \sum_{a \in S_n} I(\hat{a})$$

Adding these equations gives

$$2A(n) = \frac{1}{n!} \sum_{a \in S_n} [I(a) + I(\hat{a})]$$

$$= \frac{1}{n!} \sum_{a \in S_n} \frac{n(n - 1)}{2}$$

$$= \frac{n(n - 1)}{2}$$

and so the average number of inversions in a permutation of $1, 2, \ldots, n$ is $n(n - 1)/4$.

The number of comparisons of $KeyOf(A[j - 1])$ with $KeyOf(x)$ in $StraightInsertionSort(1, n)$ can now be counted. Let these comparisons be divided into those that succeed and those that fail. Since failure terminates the inner loop, it must happen once per iteration of the outer loop, which is exactly n times. On the other hand, every successful comparison occurs between two keys $KeyOf(A[j - 1])$ and $KeyOf(x)$ that formed an inversion in the original input, since $j - 1 < i$ and $KeyOf(A[j - 1]) > KeyOf(x)$; and every inversion shows up at some point as such a comparison. Therefore, for each permutation a in S_n,

Total number of comparisons = Total number of inversions + n

and so the worst-case complexity of $StraightInsertionSort$ is $W(n) = n(n - 1)/2 + n$, and the average complexity is $A(n) = n(n - 1)/4 + n$.

Observe that the complexity is closely related to the number of inversions. This means that it can vary dramatically with the input. In particular, if the input is known to be almost sorted (say, containing only $2n$ or $3n$ inversions), then straight insertion sort will be very efficient.

8.2   Selection Sorting

Selection sorting is another simple strategy. An entry with minimum key is repeatedly extracted from the instance, and appended to the result sequence; as in Table 8.4.

The abstract implementation of this is

> **procedure** *SelectionSort*(*Instance*: *multiset*): *sequence*;
> **var** *Result*: *sequence*;
> **begin**
>   *Initialize*(*Result*);
>   **while not** *Empty*(*Instance*) **do**
>   *x* := *DeleteMin*(*Instance*);
>   *Result* := *Append*(*Result*, *MakeList*(*x*));
>   **end**;
>   **return** *Result*;
> **end** *SelectionSort*;

Although it is true that *Result* is always a sorted permutation of the entries extracted from *Instance*, this is not the whole story: it must also be said that these are the smallest elements of *Instance*. The loop invariant for *SelectionSort* is therefore quite different from the one for *Insertion-Sort*, and in fact it is '*Result* contains an initial part of a sorted permutation of *Instance*', showing that *SelectionSort* is an incremental

Table 8.4

Instance	Result
{3.5, 6.2, 2.8, 5.0, 1.1, 4.5}	⟨ ⟩
{3.5, 6.2, 2.8, 5.0, 4.5}	⟨1.1⟩
{3.5, 6.2, 5.0, 4.5}	⟨1.1, 2.8⟩
{6.2, 5.0, 4.5}	⟨1.1, 2.8, 3.5⟩
{6.2, 5.0}	⟨1.1, 2.8, 3.5, 4.5⟩
{6.2}	⟨1.1, 2.8, 3.5, 4.5, 5.0⟩
{ }	⟨1.1, 2.8, 3.5, 4.5, 5.0, 6.2⟩

algorithm of the second kind, according to the classification introduced in Section 4.2.

Result may be a simple list, but the operations on *Instance* suggest the use of a priority queue. The data structures of Chapter 7 provide a variety of $O(n\log n)$ implementations of *SelectionSort*. One in particular stands out, as being an in-place sort of $O(n\log n)$ worst-case complexity, using no extra memory for pointers or anything else – a combination of advantages found in no other sorting algorithm. This is *heapsort*, and it is presented in Section 7.4.

A very simple $O(n^2)$ implementation of selection sort, called *straight selection*, may be found in Exercise 2.12.

8.3   Merging and Mergesort

Suppose there are two sorted sequences of entries, and they need to be *merged* into a single sorted sequence. Our primary motivation for this is a sorting algorithm, called *Mergesort*, which appears below; but merging has other applications as well, for example *batch file update* (Exercise 8.18).

When merging two sequences p and q, the first entry of the result will be the smaller of the first entries of the two sequences. After it is removed, the second entry will be the smaller of what remains, and so on, as exemplified in Table 8.5.

At this point, no more comparisons are needed, and the remaining elements of p may be moved to the back of the result list.

In abstract terms, the *FifoQueue* ADT of Section 3.2 is needed to implement this algorithm. It provides *Dequeue* (p), which deletes and returns the entry at the front of p, and *Enqueue* $(x, Result)$, which appends x to the back of *Result*. Here then is the code:

Table 8.5

p	q	*Result*
⟨2.8, 3.5, 5.0, 6.2⟩	⟨1.1, 4.5⟩	⟨ ⟩
⟨2.8, 3.5, 5.0, 6.2⟩	⟨4.5⟩	⟨1.1⟩
⟨3.5, 5.0, 6.2⟩	⟨4.5⟩	⟨1.1, 2.8⟩
⟨5.0, 6.2⟩	⟨4.5⟩	⟨1.1, 2.8, 3.5⟩
⟨5.0, 6.2⟩	⟨ ⟩	⟨1.1, 2.8, 3.5, 4.5⟩

```
procedure Merge(p, q: FifoQueue): FifoQueue;
var Result: FifoQueue;
begin
    Initialize(Result);
    while not Empty(p) and not Empty(q) do
        if KeyOf(FirstEntry(p)) ≤ KeyOf(FirstEntry(q)) then
            Enqueue(Dequeue(p), Result);
        else
            Enqueue(Dequeue(q), Result);
        end;
    end;
    if not Empty(p) then
        Result := Append(Result, p);
    else
        Result := Append(Result, q);
    end;
    return Result;
end Merge;
```

This algorithm works correctly when either or both of p and q are empty. The loop invariant is, in part, '*Result* is an initial part of the sequence which is the original p and q merged', making *Merge* a simple example of an incremental algorithm of the second kind.

The analysis of *Merge* is easy. The *FifoQueue* operations can each be implemented in $O(1)$ time, so it is realistic to take the number of comparisons between keys as the measure of complexity. Suppose that initially p contains m entries and q contains n entries. Each comparison between keys is followed by the movement of one entry to the result list, so while the loop is running the number of comparisons between keys is equal to the size of the result list. When the loop terminates, some unknown number of entries, say k, will remain on p or q, and at that moment the size of the result list is $m + n - k$, which must therefore be the total number of comparisons made. This is maximized when k is minimized. If either p or q is initially non-empty, $k \geq 1$, so the worst-case complexity of $Merge(p, q)$ is

$$W(m, n) = 0 \qquad\qquad \text{if } m = n = 0$$

$$= m + n - 1 \qquad \text{otherwise}$$

Incidentally, the corresponding formula for average complexity is

$$A(m, n) = m + n - \left(\frac{n}{m + 1} + \frac{m}{n + 1}\right)$$

but the derivation requires expertise with binomial coefficients, so is beyond the scope of this text. If $m = n$, this is never less than $m + n - 2$, which is surprisingly close to $W(m, n)$.

Mergesort.   The *Mergesort* algorithm is a classic example of divide-and-conquer. To sort an array, recursively sort its left and right halves separately, then merge them. For example,

Initial array:

3.5	6.2	2.8	5.0	1.1	4.5

After sorting each half:

2.8	3.5	6.2	1.1	4.5	5.0

After merging:

1.1	2.8	3.5	4.5	5.0	6.2

This strategy is so simple, and so efficient (as will be seen shortly), that it could well be asked, why bother with any other method? The problem here is that there seems to be no easy way to merge two adjacent sorted arrays together in place. (It is quite easy to do if the result may be built up in a separate array, but this idea will not be pursued any further here.) So each entry is made into a one-element *FifoQueue*, and the *Merge* algorithm above used to perform the merging.

```
procedure Merge(p, q: ArrayIndex): ArrayIndex;
var r: ArrayIndex;
begin
  r := dummy;
  while (p ≠ 0) and (q ≠ 0) do
    if KeyOf(A[p]) ≤ KeyOf(A[q]) then
      A[r].next := p; p := A[p].next;
    else
      A[r].next := q; q := A[q].next;
    end;
    r := A[r].next;
  end;
  if p ≠ 0 then A[r].next := p;
  else A[r].next := q;
  end;
  return A[dummy].next;
end Merge;
```

This version of *Merge* is designed for use in the merge sorting of an array *A* of entries. Array indices are used instead of pointers to implement the linked lists, with 0 playing the part of a nil pointer. Each entry contains a *next* field, holding the index of the next entry in the list, in addition to the usual key and value fields. A dummy entry, possibly *A*[0], is assumed to exist; it serves as a header for the result list. The variable *r* always points to the last entry of the result list.

Using this version of *Merge*, *Mergesort* may be implemented as follows:

```
procedure Mergesort(a, b: integer): ArrayIndex;
var left, right: ArrayIndex;
   mid: integer;
begin
   if a > b then
      return 0;
   elsif a = b then
      A[a].next := 0;
      return a;
   else
      mid := (a + b) div 2;
      left := Mergesort(a, mid);
      right := Mergesort(mid + 1, b);
      return Merge(left, right);
   end;
end Mergesort;
```

Notice that no entries actually move; only the pointers change. If the entries need to appear in the array in increasing order, mergesort is probably inferior to *Heapsort*; alternatively, a tedious rearrangement of the entries could be undertaken (Exercise 8.6).

Analysis of *Mergesort*.   Let $W(n)$ be the number of comparisons between keys made by *Mergesort*(1, *n*) in the worst case. Clearly $W(0) = W(1) = 0$, and for larger *n* the code executed is

left := Mergesort(1, $\lfloor (n + 1)/2 \rfloor$);
right := Mergesort($\lfloor (n + 1)/2 \rfloor + 1$, *n*);
return *Merge* (*left*, *right*);

The total length of the *left* and *right* lists is *n*, so *Merge*(*left*, *right*) costs $n - 1$ comparisons in the worst case. The recurrence equation is therefore

$$W(0) = 0$$
$$W(1) = 0$$
$$W(n) = W(\lfloor(n + 1)/2\rfloor) + W(n - \lfloor(n + 1)/2\rfloor) + n - 1$$

The floor function is eliminated by restricting n to the form $n = 2^k$, $k \geq 1$. Informally, this ensures that the array will break into two equal halves at each level of the recursion; algebraically,

$$\lfloor(n + 1)/2\rfloor = n - \lfloor(n + 1)/2\rfloor = 2^{k-1}$$

Substituting these values into the recurrence equation gives

$$W(2^k) = 2W(2^{k-1}) + 2^k - 1$$

which can be solved by repeated substitution:

$$
\begin{aligned}
W(2^k) &= 2W(2^{k-1}) + 2^k - 1 \\
&= 2[2W(2^{k-2}) + 2^{k-1} - 1] + 2^k - 1 \\
&= 2[2[2W(2^{k-3}) + 2^{k-2} - 1] + 2^{k-1} - 1] + 2^k - 1 \\
&= 2^3W(2^{k-3}) + 3\cdot2^k - 2^2 - 2^1 - 2^0 \\
&= \ldots \\
&= 2^iW(2^{k-i}) + i2^k - \sum_{j=0}^{i-1} 2^j
\end{aligned}
$$

Letting $i = k$ gives

$$
\begin{aligned}
W(2^k) &= 2^kW(2^0) + k2^k - \sum_{j=0}^{k-1} 2^j \\
&= k2^k - (2^k - 1)
\end{aligned}
$$

using the standard formula for the sum of a geometric progression. But now recall that $2^k = n$, and $k = \log_2 n$, and so the worst-case complexity of $Mergesort(1, n)$ is

$$W(n) = n\log_2 n - (n - 1)$$

when n is a power of 2. This is the smallest of any sorting algorithm that will be studied here, and (as will be proved in Chapter 11) is close to the best possible for any sorting algorithm based on comparisons. The average complexity analysis is beyond the scope of this book, but it turns out that $A(n) \simeq n\log_2 n - 1.2645n$ (Knuth, 1973b).

8.4 Quicksort

The sorting algorithm presented in this section, like *Mergesort*, is an application of the divide-and-conquer strategy. It was named *Quicksort* by its inventor, Hoare (1962).

Quicksort is the method of choice for general-purpose sorting, because, when implemented carefully, its average running time is smaller than other algorithms. Unfortunately, its worst-case complexity is poor, and in practice it is necessary to take precautions which reduce the probability of a worst case occurring.

The idea of *Quicksort* is to take one entry of $A[a..b]$, say $A[a]$, and move it to the position it will occupy when the sort is complete. This entry is called the *pivot*. At the same time, other entries are also moved, to guarantee that all entries to the left of the pivot are no larger than the pivot, and all entries to the right are no smaller. For example,

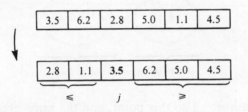

It will be seen later how to do this. For now, it is assumed that there is a function $Partition(a, b)$ that rearranges the entries in this way and returns j, the index of the place where the pivot ended up. Then once $A[a..j-1]$ and $A[j+1..b]$ are sorted recursively, the whole array will be sorted:

```
procedure Quicksort(a, b: integer);
var j: integer;
begin
    if a ≤ b then
        j := Partition(a, b);
        Quicksort(a, j - 1);
        Quicksort(j + 1, b);
    end;
end Quicksort;
```

The analysis of *Quicksort* is based on an unexpected correspondence between it and binary search trees. For example, when partitioning

| 3.5 | 6.2 | 2.8 | 5.0 | 1.1 | 4.5 |

3.5 is compared with each of the other $n - 1$ entries, to determine which side to put them, and the result is

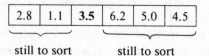

| 2.8 | 1.1 | **3.5** | 6.2 | 5.0 | 4.5 |

still to sort   still to sort

Now consider what happens when 3.5, 6.2, 2.8, 5.0, 1.1, 4.5 is inserted into an initially empty binary search tree. The first element, 3.5, becomes the root, and there are $n - 1$ comparisons between it and the other elements, as they pass through the root on their way to the left or right subtree:

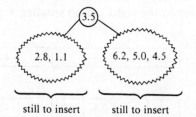

still to insert   still to insert

The costs are both $n - 1$ to this point, and the same argument applies recursively, so it can be concluded that for every permutation a in S_n, the cost of *Quicksort* on a is the same as the cost of inserting the elements of a one by one into an initially empty binary search tree.

By the analysis of Section 6.5, it follows that the worst-case complexity of *Quicksort* is $W(n) = n(n - 1)/2$. This occurs when the corresponding tree is skew, for example, when the input is already sorted. The average complexity is $A(n) = 2(n + 1)H_n - 4n \approx 1.38n\log_2 n - 4n$, which is about 38% more comparisons between keys than *Mergesort* makes in the worst case. In practice, however, the inner loops of *Quicksort* are faster than *Mergesort's*, and this gives *Quicksort* the advantage.

In his original paper, Hoare suggested a variety of ways to improve the running time of *Quicksort*. One suggestion is to stop the recursion when $n \leq 10$ (say), and use some simple sort like straight insertion instead. This increases $A(n)$, but pays off in less overhead for recursion (Exercise 8.9). Another is to choose for pivot element the median of a small sample of the input. Choosing the median of $A[a]$, $A[(a + b)$ **div** $2]$, and $A[b]$ for pivot, as suggested by Singleton (1969), will convert a sorted initial array from a worst case into a best case, and will approximately halve $W(n)$ (Exercise 8.10); also, it can be shown to reduce $A(n)$ to about $1.16n\log_2 n$ (Knuth, 1973b). It also provides a sentinel for the partitioning algorithm given below. Both improvements are recommended.

Partitioning the array.   There are several possible ways to implement *Partition*(*a*, *b*), but the following seems to be the best. Starting at *A*[*a* + 1], scan to the right and stop at the first *A*[*i*] such that *KeyOf*(*A*[*i*]) ≥ *KeyOf*(*A*[*a*]). Then *A*[*a* + 1..*i* − 1] are at their proper end, and need not be moved, but *A*[*i*] belongs at the right-hand end. Now start at *A*[*b*] and scan to the left, stopping at the first *A*[*j*] such that *KeyOf*(*A*[*j*]) ≤ *KeyOf*(*A*[*a*]). Then *A*[*j* + 1..*b*] are at their proper end, but *A*[*j*] belongs at the left-hand end:

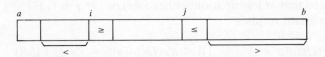

So swap *A*[*i*] with *A*[*j*], and carry on from *A*[*i* + 1] and *A*[*j* − 1]. When *i* and *j* cross, it is time to stop, and a final swap of *A*[*a*] with *A*[*j*] completes the partitioning.

The following version of *Partition*(*a*, *b*) assumes that a sentinel entry *A*[*b* + 1] exists, and that *KeyOf*(*A*[*a*]) ≤ *KeyOf*(*A*[*b* + 1]), which means that *Quicksort*(1, *n*) assumes that *A*[*n* + 1] exists with *KeyOf*(*A*[*n* + 1]) at least as large as any element of *A*. Here is *Partition*:

```
procedure Partition(a, b: integer): integer;
var i, j: integer;
begin
   i := a + 1; j := b;
   while KeyOf(A[i]) < KeyOf(A[a]) do i := i + 1; end;
   while KeyOf(A[j]) > KeyOf(A[a]) do j := j − 1; end;
   while i < j do
      Swap(A[i], A[j]);
      i := i + 1; j := j − 1;
      while KeyOf(A[i]) < KeyOf(A[a]) do i := i + 1; end;
      while KeyOf(A[j]) > KeyOf(A[a]) do j := j − 1; end;
   end;
   if a < j then Swap(A[a], A[j]); end;
   return j;
end Partition;
```

This is a little longer than it needs to be, but it is more amenable to proof than other tuned implementations known to the author. The invariant of the main loop ('**while** *i* < *j* . . .') is, in part,

$$KeyOf(A[a + 1..i − 1]) \le KeyOf(A[a]) \le KeyOf(A[j + 1..b])$$
$$\text{and } KeyOf(A[i]) \ge KeyOf(A[a]) \text{ and } KeyOf(A[j]) \le KeyOf(A[a])$$

The notation $KeyOf(A[a + 1..i - 1]) \leq KeyOf(A[a])$, for example, means that all the keys of $A[a + 1..i- 1]$ are less than or equal to $KeyOf(A[a])$. It is easy to see that the two initial loops establish this loop invariant, and that it holds at the beginning of each iteration of the main loop.

The inner loops will not allow i and j to cross, since i scans past keys strictly smaller than $KeyOf(A[a])$, and j scans past keys strictly larger than $KeyOf(A[a])$. Therefore, the furthest i can get past j is $i = j + 1$, which occurs when $i = j - 1$ at the beginning of the main loop. It may be concluded that at termination, either $i = j$ or $i = j + 1$. If $i = j$, then the loop invariant implies

$$KeyOf(A[a + 1..j - 1]) \leq KeyOf(A[a]) = KeyOf(A[j])$$
$$\leq KeyOf(A[j + 1..b])$$

and the final swap of $A[a]$ with $A[j]$ correctly completes the partitioning. In the more usual case when $i = j + 1$, the loop invariant implies

$$KeyOf(A[a + 1..j]) \leq KeyOf(A[a]) \leq KeyOf(A[j + 1..b])$$

and again the final swap of $A[a]$ with $A[j]$ is correct.

This partitioning algorithm differs somewhat from the one envisaged when analysing *Quicksort* above. First, it makes one or two sentinel comparisons in addition to the $n - 1$ comparisons counted in the analysis. They are regarded as part of the general overhead. Second, it does not place entries into subarrays in the same order as they appeared in the original array (for example, 6.2 is moved to the right of 5.0 in the example partitioning above). This does not affect $W(n)$, since, if the array is sorted initially, no entries ever move; and Exercise 8.8 shows that it does not affect $A(n)$ either.

8.5 Radix Sorting

The final sorting algorithm studied here, *radix sorting*, is radically different from the others that have been considered. Like hashing, it uses array indexing instead of comparisons to distinguish between keys.

It is assumed that the keys are d-digit numbers in base r (r is also called the *radix*). For example, if the keys are strings of lower-case letters of length 6, then $d = 6$ and $r = 26$. The example below uses decimal keys in the range $0 \leq x \leq 999$, with $d = 3$ and $r = 10$. Any digit x_i of a key satisfies $0 \leq x_i \leq r - 1$, and so may be used to index an array of r lists. The basic idea of radix sorting is to make one pass through the entries, placing each entry at the back of the x_ith list, where x_i is the ith digit of the entry's key. This is called *a spread on the ith digit*.

The most natural way to sort using spreads is to begin with a sort on the first, or most significant digit. The resulting r sublists are then sorted recursively (beginning with a spread on the second digit), and their concatenation is the final result – a kind of r-way divide-and-conquer. This algorithm is called *MSD radix sort*. It suffers from fragmentation of its entries into many small sublists.

A less obvious strategy, *LSD radix sort*, begins with a spread on the last, or least significant digit. For example, to sort

the procedure begins with a spread on the third digit:

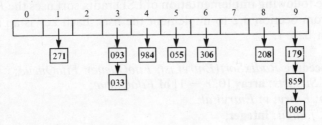

and then the lists are concatenated, giving

271 ▸ 093 ▸ 033 ▸ 984 ▸ 055 ▸ 306 ▸ 208 ▸ 179 ▸ 859 ▸ 009

The entries are now in order, if everything but the last digit of each key is ignored. This has been emphasized by emboldening these last digits. A second spread/concatenate, on the second last digit, brings the entries into order if all but the last two digits of each key are ignored:

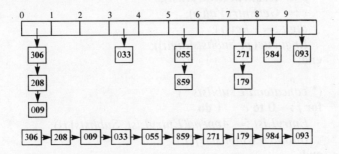

Notice how the correct order for final digits is not disturbed; they are in order on each sublist, since entries are placed at the end of the sublist during the spread. Carrying on in this way, the final spread/concatenate on the most significant digit completes the sort:

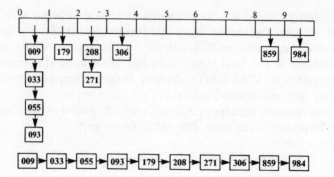

The following implementation of LSD radix sort uses the *FifoQueue* ADT from Section 3.2 to implement the lists. Each key is an array of *d* digits in base *r*.

```
procedure RadixSort(EntryList: FifoQueue): FifoQueue;
var Sublists: array [0..r - 1] of FifoQueue;
  p: Entry; v: EntryVal;
  i, j, digit: integer;
begin
  for j := 0 to r - 1 do
    Initialize (Sublists[ j]);
  end;

  for i := d to 1 by - 1 do

    (* spread on the ith digit *)
    while not Empty (EntryList) do
      p := Dequeue(EntryList);
      v := GetEntryVal(p);
      digit := v.key[i];
      Enqueue(p, Sublists[digit]);
    end;

    (* concatenate sublists *)
    for j := 0 to r - 1 do
      EntryList := Append(EntryList, Sublists[ j]);
      Initialize(Sublists[ j]);
    end;

  end;
  return EntryList;
end RadixSort;
```

The outer loop's invariant is '*EntryList* is sorted if we ignore all but digits i to d of each key'. This makes LSD radix sort an incremental algorithm of the first kind.

The complexity of LSD radix sort is a function of n, d, and r. The characteristic operation for the spread phase is the movement of one entry from the master list to a sublist. This occurs n times per spread. The characteristic operation for the concatenation phase is the append of a sublist to the new master list. This occurs r times per concatenate. So the total cost of one spread/concatenate is $O(n + r)$. Since the whole sort consists of d such phases, its complexity is $O(d(n + r))$.

For fixed d and r, LSD radix sort is $O(n)$. Note, however, that if the n keys are distinct, then $d \geq \log_r n$. This is so because, given d digits in base r, it is possible to represent at most $n = r^d$ distinct keys. So as n increases, it may be necessary to increase r, if $O(n)$ complexity is to be maintained. Another problem is that the overhead $O(dr)$ is independent of n: if n is small, a lot of time is wasted concatenating empty sublists.

8.6 Choosing a Sorting Algorithm

The sorting algorithms studied in this chapter may be summarized as shown in Table 8.6 (only the leading terms of the complexities are given).

Straight insertion is a good choice when n is small, or when the input is known to be almost sorted. It is simple, and no extra memory (for example, for pointers) is required.

Heapsort and *Mergesort* have similar characteristics: they offer $O(n\log n)$ complexity in the worst case, and in practice their running times are quite similar. *Heapsort's* output is an array, and it has the advantage of requiring no extra memory. *Mergesort's* principal advantage is that it accesses the entries sequentially, which makes it well adapted to sorting on external storage devices.

Quicksort is generally the method of choice. The partitioning algorithm can be highly tuned, and in practice this, together with its low

Table 8.6			
	Length (*lines*)	$W(n)$	$A(n)$
StraightInsertionSort	14	$0.5n^2$	$0.25n^2$
Heapsort	25	$2.0n\log_2 n$	unknown
Mergesort	37	$1.0n\log_2 n$	$1.00n\log_2 n$
Quicksort	24	$0.5n^2$	$1.38n\log_2 n$
RadixSort	27	$O(d(n + r))$	$O(d(n + r))$

average complexity, makes *Quicksort* run faster than its competitors. The improvements discussed at the end of Section 8.4 offer some protection against the poor worst case.

LSD radix sort has the potential to run in linear time, but several caveats apply. The keys must be composed of a fixed number d of base r digits. The result is a list, not a sorted array, and extra memory is needed for pointers. Most important, n must be large, or else the $O(dr)$ part will dominate the complexity.

A large number of other sorting algorithms exist, and they have been comprehensively surveyed by Knuth (1973b). Knuth also discusses the methods employed when the data to be sorted are on external storage devices.

EXERCISES

8.1 A sorting algorithm is *stable* if it preserves the relative order of entries with equal keys. Are the following sorting algorithms stable, or can they easily be made so?

(a) *StraightInsertionSort*
(b) *Quicksort*
(c) *Mergesort*
(d) *Heapsort*
(e) *RadixSort*

8.2 The following implementation of insertion sort uses binary search to find the position where the next insertion should take place:

```
procedure BinaryInsertionSort(a, b: integer);
var i, j, pos: integer;
    found: boolean;
    x: Entry;
begin
  for i := a + 1 to b do
    found := BinarySearch(A, a, i−1, KeyOf(A[i]), pos);
    x := A[i];
    for j := i − 1 to pos + 1 by − 1 do
      A[j + 1] := A[j];
    end;
    A[pos + 1] := x;
  end;
end BinaryInsertionSort;
```

(a) What is the asymptotic worst-case complexity of *BinaryInsertionSort* (1, *n*) if the characteristic operation is one comparison between keys?

(b) Repeat (a), using the assignment $A[j + 1] := A[j]$ as the characteristic operation.

8.3 What is the time complexity of *Mergesort* when its input is already sorted?

8.4 Find a file of 8 elements that is a worst case for *Mergesort*, that is, that takes $8\log_2 8 - 7 = 17$ comparisons to sort.

8.5 Use dynamic programming to eliminate the recursion from *Mergesort*. Does the method apply to *Quicksort*?

8.6 At the conclusion of *Mergesort*, the linked list gives the sorted ordering of the array elements, but they have not been moved:

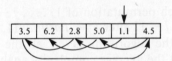

Find an $O(n)$ algorithm for rearranging the entries into sorted order. Care must be taken when swapping 1.1 and 3.5, for example, to ensure that the data structure does not forget that 3.5 is the successor of 2.8.

8.7 *Median-finding.* Consider the problem of finding the *k*th smallest element of a set of numbers. For example, if $k = \lfloor (n + 1)/2 \rfloor$ this would be finding the median element. The obvious $O(n\log n)$ solution is to put the *n* numbers into an array $A[1..n]$, sort the array, and return $A[k]$. There are several algorithms in the literature which achieve $O(n)$ complexity in the worst case; the first was by Blum *et al.* (1973). They are unfortunately rather complicated to implement. The following algorithm, based on *Quicksort*, has $O(n)$ average complexity and so is a good compromise:

(* *Pre*: $a \le k \le b$ *)
(* *Post*: *A[k] contains the element of A[a..b] that* *)
(* *it would contain if A[a..b] were sorted.* *)

```
procedure Select(a, b, k: integer);
var j: integer;
begin
  j := Partition(a, b);
  if j < k then
    Select(j + 1, b, k);
  elsif j > k then
    Select(a, j - 1, k);
  end;
end Select;
```

It turns out that this algorithm is rather hard to analyse in general, so only the special case of *Select*(1, *n*, 1) will be considered.

(a) Explain briefly how *Select*(*a*, *b*, *k*) works. Include a diagram.
(b) What is the worst-case complexity of *Select*(1, *n*, 1)?
(c) What is the average complexity of *Select*(1, *n*, 1)? The analysis of *Quicksort* can be adapted to this problem.

8.8 Show that each permutation of 1, ..., *j* − 1 is equally likely to occur in *A*[1..*j* − 1] after *j* := *Partition*(1, *n*) is complete, where *Partition* is the algorithm given at the end of Section 8.4. Conclude that the average complexity analysis of *Quicksort* holds for this version of *Partition*.

8.9 How many recursive calls to *Quicksort* are made by *Quicksort*(1, *n*)? If the recursion is stopped when *n* ≤ *k* (for example, *k* = 10), and some other sort is used on these small subarrays, what can be said about the number of recursive calls then?

8.10 In the following implementation of median-of-three quicksort, procedure *ThreeSort*(*x*, *y*, *z*) examines *x*, *y*, and *z*, swapping the smallest into *x*, the largest into *z*, and the median of the three into *y*. This takes three comparisons between keys. *Partition* (*a*, *b*) performs the usual partition of *A*[*a*..*b*] about *A*[*a*], taking *b* − *a* comparisons.

```
procedure ThreeSort(var x, y, z: Entry);
begin
  if KeyOf(x) > KeyOf(y) then Swap(x, y); end;
  if KeyOf(x) > KeyOf(z) then Swap(x, z); end;
  if KeyOf(y) > KeyOf(z) then Swap(y, z); end;
end ThreeSort;
```

```
procedure MedianQuicksort(a, b: integer);
var j, mid: integer;
begin
  if b − a + 1 ≤ 1 then
    (* do nothing *)
  elsif b − a + 1 = 2 then
    if KeyOf(A[a]) > KeyOf(A[b]) then
      Swap(A[a], A[b]);
    end;
  else
    mid := (a + b) div 2;
    ThreeSort(A[a], A[mid], A[b]);
    if a + 1 ≠ mid then
      Swap(A[a + 1], A[mid]);
    end;
    j := Partition(a + 1, b − 1);
    MedianQuicksort(a, j − 1);
    MedianQuicksort(j + 1, b);
  end;
end MedianQuicksort;
```

(a) If j is the value returned by Partition, show that the number of comparisons between keys made by MedianQuicksort(1, n) is given by the recurrence

$$T(0) = 0$$
$$T(1) = 0$$
$$T(2) = 1$$
$$T(n) = n + T(j − 1) + T(n − j)$$

(b) Assuming that the worst case occurs on the least balanced partition, use (a) to write down a recurrence equation for W(n). Solve your recurrence for the case n even, n ≥ 2, and show that in this case $W(n) = n(n + 2)/4 − 1$.

8.11 This question is concerned with the amount of extra memory used by Quicksort.

(a) find a case which shows that the runtime stack which implements the recursion in Quicksort can grow to $O(n)$ in size.

(b) Eliminate the recursion in Quicksort by storing the indices of the endpoints of unsorted subarrays in a stack. After Partition produces two new subarrays, stack one and move on to sort the other.

(c) Show that, if the larger of the two subarrays is stacked and the smaller is sorted, then the size of the stack is always $O(\log n)$.

8.12 Produce a highly tuned version of *Quicksort* for production use. You should implement median-of-three *Quicksort*, recursion elimination, stacking of smaller subarrays, and insertion sort of small subarrays (this requires a sentinel, remember). Save procedure calls wherever possible by copying their bodies into the main program. Carefully test your implementation, then perform an empirical comparison of its performance against basic Quicksort. Was your effort worthwhile?

8.13 Consider modifying *Quicksort* by choosing the pivot element at random from $A[a..b]$.

(a) How does the overhead of this method (that is, the cost of calling the random number generator) compare with the total cost of the sort?

(b) In what sense is the worst case less likely to occur if this is done?

8.14 Radix sort uses two characteristic operations: the movement of one entry from the master list to a sublist, and the concatenation of a sublist to the master list. In this question it is assumed that these two operations take equal time, so that the time complexity of radix sort is $dn + dr$ characteristic operations.

Suppose that each key is c bits in length and is divided into digits each w bits in length. That is, $d = c/w$ and $r = 2^w$. For fixed c and n, how sensitive is radix sort to the choice of w? How can w be chosen to minimize the number of characteristic operations performed?

8.15 If r is large, radix sort wastes a lot of time examining empty sublists when rebuilding the master list. Can you find a way to examine only the non-empty sublists?

8.16 It often happens that the keys to be sorted are strings of characters with the usual lexicographical ordering, for example, $alp < alpha < beta$. Such keys are easily handled by comparison-based sorting algorithms, but the varying length is a problem for LSD radix sort: the obvious approach, padding each string to a maximum length with blanks, is inefficient and inconvenient. Investigate ways to radix sort character strings, aiming for a complexity on the order of the total length of all the strings. Two ideas: look again at MSD radix sort, and consider an initial sort of the strings by their length.

8.17 In sorting applications where many equal keys are expected, it may be worthwhile to adapt the sorting algorithms to take advantage of their presence. One way to do this is to use a comparison with a three-way outcome (<, = or >). Then, in the cases where two keys are found to be equal, the two entries may be replaced with one 'super-entry' that henceforward represents both. This effectively reduces the size of the instance by 1. For example, consider the following straight insertion sort:

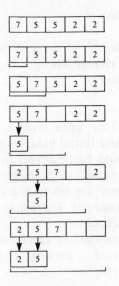

In principle, this idea can be applied to any comparison-based sorting algorithm, but it will be more attractive if extra data structures, like the linked lists used above, can be avoided. Do any of the sorting algorithms of this chapter lend themselves to this?

8.18 A bank maintains a large file of account records, sorted by account number. During the day, a number of transactions occur on these accounts, but, since they are stored on a magnetic tape, the accounts cannot be updated as the transactions occur. When the bank's doors close at 3 p.m., the transactions are collected together, sorted by account number, and then merged with the account file to produce an updated account file:

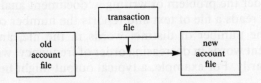

The account and transaction records have the following types:

```
type Account =
record
    number: integer;      (* account number *)
    balance: integer;     (* current balance in cents *)
    info: InfoType;       (* customer name, etc. *)
end;

type Transaction =
record
    number: integer;   (* account number *)
    type: (open, change, close);   (* type of transaction *)
    amount: integer;
end;
```

A transaction of type **open** creates a new account with the specified number and initial balance. A **change** transaction adds *amount* (which could be negative) to the balance of the given account. A **close** transaction closes an account, provided that its balance is 0. If there are no transactions for an account, it is copied through unchanged. There may be several transactions, of any type, on one account.

There are a number of error conditions that need to be detected. In each case, a message is printed and the offending transaction is ignored:

open: account already exists
change: account does not exist
change: balance insufficient to cover withdrawal
close: account does not exist
close: account has non-zero balance

Write a program that reads a sorted accounts file and a sorted transactions file, performs the transactions, prints any error messages, and writes out the new accounts file. You may assume that all files are terminated with a record whose number is *infinity*, a special value that is larger than any account number. What is the loop invariant of your program? Be warned that this problem is notoriously difficult to solve correctly.

8.19 Consider the problem of writing a 'document analysis' program, which reads a file of text and reports the number of words in the file, the number of distinct words in the file, and the k most frequent words in decreasing order of frequency, with ties broken arbitrarily. For example, a typical output might be

File contains 2586 words, 931 distinct.

37 *the*
37 *metempsychosis*
32 *and*
31 *a*

The value of k is a parameter of the program. If there are less than k distinct words, all are to be printed. (A word is a non-empty sequence of letters, digits, and hyphens, delimited by any other character or by end of line. Other characters are ignored. Upper and lower case are equivalent; all output is to be in lower case.)

There are a number of solutions to this problem, of varying complexities. Aim to produce a solution that is efficient on the average. Determine the asymptotic complexity of your solution as a function of

c: the number of characters in the file;
m: the number of words in the file;
n: the number of distinct words in the file;
k: the number of words printed at the end.

These quantities satisfy $c \geq m \geq n \geq k$.

Chapter 9

Disjoint Sets

The subject of this chapter is the *disjoint sets* ADT. It is encountered much less frequently than symbol tables and priority queues, yet its applications are diverse: finding minimum spanning trees (Section 10.9), testing whether two finite automata are equivalent (see Aho *et al.*, 1974), unifying logical predicates (Paterson and Wegman, 1978), and others. It is a curious ADT, with implementations unlike any others.

9.1 Specification

A *disjoint sets structure* is a set of sets of entries. An entry contains no information except its name and which set it lies in. An entry may be in at most one set at any one time, which makes the sets disjoint. For example, if $a, b, \ldots, f$ are the names of entries, then $\{\{a, e\}, \{b, c, f\}, \{d\}\}$ is a disjoint sets structure. Here is a specification of the corresponding ADT:

definition module *DisSets*;

> **type** *Entry*;   (* *an entry* *)
> **type** *SetType*;   (* *a set of entries* *)
> **type** *DisjointSets*;   (* *a set of sets of entries* *)
>
> **procedure** *New* ( ): *Entry*;
> **procedure** *Initialize* (**var** *D*: *DisjointSets*);
> **procedure** *MakeSet*(*x*: *Entry*; **var** *D*: *DisjointSets*);
> **procedure** *Find* (*x*: *Entry*; **var** *D*: *DisjointSets*): *SetType*;
> **procedure** *Union*(*v*, *w*: *SetType*; **var** *D*: *DisjointSets*);
>
> **end** *DisSets*.

The operation *New* creates a new entry. *Initialize*(D) initializes D to contain no sets of entries:

Initialize(D)   { }

The operation *MakeSet*(x, D) adds the set $\{x\}$, where x is an entry, to D:

MakeSet(a, D)	$\{\{a\}\}$
MakeSet(b, D)	$\{\{a\}, \{b\}\}$
MakeSet(c, D)	$\{\{a\}, \{b\}, \{c\}\}$
MakeSet(d, D)	$\{\{a\}, \{b\}, \{c\}, \{d\}\}$

The operation *Find*(x, D), where x is an entry lying in one of the sets of D, returns the set containing x:

Find(c, D) = $\{c\}$
Find(a, D) = $\{a\}$

Finally, the operation *Union*(v, w, D) replaces the two sets v and w in D with their union:

Union(*Find*(a, D), *Find*(c, D), D)	$\{\{a, c\}, \{b\}, \{d\}\}$
Union(*Find*(d, D), *Find*(a, D), D)	$\{\{a, c, d\}, \{b\}\}$

Now *Find*(c, D) = *Find*(a, D) = *Find*(d, D) = $\{a, c, d\}$. The effect of the operation *Union*(v, w, D) when $v = w$ will be left undefined; it should always be checked that $v \neq w$ before attempting such a union. If the disjoint sets structure has n entries, a maximum of $n - 1$ *Union* operations are possible before they all lie in one set.

This abstract data type arises whenever things which are initially separate are gradually joined together as time progresses. For example, consider the growth of the railway network of Britain and Ireland. In the year 1800, before the railway was invented, the cities of Britain and Ireland were unconnected by rail:

$$D = \{ \, \{London\}, \, \{Birmingham\}, \, \{Liverpool\}, \, \{Manchester\},$$
$$\{Edinburgh\}, \, \{Belfast\}, \, \{Dublin\} \, \}$$

The first railway connected the cities of Liverpool and Manchester in the year 1830:

$D = \{\{London\}, \{Birmingham\}, \{Liverpool, Manchester\},$
$\quad\quad \{Edinburgh\}, \{Belfast\}, \{Dublin\}\}$

The reader can now easily interpret the ADT operations. Using the disjoint sets structure shown, it can be determined whether cities a and b are connected by rail (either directly or via other cities) with the boolean test $Find(a, D) = Find(b, D)$. When a new railway is built between cities a and b, the operation $Union(Find(a, D), Find(b, D), D)$ will update the structure accordingly. At the time of writing, the railway network (Figure 9.3) is described by

$D = \{\{London, Birmingham, Liverpool, Manchester, Edinburgh\},$
$\quad\quad \{Belfast, Dublin\}\}.$

The disjoint sets ADT is also related to the concept of an *equivalence relation*, defined in Section 10.3. The sets are the equivalence classes of some equivalence relation R. The operation $Find(x, D)$ determines which class x lies in, so that the test $Find(x, D) = Find(y, D)$ determines whether $\langle x, y \rangle \in R$. The operation $Union(Find(x, D), Find(y, D), D)$ informs the ADT that, from now on, x and y are to be considered equivalent; so clearly their classes must be united.

9.2   The Galler–Fischer Representation

One simple way to represent the disjoint sets is to store in each entry a value which indicates which set the entry lies in. For example, the structure $D = \{\{a, b, c, d\}, \{e, f\}, \{g\}\}$ could be represented by

Then $Find(e, D)$ would simply return 2, etc. Unfortunately, a *Union* operation would have to change all the values of one set to the values of the other, which in the worst case would take $O(n)$ time.

There is another, very clever data structure for representing disjoint sets, which is due to Galler and Fischer (1964). Each set is a tree with pointers going from children to parents – the reverse of the usual direction. For example, if $D = \{\{a, b, c, d\}, \{e, f\}, \{g\}\}$, the representation might be the forest

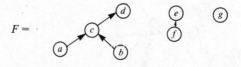

Each node is an entry. Type *Entry* is realized as a pointer to a record containing just one field: a pointer to its parent. *SetType* is realized as a pointer to the root of a tree. With this representation, the operations are remarkably simple to implement. The operation $Find(x, D)$ follows the parent pointers to the root of the tree containing x. $Union(v, w, D)$ simply makes w the parent of v, so that subsequent *Find* operations will terminate at w:

```
procedure MakeSet(x: Entry; var D: DisjointSets);
begin
    x^.parent := nil;
end MakeSet;


procedure Find(x: Entry; var D: DisjointSets): SetType;
var y: Entry;
begin
    y := x;
    while y^.parent ≠ nil do
        y := y^.parent;
    end;
    return CAST(SetType, y);
end Find;
```

procedure *Union*(*v*, *w*: *SetType*; **var** *D*: *DisjointSets*);
begin
    v^.*parent* := *CAST*(*Entry*, *w*);
end *Union*;

It happens that *D* itself is not used by these operations; no information is stored apart from the entries. For example, here are some *Union* operations in action:

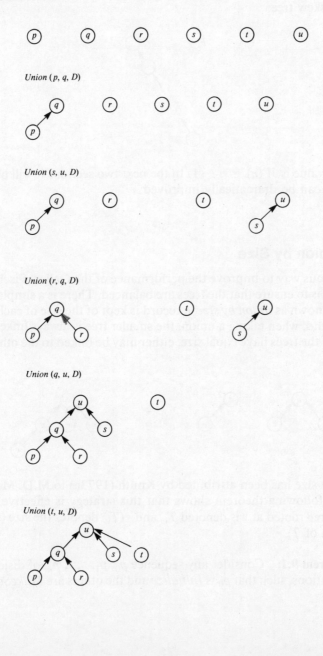

Notice that a node may have arbitrarily many children.

The *MakeSet* and *Union* operations have $O(1)$ complexity. For the *Find* operation, the number of pointers traversed is chosen as the measure of complexity, or in other words, the number of times the operation $y := y^\wedge.parent$ is executed. Clearly the cost of *Find*(x) is $d(x)$, the depth of x in its tree. If the height of a forest is defined to be the height of the tallest tree in it, then the worst-case complexity of *Find*(x), when x lies in the forest F, is $h(F) - 1$. This is maximized for fixed n when F consists of a single skew tree:

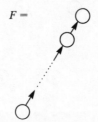

when its value is $W(n) = n - 1$. In the next two sections it will be shown how this can be dramatically improved.

9.3 Union by Size

The obvious way to improve the performance of the Galler–Fischer data structure is to ensure that the trees are balanced. There is a simple way to do this, known as *union by size*: a record is kept of the size of each tree in its root, and, when taking a union, the smaller tree is always linked to the larger. (If the trees have equal size, either may be linked to the other.) For example:

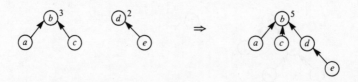

Union by size has been attributed by Knuth (1973a) to M.D. McIlroy.

The following theorem shows that this strategy is effective. Recall that the tree rooted at v is denoted T_v, and $s(T_v)$ denotes the size (number of nodes) of T_v.

Theorem 9.1: Consider any sequence $p_0, p_1, \ldots, p_m$ of disjoint sets operations, such that p_0 is *Initialize* and the others are *MakeSet, Find,* and *Union*, employing union by size. Let x be any node in existence after p_m. Then $2^{h(T_x)-1} \leq s(T_x)$.

Proof: As usual with proofs of data structure invariants, the proof is by induction on m, the length of the operation sequence.

Basis step: $m = 0$. Then the ADT is empty, and the theorem is vacuously true.

Inductive step: $m > 0$. The inductive hypothesis says that, before p_m begins, $2^{h(T_x)-1} \leq s(T_x)$ for all nodes x. It must be shown that this remains true after p_m is complete.

If p_m is *MakeSet*(x, D), it introduces a new tree T_x of size $s(T_x) = 1$ and height $h(T_x) = 1$, which satisfies the condition. If p_m is *Find*(x, D), there is no change in the structure.

Finally, suppose that p_m is the operation *Union*(v, w, D). Without loss of generality, it may be assumed that $s(T_v) \leq s(T_w)$, so that v is linked to w, creating the new tree

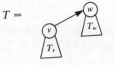

$$T =$$

Clearly, $h(T) = \max(1 + h(T_v), h(T_w))$, and from this it can be shown that $2^{h(T)-1} \leq s(T)$ as follows:

$$2^{h(T)-1} = 2^{\max(1+h(T_v),\ h(T_w))-1}$$
$$= \max(2^{h(T_v)-1+1},\ 2^{h(T_w)-1})$$
$$\leq \max(2s(T_v), s(T_w))$$

by the inductive hypothesis applied to the nodes v and w. Now from $s(T) = s(T_v) + s(T_w)$, and $s(T_v) \leq s(T_w)$, it may be concluded that $2s(T_v) \leq s(T)$ and $s(T_w) \leq s(T)$. Consequently,

$$2^{h(T)-1} \leq \max(s(T), s(T)) = s(T)$$

and the theorem is proved.   ∎

Taking logarithms, in a forest built by *MakeSet* and *Union* operations, employing union by size, every tree T must satisfy $h(T) - 1 \leq \log_2 s(T)$. Since $s(T) \leq n$, the cost of any *Find* operation is at most $\log_2 n$.

To summarize, then, the implementation of the disjoint sets ADT using trees and union by size has a worst-case complexity of $O(1)$ for *Initialize*, *MakeSet*, and *Union*, and $O(\log n)$ for *Find*. Its efficiency is comparable with others in this book for symbol tables and priority queues, and the code is exceptionally simple.

9.4   Path Compression

This section presents a way to reduce the cost of find operations, by exploiting more fully the fact that a node may have arbitrarily many children. After finding that the root of the tree containing x is y, the path from x to y is traversed a second time, setting all pointers to point directly to y:

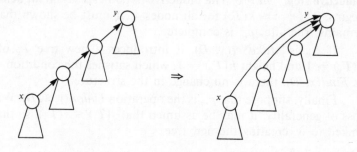

Subsequent finds will now run faster. This is called *path compression*, and it has been attributed by Knuth (1973a) to A. Tritter. The code is given in Implementation Module 9.1.

It turns out that path compression, in conjunction with union by size, reduces the cost of *Find* operations considerably, to the point where they are virtually $O(1)$ each, in the amortized sense. The proof of this is quite difficult, and the remainder of this section is devoted to it.

Path compression cannot reduce the cost of the first *Find* in a sequence of operations, so there is no improvement in worst-case complexity expected. Instead it is hoped to reduce the total cost of a sequence of operations, and this brings the problem into the realm of amortized complexity. As before, the measure of complexity will be the number of edges traversed during the scan from x to the root. The cost of the second (compressing) scan is ignored. This is realistic, because the second scan traverses the same path.

In the following discussion, p is a sequence of disjoint sets operations beginning with *Initialize*, and containing $m_1 = n$ *MakeSet*, m_2 *Find*, and m_3 *Union* operations in any order. Let x be any node in existence after operation sequence p is complete, and define $r(x)$, the *rank* of x, as follows:

(1) Execute p with path compression turned off;
(2) Let $r(x) = h(x) - 1$, where $h(x)$ is the height of x in the forest resulting from (1).

For example, here is an operation sequence p and the forest resulting from (1). For brevity, the *Initialize* and *MakeSet* operations are omitted.

Each node contains its rank, and is displayed at an appropriate level in the diagram:

Union(a, d, D)
Union(h, f, D)
Union(i, j, D)
Find(h, D)
Union(g, e, D)
Union(f, e, D)
Find(h, D)
Union(b, c, D)
Union(c, d, D)
Union(d, e, D)

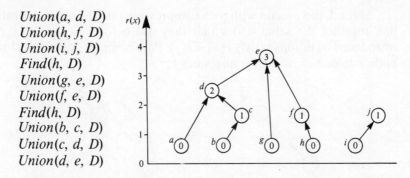

The values $r(x)$ will be used in defining $\Phi(D)$, which is unusual, because $\Phi(D)$ is supposed to be a function of the current state D, yet the $r(x)$ are determined by the final state. This is justified by observing that, once p is fixed, the $r(x)$ are constants. In effect, p is run with path compression off, the $r(x)$ are determined, D is reset to empty, and p run a second time with path compression on, using the $r(x)$ to help in analysing this second run.

In the diagram just given, the edges all point upwards (in other words, $r(x) < r(x.parent)$ for all non-root nodes x). This must be so, because $r(x) = h(x) - 1$, and the height of a node is always strictly greater than the height of each of its children. But what if the nodes are drawn in these positions (determined by the constants $r(x)$) at some intermediate moment in p, perhaps with path compression on? Would the edges point upwards then?

For example, if the sequence p given above is run, employing path compression, and is stopped after $Union(c, d, D)$, the picture is

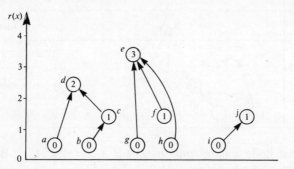

There are fewer edges, but they all point upwards.

The proof that $r(x) < r(x.parent)$ at all times for all non-root nodes x, with or without path compression, is in two parts. First, turn path compression off, stop p at some intermediate moment, and consider any edge $x \rightarrow y$. At this moment, $h(x) < h(y)$, and since x is not a root, its height cannot change from now on. The height of y cannot decrease (path compression is off, remember), so $h(x) < h(y)$ at the end of p, hence $r(x) < r(y)$.

Second, run p again with path compression on. The union operations link together the same nodes that they did before, so the links $x \rightarrow y$ introduced by unions satisfy $r(x) < r(y)$. Path compression always links a node x to one of its proper ancestors y:

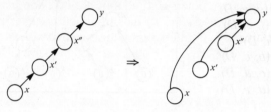

An inductive argument may assume that $r(x) < r(x')$, $r(x') < r(x'')$, etc., and so $r(x) < r(y)$.

The picture of D at some intermediate moment, with path compression on, is becoming clear: the nodes in fixed positions, the edges pointing upwards. The final element in the picture is a sequence of numbers $A_0, A_1, \ldots, A_k, A_{k+1}$. These numbers can be chosen freely, subject only to the condition

$$0 = A_0 < A_1 < \ldots < A_k \leq \lfloor \log_2 n \rfloor < A_{k+1}$$

The A_i are horizontal lines cutting across the picture. If $k = 1$, for example, with $A_0 = 0$, $A_1 = 3$, and $A_2 = 4$,

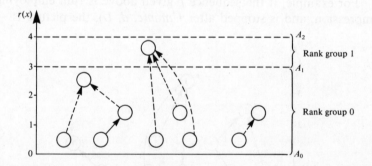

It is said that node x is in *rank group* i if $A_i \leq r(x) < A_{i+1}$. By Theorem 9.1, union by size guarantees that $0 \leq r(x) \leq \lfloor \log_2 n \rfloor$, so every node is in exactly one rank group.

As shown in the diagram just given, the edges of D are divided into two groups: *dashed* and *solid*. Edges that connect nodes lying in different rank groups are shown dashed. Edges leading into root nodes are also dashed. The remaining edges are solid.

As an aid to analysis, a *count* field is introduced into each node, holding a non-negative integer. Actual implementations do not have this field; it is only an analytical device. Define

$$\Phi(D) = -\sum_{x \in F} x.count$$

It is rare to encounter a potential function that takes on negative values.

The operation *MakeSet*(x, D) has an actual complexity of 1 (say). *x.count* is initialized to 0, and so the amortized complexity is 1 also.

The operation *Union*(v, w, D) also has actual complexity equal to 1. No changes are made to the count fields, so again the amortized complexity is 1.

The operation *Find*(x, D) traverses a path composed of dashed and solid edges. Its actual complexity is the number of edges on this path. However, whenever a solid edge $y \to z$ is traversed, 1 is added to *y.count*. This decreases the potential by 1, cancelling the cost of traversing the solid edge, and so the amortized complexity of *Find*(x, D) is the number of dashed edges traversed. For example, consider

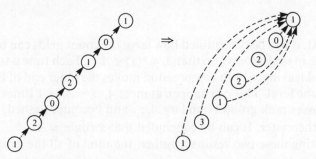

where the count values are shown inside the nodes. The actual complexity is 6, but 3 count fields were incremented, for an amortized complexity of 3.

Since the edges point upwards, a path can cross each of the k rank group boundaries at most once, giving at most k dashed edges; but there is also the final dashed edge leading into the root. It can be concluded that the amortized complexity of *Find*(x, D) is at most $k + 1$.

This completes the analysis of the operations. The total actual complexity of any sequence of m_1 *MakeSet*, m_2 *Find*, and m_3 *Union* operations satisfies

$$\sum_{i=1}^{m} t_i = \sum_{i=1}^{m} a_i - \Phi(D_m) + \Phi(D_0)$$
$$\leq m_1 + m_2(k + 1) + m_3 - \Phi(D_m)$$

since $\Phi(D_0) = 0$. It remains to determine $-\Phi(D_m)$, the total of all the count fields when the sequence ends.

First, it will be shown that in any union-by-size forest D containing n nodes, there are at most $n/2^r$ nodes of rank r. Let $x_1, x_2, \ldots, x_j$ be the nodes of rank r in D. Since these nodes all have height $r + 1$, one cannot be a proper descendant of another, so the subtrees rooted at these nodes are disjoint. By Theorem 9.1, each subtree contains at least 2^r nodes, making a total of $j\,2^r$ nodes. But this cannot exceed n, so $j \le n/2^r$.

Summing this over the ranks $A_i, \ldots, A_{i+1} - 1$, the total number of nodes in rank group i is at most

$$\sum_{r=A_i}^{A_{i+1}-1} \frac{n}{2^r} = \frac{n}{2^{A_i}} \sum_{r=0}^{A_{i+1}-1-A_i} \frac{1}{2^r}$$

$$< \frac{n}{2^{A_i}} \sum_{r=0}^{\infty} \frac{1}{2^r}$$

$$= \frac{2n}{2^{A_i}}$$

Next, it will be determined how large the count fields can be. Let x be any node in rank group i, so that $A_i \le r(x) < A_{i+1}$. Each time a solid edge is traversed leaving x, path compression moves the other end of the edge up at least one level. This can happen at most $A_{i+1} - A_i - 1$ times before the edge crosses rank group boundary A_{i+1} and becomes dashed; it remains dashed thereafter. It can be concluded that $x.count \le A_{i+1} - A_i - 1$.

Putting these two results together, the total of all the count fields of the nodes of rank group i can be at most $(2n/2^{A_i}) \cdot (A_{i+1} - A_i - 1)$. Summing this over all rank groups gives

$$-\Phi(D_m) = \sum_{x \in D_m} x.count$$

$$\le \sum_{i=0}^{k} \frac{2n}{2^{A_i}} (A_{i+1} - A_i - 1)$$

and the total complexity of any sequence of $m_1 = n$ MakeSet operations, m_2 Find operations, and m_3 Union operations satisfies

$$T \le n + m_2(k + 1) + m_3 + \sum_{i=0}^{k} \frac{2n}{2^{A_i}} (A_{i+1} - A_i - 1)$$

The numbers A_i can now be chosen freely so as to minimize this expression. Choosing $k = 0$, $A_0 = 0$, and $A_1 = \lfloor \log_2 n \rfloor + 1$,

$$T \leq n + m_2 + m_3 + 2n \lfloor \log_2 n \rfloor$$

with the total cost of traversing solid edges dominant. At the other extreme, choosing $k = \lfloor \log_2 n \rfloor$, and $A_i = i$ for all i, then $A_{i+1} - A_i - 1 = 0$, and so

$$T \leq n + m_2(\lfloor \log_2 n \rfloor + 1) + m_3$$

with the cost of the dashed edges dominant (not surprisingly, since there are no solid edges). Finally, there is an extraordinary intermediate choice. Let

$$A_0 = 0$$
$$A_{i+1} = 2^{A_i}$$

for all i, and let k be such that $A_k \leq \lfloor \log_2 n \rfloor < A_{k+1}$. This gives

$$T \leq n + m_2(k + 1) + m_3 + \sum_{i=0}^{k} \frac{2n}{2^{A_i}}(A_{i+1} - A_i - 1)$$

$$\leq n + m_2(k + 1) + m_3 + \sum_{i=0}^{k} \frac{2n}{2^{A_i}} A_{i+1}$$

$$= n + m_2(k + 1) + m_3 + \sum_{i=0}^{k} 2n$$

$$= n + (2n + m_2)(k + 1) + m_3$$

In practice, k is virtually a small constant, because the A_i grow at a truly alarming rate: $A_0 = 0$, $A_1 = 1$, $A_2 = 2$, $A_3 = 4$, $A_4 = 16$, $A_5 = 65\,536$, $A_6 = 2^{65\,536}$. For example, if $n = 2^{65\,536} - 1$ (a truly enormous number), $A_4 \leq \lfloor \log_2 n \rfloor < A_5$, so that $k = 4$. The total complexity is therefore virtually linear in the number of operations.

This analysis is due to Hopcroft and Ullman (1973); the presentation is adapted from Purdom and Brown (1985). An even tighter bound has been given by Tarjan (1975).

EXERCISES

9.1 Find a sequence of *MakeSet*, *Union*, and *Find* operations which proves that the time complexity bounds given in Section 9.3, for union by size without path compression, cannot be improved.

9.2 Show that the following tree will never be constructed by unions that employ union by size:

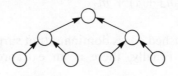

9.3 Given the tree:

$$T = \quad \textcircled{a} \rightarrow \textcircled{b} \rightarrow \textcircled{c} \rightarrow \textcircled{d} \rightarrow \textcircled{e} \rightarrow \textcircled{f} \rightarrow \textcircled{g}$$

suppose the operations *Find*(*a*, *D*), *Find*(*b*, *D*), . . . , *Find*(*g*, *D*) are executed in any order, employing path compression. Define the cost of the operation *Find*(*x*, *D*) to be the number of edges traversed on the first pass (as usual). For example in *T*, *Find*(*g*, *D*) cost 0, *Find*(*a*, *D*) costs 6, and a second *Find*(*a*, *D*) costs 1.

(a) Irrespective of the order of the operations, what will the tree look like finally?

(b) In what order should the seven *Find* operations be performed so as to minimize their total cost? Prove your result.

9.4 Consider any sequence of *MakeSet*, *Union*, and *Find* operations in which all of the *Union* operations precede all of the *Find* operations. Show that, employing path compression with or without union by size, the total cost of the sequence is linear in its length. *Hint*: let Φ be the number of nodes that possess a grandparent.

9.5 Consider extending the disjoint sets ADT to include the operations

Delete(*x*: *Entry*: *D*: *DisjointSets*);
FindAll(*S*: *SetType*; *D*: *DisjointSets*): *EntryList*;

where *Delete* (*x*, *D*) deletes entry *x* from whatever set it lies in, and *FindAll*(*S*, *D*) returns a list of all the entries in *S*. Implement this extended ADT in a way which preserves the good complexity bounds that have been derived for the other operations.

9.6 Show that, in the analysis of Section 9.4, the sequence of numbers A_i could be defined by

$$A_0 = 0$$
$$A_{i+1} = 2^{A_i} + A_i + 1$$

without jeopardising the analysis. What effect does this refinement have on the value of *k*?

9.7 Investigate the amortized complexity of the disjoint sets ADT when path compression but not union by size is employed.

Implementation Module 9.1   Implementation of the disjoint sets ADT, using both union by size and path compression.

```
implementation module DisSets;

    from SYSTEM import CAST;
    from System import Allocate;

    type Entry = pointer to node;
    type SetType = pointer to node;
    type DisjointSets = pointer to record end;

    type node =
    record
        parent: Entry;
        size: integer;
    end;

    procedure New( ): Entry;
    var x: Entry;
    begin
        Allocate (x, SIZE(x^));
        return x;
    end New;
```

```
    procedure Initialize (var D: DisjointSets);
    begin
    end Initialize;

    procedure MakeSet(x: Entry; var D: DisjointSets);
    begin
      x^.parent := nil;
      x^.size := 0;
    end MakeSet;

    procedure Find(x: Entry; var D: DisjointSets): SetType;
    var y, z, tmp: Entry;
    begin
      y := x;
      while y^.parent ≠ nil do
        y := y^.parent;
      end;
      z := x;
      while z^.parent ≠ nil do
        tmp := z^.parent;
        z^.parent := y;
        z := tmp;
      end;
      return CAST(SetType, y);
    end Find;

    procedure Union(v, w: SetType; var D: DisjointSets);
    begin
      if v^.size ≤ w^.size then
        v^.parent := CAST(Entry, w);
        w^.size := v^.size + w^.size;
      else
        w^.parent := CAST(Entry, v);
        v^.size := v^.size + w^.size;
      end;
    end Union;

end DisSets.
```

Chapter 10

Graph Algorithms

Graphs model the real world. Problems as diverse as minimizing the cost of microwave communications networks, generating efficient assembly code for evaluating expressions, measuring the reliability of telephone networks, determining the time-critical parts of large projects, and many others, are naturally formulated with graphs.

For example, consider the problem of finding the shortest route between two towns on a map. The information needed to solve this problem can be clearly represented as a *graph*:

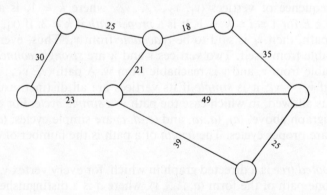

Lines represent roads, nodes represent intersections and towns, and the number attached to each line is the length of each road, or perhaps an estimate of the time it would take to travel it.

Many important problems about graphs have never been efficiently solved; for others there are elegant algorithms whose correctness requires careful study. A comprehensive account of these problems would fill volumes; only a few central ones can be treated here.

10.1   Definitions

In this section some basic definitions for directed and undirected graphs
are presented. The definitions are approximately standard, but the reader
must be prepared for minor variations among authors.

A *directed graph* or *digraph* $G = \langle V, E \rangle$ is a set V of *vertices* together
with a set E of *edges*. Each edge is a sequence of two vertices, and is represented diagrammatically by an arrow from the first vertex to the second.
For example,

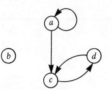

$$V = \{a, b, c, d\}$$
$$E = \{\langle a, a \rangle, \langle a, c \rangle, \langle c, d \rangle, \langle d, c \rangle\}$$

is a digraph with four vertices and four edges. This definition permits
self-loops (edges of the form $\langle v, v \rangle$), but prohibits *parallel edges* (two equal
edges $\langle v, w \rangle$ in E). If $\langle v, w \rangle \in E$, v is then said to be a *predecessor*
of w, and w is a *successor* of v. The *indegree* of w is the number of its
predecessors, and the *outdegree* of v is the number of its successors.

A sequence of vertices $\langle v_1, v_2, \ldots, v_k \rangle$, where $k \geq 1$, is a *path* if
$\langle v_i, v_{i+1} \rangle \in E$ for $1 \leq i \leq k - 1$. It is a *proper path* if $k \geq 2$. If $\langle v_1, v_2, \ldots, v_k \rangle$ is a path, then v_k is said to be *reachable* from v_1. Thus, every vertex
is reachable from itself. Two vertices v and w are *strongly connected* if w
is reachable from v, and v is reachable from w. A path $\langle v_1, v_2, \ldots, v_k \rangle$ is
a *cycle* if $v_1 = v_k$; it is *simple* if its vertices are all distinct, except that
$v_1 = v_k$ is allowed, in which case the path is a *simple cycle*. For example,
in the digraph above, $\langle a \rangle$, $\langle a, a \rangle$, and $\langle c, d, c \rangle$ are simple cycles; $\langle a, a \rangle$ and
$\langle c, d, c \rangle$ are proper cycles. The *length* of a path is the number of edges on
it.

A *rooted tree* is a directed graph in which, for every vertex v, there is
exactly one path of the form $\langle a, \ldots, v \rangle$, where a is a distinguished vertex
called the *root* of the tree. A *subgraph* of a directed graph $G = \langle V, E \rangle$ is
a digraph $G' = \langle V', E' \rangle$ such that $V' \subset V$ and $E' \subset E$. A *spanning tree* of
a digraph $G = \langle V, E \rangle$ is a subgraph $T = \langle V', E' \rangle$ of G such that T is a
rooted tree, and $V' = V$.

The complexity of graph algorithms will be determined as a function
of n, the number of vertices, and m, the number of edges. Typically, there
will be one characteristic operation related to vertices, and another
related to edges; the number of each will be determined and their sum
reported.

Graphs.   An *undirected graph* or just *graph* $G = \langle V, E \rangle$ is a set V of vertices and a set E of edges. Each edge is a two-element set of distinct vertices. For example,

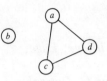

$$V = \{a, b, c, d\}$$
$$E = \{\{a, c\}, \{c, d\}, \{a, d\}\}$$

is a graph with four vertices and three edges. This definition prohibits self-loops and parallel edges. If $\{v, w\} \in E$, then the vertices v and w are said to be *adjacent*. The *degree* of vertex v is the number of vertices adjacent to v.

A sequence of $k \geq 1$ vertices $\langle v_1, v_2, \ldots, v_k \rangle$ is a *path* if $\{v_i, v_{i+1}\} \in E$ for $1 \leq i \leq k - 1$. It is a *proper path* if $k \geq 2$; it is a *cycle* if $k \geq 3$ and $v_1 = v_k$; and it is *simple* if its vertices are all distinct, except that $v_1 = v_k$ is allowed. The *length* of a path is the number of edges on it.

A *tree* (or *free tree*) is a graph in which, for every pair of vertices v, w, there is exactly one simple path of the form $\langle v, \ldots, w \rangle$. A *subgraph* of a graph $G = \langle V, E \rangle$ is a graph $G' = \langle V', E' \rangle$ such that $V' \subset V$ and $E' \subset E$. A *spanning tree* of a graph $G = \langle V, E \rangle$ is a subgraph $T = \langle V', E' \rangle$ of G such that T is a tree, and $V' = V$.

If $\langle v_1, v_2, \ldots, v_k \rangle$ is a path, v_1 and v_k are said to be *connected*. A graph is connected if every pair of vertices in it is connected. Otherwise, the graph is made up of a number of *connected components*: maximal subgraphs which are connected. The graph G above has two connected components.

10.2 Specification and Representation

The following ADT provides operations for creating a digraph by initializing it to empty, inserting new vertices, and inserting an edge between two existing vertices. Vertices and edges may have associated values, such as edge costs for example. All the digraphs of this chapter may be built with a sequence of these operations.

Although one can think of a number of operations to apply to graphs – modifying them, enquiring whether a certain edge is present, and so on – the main interest here will be in traversing a fixed graph in various ways. Accordingly, the following ADT concentrates on operations which implement the traversals needed:

definition module *Digraph*;

   type *Digraph*;
   type *Vertex*;
   type *Edge*;

  var *NilVertex*: *Vertex*; *NilEdge*: *Edge*;

  procedure *InitDigraph*(**var** *G*: *Digraph*);
  procedure *InsertVertex*(*val*: *VertexVal*; **var** *G*: *Digraph*): *Vertex*;
  procedure *InsertEdge*(*v*, *w*: *Vertex*; *val*: *EdgeVal*; **var** *G*: *Digraph*):
    Edge;
  procedure *GetVertexVal*(*v*: *Vertex*; **var** *val*: *VertexVal*);
  procedure *SetVertexVal*(*v*: *Vertex*; *val*: *VertexVal*);
  procedure *GetEdgeVal*(*e*: *Edge*; **var** *eval*: *EdgeVal*);
  procedure *SetEdgeVal*(*e*: *Edge*; *val*: *EdgeVal*);

  procedure *FirstVertex* (**var** *G*: *Digraph*): *Vertex*;
  procedure *NextVertex* (*v*: *Vertex*; **var** *G*: *Digraph*): *Vertex*;
  procedure *FirstEdge*(*v*: *Vertex*; **var** *G*: *Digraph*): *Edge*;
  procedure *NextEdge* (*v*: *Vertex*; *e*: *Edge*; **var** *G*: *Digraph*): *Edge*;
  procedure *Endpoint*(*e*: *Edge*; **var** *G*: *Digraph*): *Vertex*;

end *Digraph*.

The *FirstVertex* and *NextVertex* operations allow for visiting all the vertices of *G* in an unspecified order, using the code

```
v := FirstVertex(G);
while v ≠ NilVertex do

    v := NextVertex(v, G);
end;
```

Both operations return *NilVertex* when there is no suitable vertex. The operations *FirstEdge* and *NextEdge* allow for visiting all the edges leading out of a given vertex, again in an unspecified order. The operation *Endpoint* returns the endpoint of an edge (that is, the vertex it points to). Thus, to visit each successor *w* of a given vertex *v*:

```
e := FirstEdge (v, G);
while e ≠ NilEdge do
    w := Endpoint(e, G);
    e := NextEdge (v, e, G);
end;
```

Unlike symbol tables and priority queues, this ADT is quite easy to implement so that all operations are $O(1)$ in the worst case. The representation is called *adjacency lists*. A linked list of records denoting edges is grown out of each vertex. Each contains a pointer to the endpoint of the edge. For example, here is a digraph and its adjacency lists representation:

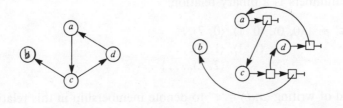

An ADT implementation using adjacency lists is given in Implementation Module 10.1. The edges leading out of a vertex *v* are linked together through their *nextedge* fields, beginning with *v^.firstedge*, and ending with a nil pointer. The vertices are linked together through their *nextvertex* fields. Type *Digraph* is a pointer to the first vertex on this list, and a nil pointer terminates the list. (Alternatively, the vertex records could be stored sequentially in an array; type *Vertex* would then be an array index.)

A variant of the *Digraph* ADT may be used for undirected graphs as well. It must simply be ensured that *InsertEdge* (*v*, *w*, *val*, *G*) adds two new edges: one from *v* to *w*, and one from *w* back to *v*. The name *Graph* may be given to this variant of the ADT.

10.3   Relations and Digraphs

Since directed graphs, undirected graphs, and directed graphs without cycles will be studied, it is worth asking why these variants of the basic idea arise. The best way to answer this question is to look at the mathematical theory of *relations*, which underlies all kinds of graphs.

Begin with a set *S*, and define the *Cartesian product* of *S* with itself, $S \times S$, to be the set of all two-element sequences of elements of *S*. For example, if $S = \{a, b, c, d\}$, then

$$S \times S = \{ \langle a, a \rangle, \langle a, b \rangle, \langle a, c \rangle, \langle a, d \rangle,$$
$$\langle b, a \rangle, \langle b, b \rangle, \langle b, c \rangle, \langle b, d \rangle,$$
$$\langle c, a \rangle, \langle c, b \rangle, \langle c, c \rangle, \langle c, d \rangle,$$
$$\langle d, a \rangle, \langle d, b \rangle, \langle d, c \rangle, \langle d, d \rangle \}$$

A *binary relation* (or just *relation*) R on S is a subset of $S \times S$. For example, $R = \{\langle a, a \rangle, \langle b, b \rangle, \langle b, c \rangle, \langle c, b \rangle\}$ is a binary relation on the set S given above. Thus, from a formal point of view, a digraph $G = \langle V, E \rangle$ is just a relation, taking $V = S$ and $E = R$.

Relations are commonly met with as boolean conditions between numbers. For example, the '$\leq$' (less than or equal to) condition between whole numbers is a binary relation:

$$\text{'}\leq\text{'} = \{\langle 0, 0 \rangle, \langle 0, 1 \rangle, \langle 0, 2 \rangle, \ldots$$
$$\langle 1, 1 \rangle, \langle 1, 2 \rangle, \ldots$$
$$\langle 2, 2 \rangle, \ldots\}$$

Instead of writing $\langle a, b \rangle \in \text{'}\leq\text{'}$ to denote membership in this relation, the simpler notation $a \leq b$ is conventionally used. In the same way, the notation $a \, R \, b$ will be used instead of the formal $\langle a, b \rangle \in R$ for other relations as well.

No restriction is made as to which pairs may appear in a relation, and in general the corresponding digraph may be a random collection of vertices and edges. In practice, however, certain patterns or properties appear frequently in applications, especially the following five.

Reflexivity. A binary relation R is reflexive if $x \, R \, x$ for all x in S. In digraph terms, every vertex has a self-loop:

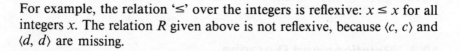

For example, the relation '$\leq$' over the integers is reflexive: $x \leq x$ for all integers x. The relation R given above is not reflexive, because $\langle c, c \rangle$ and $\langle d, d \rangle$ are missing.

Irreflexivity. A relation R is *irreflexive* if $x \, R \, x$ is false for all x. There are no self-loops in the corresponding digraph. For example, the relation '$<$' over the integers is irreflexive: $x < x$ is false for all integers x.

Symmetry. A relation R is symmetric if $x \, R \, y$ implies $y \, R \, x$, for all x and y. In digraph terms, all edges except self-loops occur in pairs:

For example, the equality relation is symmetric: $x = y$ implies $y = x$ for all x and y. The relation R given above is also symmetric.

Antisymmetry.   A relation is antisymmetric if $x \, R \, y$ and $y \, R \, x$ together imply $x = y$, for all x and y. The relation '$\leq$' is antisymmetric: $x \leq y$ and $y \leq x$ together imply $x = y$, for all x and y. The reader may prefer to think of antisymmetry in its contrapositive form: $x \neq y$ implies $x \, R \, y$ is false or $y \, R \, x$ is false. The corresponding digraph can have no edge pairs like the one above.

Transitivity.   A relation R is transitive if $x \, R \, y$ and $y \, R \, z$ implies $x \, R \, z$, for all x, y, and z. In digraph terms, the endpoints of all proper paths are connected by an edge:

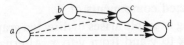

In this diagram the presence of the solid edges implies the presence of the dashed ones. The edge $\langle a, d \rangle$ must be present, since $\langle a, b \rangle$ and $\langle b, d \rangle$ are present. Most interesting relations are transitive. For example, '$\leq$' is transitive: $x \leq y$ and $y \leq z$ implies $x \leq z$.

Two particular combinations of these properties are so frequently met with, that they deserve special attention: equivalence relations and partial orders.

Equivalence relations.   An *equivalence relation* is a reflexive, symmetric and transitive relation. Informally, equivalence relations arise when the idea needs to be expressed that two things are essentially the same, but not necessarily strictly equal. The archetypal equivalence relation is $=$, the equality relation, but there are others. The fundamental fact about any equivalence relation R is that it partitions its domain S into pairwise disjoint subsets E_x of the form

$$E_x = \{y \mid y \, R \, x\}$$

called the *equivalence classes* of R. For example, the equivalence relation

$$R = \{\langle a, a \rangle, \langle b, b \rangle, \langle b, c \rangle, \langle c, b \rangle, \langle c, c \rangle\}$$

partitions its domain into the equivalence classes $\{a\}$ and $\{b, c\}$. This result will not be proved here (see, for example, Stanat and McAllister (1977) for a full discussion of relations). Instead, several examples will be given.

Consider the relation 'is connected to' between vertices of an undirected graph, for example

$G =$

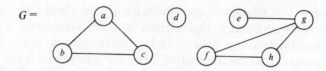

It is easy to check that this is an equivalence relation: vertex x is connected to x for all x; x is connected to y implies that y is connected to x; x is connected to y and y is connected to z together imply that x is connected to z (via the path $\langle x, \ldots, y, \ldots, z \rangle$). The equivalence classes are of the form $E_x = \{ y \in V \mid y \text{ is connected to } x \}$ and, for G above, they are $E_a = \{a, b, c\}$, $E_d = \{d\}$, and $E_f = \{e, f, g, h\}$. These are just the vertices of the connected components of G.

A more interesting example arises in directed graphs. Define $x \leftrightarrow y$ if there is a path from x to y and from y to x. Alternatively, the relation could be defined by saying that it holds when $x = y$ or there is a cycle containing x and y. It is left to the reader to verify that '$\leftrightarrow$' is an equivalence relation. Here is an example of a digraph G, with the equivalence classes grouped inside dashed circles:

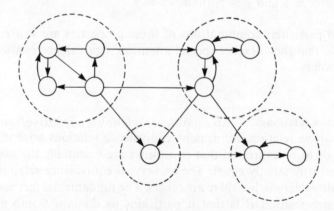

The graph can now be factored into the parts within the equivalence classes, and the part outside. For the outside part a new digraph can be drawn whose vertices are equivalence classes:

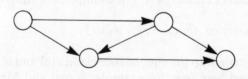

It is not hard to see that this *reduced digraph* must be acyclic. The subgraphs whose vertices are the equivalence classes of this relation are strongly connected, and they are known as the *strongly connected*

components of G. An algorithm for finding them will be studied in Section 10.7.

Partial orders.   A *partial order* is a reflexive, antisymmetric, and transitive relation. The archetypal partial order is '≤', but there are others.

An important fact about partial orders (in fact, all antisymmetric and transitive relations) is that their digraphs are acyclic. This can be proved as follows. Suppose, on the contrary, that there is a proper cycle $\langle x, y, \ldots, x \rangle$ in the digraph corresponding to an antisymmetric and transitive relation R. Immediately $x R y$; and from transitivity applied to the path $\langle y, \ldots, x \rangle$ it may be concluded that $y R x$. But then antisymmetry implies $x = y$, a contradiction.

Knowledge of antisymmetry and transitivity is valuable information for algorithms which traverse digraphs, since they need not guard against the danger of looping endlessly around a cycle. Such algorithms will be studied in Section 10.4.

Representing relations.   Suppose now that a relation R is to be represented as a digraph G, and that R has one or more of the five properties defined above. Can this knowledge be used to simplify the representation? It turns out that it can.

Consider a relation R which is known to be reflexive. The self-loops can be omitted from G, and simply assumed to be there. Similarly, if R is transitive, the edges implied by transitivity can be omitted. For example, consider this heap-ordered tree:

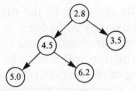

The only pairs represented explicitly are the four shown: $2.8 \le 4.5$, $4.5 \le 5.0$, $4.5 \le 6.2$, and $2.8 \le 3.5$. Yet since it is known that '≤' is reflexive and transitive, a larger relation is being represented whose digraph is

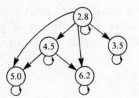

A different kind of simplification can be made if R is known to be symmetric. The following replacement can be made:

The digraph has become a graph.

To summarize this section: digraphs may be used to represent arbitrary relations; directed acyclic graphs arise when the relation is antisymmetric and transitive; and undirected graphs are the natural representation for symmetric relations.

10.4   Directed Acyclic Graphs

It is the possibility of cycles that makes graphs more difficult to deal with than trees. A cycle creates the risk of infinite loops; and, more subtly, there is no natural place to begin on a cycle. For these reasons, the *directed acyclic graph*, or *dag*, which is a directed graph with no cycles, will first be considered.

Dags arise whenever certain activities must be carried out in some order, but not just any order. For example, the dag:

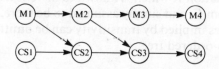

represents the prerequisite structure of the mathematics and computer science courses at the University of Sydney. It shows, for example, that both M2 and CS2 must be completed before CS3 is undertaken. Clearly, a sensible prerequisite structure will always be acyclic.

A *topological ordering* of the vertices of a digraph is a way to visit the vertices, one by one, in a sequence that satisfies all the prerequisite constraints. For example, M1, CS1, CS2, M2, M3, M4, CS3, CS4 is one of 47 possible topological orderings for the vertices of the digraph given above. Formally, a topological ordering of the vertices of a directed graph $G = \langle V, E \rangle$ is a sequence $\langle v_1, v_2, \ldots, v_n \rangle$, such that $V = \{v_1, v_2, \ldots, v_n\}$ and, for all $\langle v_i, v_j \rangle$ in E, v_i precedes v_j in the sequence.

The idea of modelling constrained activities with a dag, then using a topological ordering to solve the problem of performing the activities correctly, arises frequently. Consider evaluating the arithmetic expression

$$(a - b * c) + (d - e)$$

The addition cannot be performed before the results of the subtractions are known, but either subtraction may be performed first. These constraints are expressed by the following dag:

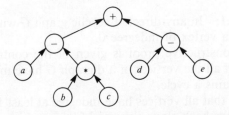

For example, $b \rightarrow *$ means that $*$ cannot be performed until b is known. Notice that this dag does not say which argument of $-$ is subtracted from the other; for that, an ordering on incoming edges would need to be specified.

When the dag is a tree with its edges pointing towards the root, a postorder traversal will yield a topological ordering. In this example, the ordering is $a\ b\ c\ *\ -\ d\ e\ -\ +$. However, more complex expressions do arise. Consider the efficient evaluation of the two roots of a quadratic equation:

$(-b + \mathrm{sqrt}(b * b - 4 * a * c))/2a$ and
$(-b - \mathrm{sqrt}(b * b - 4 * a * c))/2a$

The corresponding dag is no longer a tree:

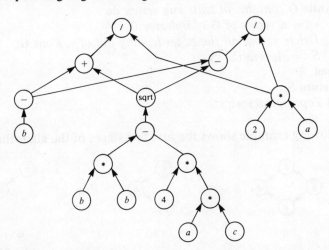

To evaluate this expression correctly, the dag must be traversed in topological order.

It should be clear that, if a digraph has a cycle, there can be no topological ordering of its vertices; but the converse statement, that the vertices of every dag can be topologically ordered, is less obvious. The following theorem, first published by Szpilrajn (1930), is the first step in the proof of this fact.

Theorem 10.1:   In any directed acyclic graph G with $n \geq 1$ vertices, there exists a vertex of indegree 0.
Proof: A constructive proof is given of the contrapositive, which states that, if all the vertices of a digraph G have indegree at least 1, then G contains a cycle.

Assume that all vertices have indegree at least 1. Starting at any vertex v_1, trace back along any one of its incoming edges to a vertex v_2. From v_2 trace back to v_3, and so on. Since all vertices have indegree at least 1, this process need never stop; but since G is finite, eventually a vertex must be reached that has been passed through before. So G contains a cycle.   ∎

The vertex of indegree 0 that this theorem provides is a suitable first element of a topological ordering, since it is not constrained to follow any other vertex. This leads to an efficient algorithm, known as *topological sort*, for finding a topological ordering of the vertices of a dag G:

```
procedure TopologicalSort(G: Digraph): List;
var S: List;
begin
    Initialize (S);
    while G contains at least one vertex do
        v := a vertex of G of indegree 0;
        Delete v, and all the edges leading out of v, from G;
        S := Append(S, v);
    end;
    return S;
end TopologicalSort;
```

The following example shows the first few stages of the algorithm:

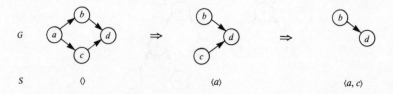

Eventually G becomes empty and $S = \langle a, c, b, d \rangle$. After a is deleted, both b and c have indegree 0, and the algorithm is free to choose either.

Topological sort resembles selection sort, in that a smallest element is repeatedly deleted in both algorithms; so it is an incremental algorithm of the second kind, in the classification of Section 4.2. This suggests that the loop invariant should be 'S may be extended to a topological ordering of the vertices of G'. Unfortunately, it is not yet definite that a topological ordering of G exists, so even if $S = \langle \rangle$ it cannot be proved that this condition holds. The following loop invariant cleverly avoids this problem.

Theorem 10.2   (Loop invariant of topological sort): Let $G = \langle V, E \rangle$ be a directed acyclic graph. Then, at the beginning of the kth iteration of *TopologicalSort(G)*, $S = \langle v_1, v_2, \ldots, v_{k-1} \rangle$ has the following property: for all edges $\langle v_i, v_j \rangle$ in E, if v_j is in S, then v_i precedes v_j in S.

Proof: by induction on k. Let $S_k = \langle v_1, v_2, \ldots, v_{k-1} \rangle$ be the value of S at the beginning of the kth iteration, and let G_k be the value of G.

Basis step: $k = 1$. Then $S_1 = \langle \rangle$, so the theorem is vacuously true.

Inductive step: The inductive hypothesis concerning S_k is as above; it must be proved that it is true of $S_{k+1} = \langle v_1, v_2, \ldots, v_k \rangle$, where v_k is the vertex selected by the algorithm during the kth iteration. Now v_k exists, by Theorem 10.1 applied to the directed acyclic graph G_k. Since v_k has indegree 0 in G_k, in the original digraph G it must be the case that all of v_k's predecessors lie in $\{v_1, v_2, \ldots, v_{k-1}\}$, which means that, for all $\langle v_i, v_k \rangle$ in E, v_i precedes v_k in S_{k+1}. So the theorem holds for $S_{k+1} = \langle v_1, v_2, \ldots, v_k \rangle$. ∎

At termination, the loop invariant implies that S_{n+1} is a topological ordering of the vertices of G. It can be concluded not only that topological sort is correct, but also that the vertices of any dag may be topologically ordered.

Implementation and analysis of topological sort.   The following implementation of topological sort, due to Knuth (1973a), uses the *Digraph* ADT of Section 10.2. Type *VertexValue* is a record containing an *indegree* field, which holds the current indegree of the vertex, and simulates the deletion of edges from G by gradually decreasing. When the indegree reaches 0, the vertex is ready for inclusion in the result list S.

The implementation uses the *SimpleSet* ADT of Section 3.1 to hold those vertices that have indegree 0, but that have not yet been included in the result list; this cleverly avoids any need to search for these vertices, except to begin with. It also uses the *List* ADT of Section 3.2 to hold the result list. (Since these ADTs share some names, for example, *Initialize* and *New*, in practice these names need to be qualified with the appropriate module name. For ease of reading these qualifications have been deleted from the following otherwise executable code.)

```
procedure TopologicalSort(G: Digraph): List;
var S: List;
    Q: SimpleSet;
    v, w: Vertex;
    val, wval: VertexVal;
    e: Edge; eval: EdgeVal;
begin
  Initialize(S);
  Initialize(Q);
  v := FirstVertex(G);
  while v ≠ NilVertex do
    GetVertexVal(v, val);
    if val.indegree = 0 then
      Insert(New(v), Q);
    end;
    v := NextVertex(v, G);
  end;

  while not Empty(Q) do
    v := ValueOf(DeleteAny(Q));
    S := Append(S, MakeList(New(v)));
    e := FirstEdge(v, G);
    while e ≠ NilEdge do
      w := Endpoint(e, G);
      GetVertexVal(w, wval);
      wval.indegree := wval.indegree − 1;
      SetVertexVal(w, wval);
      if wval.indegree = 0 then
        Insert(New(w), Q);
      end;
      e := NextEdge(v, e, G);
    end;
  end;

  return S;
end TopologicalSort;
```

The initialization is $O(n)$, or if the *indegree* fields must be initialized, it is $O(n + m)$. The main loop is also $O(n + m)$, since it visits every vertex once and traverses every edge once.

Critical paths.   A number of problems on directed acyclic graphs may be solved efficiently by visiting the vertices in topological order. The *critical path problem* is one.

Consider a large project, like the construction of a building. The project divides into a number of subprojects: laying the foundations, building the walls, installing the electrical wiring, and so on. Each subproject takes some amount of time to complete; each cannot begin until certain other subprojects are complete. This can all be represented by a dag with a cost on each edge. For example,

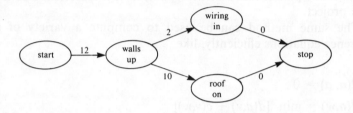

represents a simple building project, in which it takes 12 units of time to get the walls up, at which point the roof construction and wiring may proceed independently, taking 10 and 2 units of time, respectively. An edge ⟨*v*, *w*⟩ represents a subproject, and its label, *c*(*v*, *w*), represents the cost in units of time of the subproject. Vertices represent states, or moments in time between subprojects. Projects have a natural *start state*, when nothing has been done, and a natural *stop state*, when all is complete, so the existence of a unique *start vertex* which is an ancestor of every vertex, and unique *stop vertex* which is a descendant of every vertex, will be assumed.

The natural question to ask is, 'what is the earliest possible time this project can be finished?' In the example above, this is clearly 22 units of time after commencement. Let *a* be the start vertex, and for every vertex *v* of *G*, let *d*(*a*, *v*) be the earliest possible time *v* can be reached. If *b* is the stop vertex, *d*(*a*, *b*) must be found. A vertex *w* will be reached at the earliest possible time if all of its predecessor vertices are reached at their earliest possible times, and the subprojects leading from them to *w* are commenced immediately. Since all of these subprojects must be completed before continuing past *w*, the recurrence equation

$$d(a, a) = 0$$
$$d(a, w) = \max_{v \in P(w)} [d(a, v) + c(v, w)]$$

holds, where $P(w)$ is the set of predecessors of *w*. Note that every vertex except a must have at least one predecessor, since it has a for a proper ancestor, so the max operation is performed over a non-empty set and hence is well-defined.

This recurrence equation leads to an obvious recursive algorithm for calculating $d(a, v)$ for all v. It is more efficient, however, to employ the dynamic programming principle, and compute the $d(a, v)$ by visiting the vertices in topological order. If the value of a predecessor v for which $d(a, w) = d(a, v) + c(v, w)$ is recorded in each vertex w, then at termination a path can be reconstructed from b back to a of total cost $d(a, b)$. Such a path is called a *critical path*, since it represents a bottleneck in the project.

The same method can be used to compute a variety of other recurrence equations efficiently, like

$$d(a, a) = 0$$
$$d(a,w) = \min_{v \in P(w)} [d(a,v) + c(v,w)]$$

for example, which calculates shortest paths. Exercise 10.8 discusses another useful recurrence.

In the following algorithm, the following types are used for the values of vertices and edges:

```
type VertexVal =
record
    visited: boolean;
    indegree: integer;
    distance: integer;
    parent: Vertex;
end;

type EdgeVal =
record
    cost: integer;
end;
```

The *distance* field in each vertex v holds a value which increases to a final value of $d(a, v)$. The field is initially undefined, and becomes defined when v's *visited* field is set to true. The predecessor v of w for which $d(a, w) = d(a, v) + c(v, w)$ is stored in w's *parent* field. The *cost* field of each edge holds the cost of the edge. In other respects the algorithm follows closely the implementation of topological sorting given above.

```
procedure CriticalPath(G: Digraph; a: Vertex);
var Q: SimpleSet; v, w: Vertex;
val, wval: VertexVal; e: Edge; eval: EdgeVal;
begin
  v := FirstVertex(G);
  while v ≠ NilVertex do
    GetVertexVal(v, val);
    val.visited := false;
    SetVertexVal(v, val);
    v := NextVertex(v, G);
  end;
  GetVertexVal(a, val);
  val.visited := true;
  val.parent := NilVertex;
  val.distance := 0;
  SetVertexVal(a, val);
  Initialize(Q); Insert(New(a), Q);
  while not Empty(Q) do
    v := ValueOf(DeleteAny(Q));
    GetVertexVal(v, val);
    e := FirstEdge(v, G);
    while e ≠ NilEdge do
      w := Endpoint(e, G);
      GetEdgeVal(e, eval);
      GetVertexVal(w, wval);
      if not wval.visited then
        wval.visited := true;
        wval.distance := val.distance + eval.cost;
        wval.parent := v;
      elsif wval.distance < val.distance + eval.cost then
        wval.distance := val.distance + eval.cost;
        wval.parent := v;
      end;
      wval.indegree := wval.indegree − 1;
      SetVertexVal(w, wval);
      if wval.indegree = 0 then
        Insert(New(w), Q);
      end;
      e := NextEdge(v, e, G);
    end;
  end;
end CriticalPath;
```

This algorithm, like topological sort, is $O(n + m)$.

10.5   Shortest Paths and Breadth-first Search

The problem of finding a shortest path between two points is basic to navigation. Let G be a directed graph, and let each edge $\langle v, w \rangle$ of G have a non-negative cost, denoted $c(v, w)$; the costs could represent distances, times of travel, construction costs, and so on. The cost of a path is the sum of the costs of its edges, or, if the path has no edges, its cost is naturally defined to be 0. Given two vertices a and b, a path of minimum cost from a to b must be found. Such a path is called a *shortest path*, and its cost is denoted $d(a, b)$.

The undirected graph

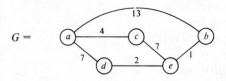

will be used as an example. Each undirected edge corresponds to two directed edges in the obvious way, so giving plenty of edges without the diagram being cluttered with arrows. A shortest path from a to b is $\langle a, d, e, b \rangle$, with cost $d(a, b) = 7 + 2 + 1 = 10$. It is convenient to draw G against a horizontal axis, with each vertex v appearing at its distance $d(a, v)$:

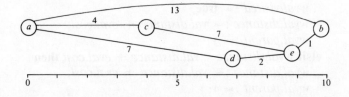

When a shortest path from a to b is found, it turns out that shortest paths from a to many other vertices are seemingly inevitably produced as a by-product. Making a virtue of necessity, it is proposed to find a shortest path from a to every vertex v of G that is reachable from a. The following theorem characterizes this set of shortest paths.

> **Theorem 10.3:**   Let G be a digraph with non-negative edge costs, and let a be a vertex of G from which every vertex of G may be reached. Then there exists a spanning tree T of G, rooted at a, which contains a shortest path from a to every vertex of G.

Proof: Since, for every vertex v, there is at least one path from a to v, there must be at least one shortest path. Any cycles on this path must have cost 0 and may be dropped. The problem is to assemble these cycle-free shortest paths into a tree. An algorithm for doing this is sketched.

Initialize T to $\langle\{a\}, \{\ \}\rangle$. Choose any vertex v not yet in T, and let $P = \langle a, \ldots, x, \ldots, v\rangle$ be a cycle-free shortest path from a to v, where x is the last vertex in P which is currently in T. Now T already contains a shortest path to x, so $\langle a, \ldots, x\rangle$ is not needed and T is extended to v by adding $\langle x, \ldots, v\rangle$ to it. Repeat until T extends to every vertex. ∎

Such a tree is called a *shortest path spanning tree*. For example, the graph G above has shortest path spanning tree

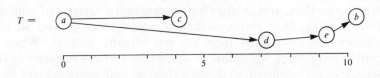

rooted at a. The problem, then, is to find a shortest path spanning tree of a given digraph.

If the digraph is acyclic, this problem may be solved in linear time using topological sort (Section 10.4). Because there are no cycles in a shortest path spanning tree, a linear algorithm for cyclic digraphs is naturally expected to exist as well. However, no such algorithm is known.

Dijkstra's algorithm.   One way to build a tree, rooted at a, with a distance from a assigned to every vertex, is repeatedly to apply the following *propagation step*: choosing any leaf of the tree, whose distance from a is known, the tree is extended to each successor w of v, using v's distance plus $c(v, w)$ for the distance of w:

When a propagation step reaches a vertex w, thereby discovering a new path $\langle a, \ldots, v, w\rangle$ from a to w, it might find a record in w of a previously discovered path from *a* to *w*. If the new path is no shorter than the old path, the new path can be forgotten; otherwise the old path is forgotten and the existence of the new path is recorded in *w*.

But now, what if *v*'s distance is reduced in this way after many paths have already been propagated out of *v*? Then all the distances of these propagations must be reduced too, and this seems to be expensive and complicated. Accordingly, a propagation step at *v* will be allowed only when it is clear that *v*'s distance has settled down to its final value, $d(a, v)$. If this policy can be enforced, a propagation step will never need to be revised.

The following algorithm, due to Dijkstra (1959), is based on these ideas. For each vertex *w*, the cost of a shortest path from *a* to *w* discovered so far is recorded in *w.distance*, and the predecessor of *w* on this path is recorded in *w.parent*. In order to choose the right vertex *v* to propagate from at each stage, the algorithm maintains a set *Q* of interesting vertices, and chooses for propagation a vertex *v* of minimum *v.distance* in *Q*. That vertex is then removed from *Q*, and all of its successors are inserted if they are not already present. When the algorithm terminates, $w.distance = d(a, w)$ for vertices *w* reachable from *a*, and the edges $\langle w.parent, w \rangle$ define a shortest path spanning tree for the reachable vertices, rooted at *a*.

>   a.distance := 0;
>   a.parent := **nil**;
>   Q := {a};
>   **while not** *Empty* (Q) **do**
>   *Extract a vertex v from Q of minimum v.distance*;
>   **for** *each vertex w adjacent to v* **do**
>   *Propagate v.distance* + c(v, w) *to w*;
>   Q := Q ∪ {w};
>   **end**;
>   **end**;

This algorithm is now traced on the graph

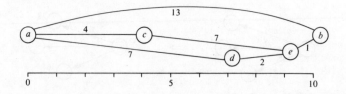

Edges $\langle v.parent, v \rangle$ leading into vertices *v* that have been extracted from *Q* will be shown as solid arrows; they are part of the final tree *T*. Edges leading into vertices of *Q* are candidates for inclusion in *T*, and are shown as dashed arrows. Other edges are not shown. Whenever the value of *v.distance* is defined, it is shown adjacent to *v*. The situation at the start of the first iteration is

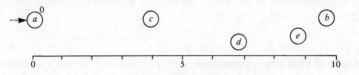

with *a* being the only vertex in *Q*. Thereafter

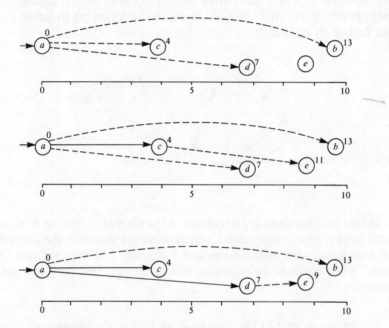

Notice at this point how the old path ⟨*a, c, e*⟩ was abandoned in favour of the new, shorter path ⟨*a, d, e*⟩. Continuing,

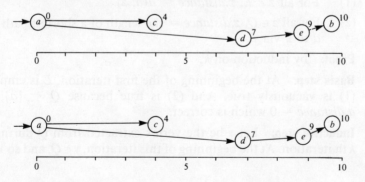

and the algorithm terminates, since Q is now empty. The algorithm found the right tree in this example, but of course its correctness is far from clear; in fact, one of the main reasons why this text devotes so much time to formal correctness is its value as an aid to understanding Dijkstra's algorithm.

Correctness of Dijkstra's algorithm.   While Dijkstra's algorithm is running, it partitions the vertices of G into three sets: L, the set of vertices that have been extracted from Q; Q itself; and R, the vertices not yet encountered. It is said that path P from a to v goes *via L* if all the vertices in P, except v, are in L. For example, in the following diagram P_1 goes via L, but P_2 does not:

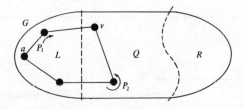

It should be clear from the operation of the algorithm that, as soon as one path from a to w is discovered, *w.parent* always points to the predecessor of w on some path from a to w, and *w.distance* is always the cost of this path. What needs to be shown is that eventually this path is a shortest path.

> **Theorem 10.4 (Loop invariant of Dijkstra's algorithm):** At the beginning of the kth iteration of Dijkstra's algorithm, the following two conditions hold:
>
> (1)   For all $z \in L$, $z.distance = d(a, z)$.
>
> (2)   For all $z \in Q$, $z.distance =$ the length of a shortest path from a to z via L.
>
> **Proof:**   by induction on k.
>
> **Basis step:**   At the beginning of the first iteration, L is empty so (1) is vacuously true. And (2) is true because $Q = \{a\}$, and $a.distance = 0$ which is correct.
>
> **Inductive step:**   Let v be the vertex extracted from Q during the kth iteration. At the beginning of this iteration, $v \in Q$, and so $v.dis$-

tance is the cost of a shortest path from a to v via L. It must be shown that there is no shorter path to v via vertices not in L, so as to justify the inclusion of v into L.

Consider any path P from a to v that does not go via L. P contains at least one vertex which is not in L, and not equal to v. Let x be the first such vertex on P:

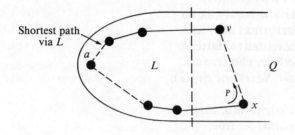

Since x is adjacent to L, $x \in Q$. So $x.distance$ is the cost of a shortest path to x via L, by the inductive hypothesis. But P contains a path from a to x via L, so the cost of P is at least as great as $x.distance$. Now $x.distance \geq v.distance$, since the algorithm chose v, not x. It can be concluded that the cost of P is at least as great as $v.distance$. Therefore v may be included into L, with (1) holding at the beginning of the next iteration. Clearly (2) is preserved also, because the algorithm updates $w.distance$ to reflect the discovery of path $\langle a, \ldots, v, w \rangle$ for all w. ∎

At termination, $L = V$ (assuming all vertices are reachable from a), and (1) says that for all $z \in V$, $z.distance = d(a, z)$ as required. It follows that Dijkstra's algorithm is correct. The careful choice of v at each stage is the hallmark of an incremental algorithm of the second kind (Section 4.2).

Implementation and analysis of Dijkstra's algorithm.   It is clear that the set Q should be implemented as a priority queue whose keys are distances and whose values are vertices. When a new path from a to w is found which is shorter than a previous one, w's distance decreases while it is in Q; so the *DecreaseKey* operation, introduced in Section 7.1 is required.

In the following implementation of Dijkstra's algorithm, each vertex has a *visited* field which is true if the vertex has been visited, in which case the *parent* field contains the predecessor on the shortest path to this vertex found so far, and the *entry* field is the vertex's entry in the priority queue:

```
procedure Dijkstra(G: Digraph; a: Vertex);
var Q: PriorityQueue;
    v, w: Vertex; val, wval: VertexVal;
    e: Edge; eval: EdgeVal;
    newdist: integer;
begin
    v := FirstVertex(G);
    while v ≠ NilVertex do
        GetVertexVal(v, val);
        val.visited := false;
        SetVertexVal(v, val);
        v := NextVertex(v, G);
    end;
    GetVertexVal(a, val);
    val.visited := true;
    val.parent := NilVertex;
    val.entry := New(0, a);
    SetVertexVal(a, val);
    Initialize(Q);
    Insert(val.entry, Q);
    while not Empty(Q) do
        v := ValueOf(DeleteMin(Q));
        GetVertexVal(v, val);
        e := FirstEdge(v, G);
        while e ≠ NilEdge do
            w := Endpoint(e, G);
            GetEdgeVal(e, eval);
            GetVertexVal(w, wval);
            newdist := KeyOf(val.entry) + eval.cost;
            if not wval.visited then
                wval.visited := true;
                wval.parent := v;
                wval.entry := New(newdist, w);
                SetVertexVal(w, wval);
                Insert(wval.entry, Q);
            elsif newdist < KeyOf(wval.entry) then
                wval.parent := v;
                SetVertexVal(w, wval);
                DecreaseKey(wval.entry, newdist, Q);
            end;
            e := NextEdge(v, e, G);
        end;
    end;
end Dijkstra;
```

In the following analysis, it will be assumed that every vertex of G is reachable from a. The complexity of this algorithm is just the total complexity of the operations on Q. Since every vertex is inserted once and deleted once, there must be n *Insert* and n *DeleteMin* calls. Each iteration of the inner loop corresponds to one edge of G, so the body of the inner loop is executed exactly m times. Inside the inner loop, either one *Insert*, one *DecreaseKey*, or nothing is performed. There are $n - 1$ insertions performed in the inner loop, so there are a maximum of $m - (n - 1)$ *DecreaseKey* operations. The worst-case complexity of Dijkstra's algorithm is therefore

$$W(n, m) = O(n \cdot \text{cost of } Insert + n \cdot \text{cost of } DeleteMin + m \cdot \text{cost of } DecreaseKey)$$

where the maximum size of the priority queue is n.

It is an interesting exercise to look through the summary of priority queue implementations given in Section 7.7, to find the one best suited to Dijkstra's algorithm. The unsorted linked list gives

$$W(n, m) = O(n \cdot 1 + n \cdot n + m \cdot 1)$$
$$= O(n^2)$$

since $m \leq n^2$. The 2-3 tree and the heap give

$$W(n, m) = O(n \cdot \log n + n \cdot \log n + m \cdot \log n)$$
$$= O(m \log n)$$

since $m \geq n - 1$ in a connected digraph. But the winner is the Fibonacci heap, with

$$W(n, m) = O(n \cdot 1 + n \cdot \log n + m \cdot 1)$$
$$= O(n \log n + m)$$

It will be shown in Chapter 11 that this is the best possible asymptotic complexity that could be hoped for: there is no more efficient way to implement Dijkstra's algorithm.

Breadth-first search.   Consider now a directed graph whose edges do not have costs. A path may be required from a to b of minimum *length* (number of edges).

If each edge is assigned a cost of 1, the cost of any path will equal its length, and Dijkstra's algorithm may be used to solve this problem. A number of simplifications are possible in this special case, however:

```
procedure BreadthFirstSearch(G: Digraph; a: Vertex);
var Q: FifoQueue;
    p: Entry; v, w: Vertex;
    e: Edge; val, wval: VertexVal;
begin

v := FirstVertex(G);
while v ≠ NilVertex do
    GetVertexVal(v, val);
    val.visited := false;
    val.parent := NilVertex;
    SetVertexVal(v, val);
    v := NextVertex(v, G);
end;

GetVertexVal(a, val);
val.visited := true;
SetVertexVal(a, val);
Initialize(Q);
Enqueue(New(a), Q);
while not Empty(Q) do
    GetEntryVal(Dequeue(Q), v);
    e := FirstEdge(v, G);
    while e ≠ NilEdge do
        w := Endpoint(e, G);
        GetVertexVal(w, wval);
        if not wval.visited then
            wval.visited := true;
            wval.parent := v;
            SetVertexVal(w, wval);
            Enqueue(New(w), Q);
        end;
        e := NextEdge(v, e, G);
    end;
end;
end BreadthFirstSearch;
```

Since the *FifoQueue* operations are all $O(1)$, this algorithm is $O(n + m)$.

Let $P_1 = \langle a, \ldots, v_1, w \rangle$ be the first path from a to w discovered by Dijkstra's algorithm in the case when all edges have cost 1. It will be shown that this is a shortest path from a to w. Let $P_2 = \langle a, \ldots, v_2, w \rangle$ be another path from a to w discovered by Dijkstra's algorithm. At the time P_1 was discovered, v_1 had just been extracted from Q, so v_1. *distance* $= d(a, v_1)$, and the cost of P_1 is $d(a, v_1) + 1$. Similarly, the cost of P_2

is $d(a, v_2) + 1$. But, since P_1 was discovered before P_2, v_1 was extracted from Q before v_2, so $d(a, v_1) \leq d(a, v_2)$. Therefore the length of P_1 is no greater than the length of P_2.

It follows that the *DecreaseKey* part of Dijkstra's algorithm will never be executed in this special case. During each iteration of the main loop, then, some vertex of distance x, say, is extracted from Q, and some other vertices of distance $x + 1$ are inserted. From this, it can easily be shown by induction that, at any moment, all of the entries of Q have distance x or $x + 1$, for some x, and that the distance of every vertex inserted is the larger of these two numbers. The priority queue may therefore be replaced with the first-in-first-out queue introduced in Section 3.2.

10.6   Depth-first Search

A generalization of the preorder traversal of a tree, known as *depth-first search*, provides perhaps the simplest way to traverse a graph or digraph: beginning at a given vertex v, v is visited and then the graph is traversed, beginning at each successor of v in turn. The algorithm avoids visiting any vertex twice (thereby also avoiding infinite loops) by marking each vertex after it has been visited, and refusing to revisit marked vertices. A boolean field called *visited* in each vertex is used to hold this mark. Here is the algorithm:

```
procedure Dfs(G: Digraph; v: Vertex);
var w: Vertex;
    e: Edge;
    val: VertexVal;
begin
    Visit(v);
    GetVertexVal(v, val);
    val.visited := true;
    SetVertexVal(v, val);
    e := FirstEdge (v, G);
    while e ≠ NilEdge do
        w := Endpoint(e, G);
        GetVertexVal(w, val);
        if not val.visited then
            Dfs(G, w);
        end;
        e := NextEdge(v, e, G);
    end;
end Dfs;
```

The precondition includes '*v* is unvisited', and the postcondition includes 'all descendants of *v* are visited'.

Procedure *Dfs* will visit every unvisited descendant of *v*, but there is no guarantee that this will cover all the vertices of *G*. To visit them all, *Dfs* must be called repeatedly until no unvisited vertices are left. The following algorithm does this; it also initializes the *visited* fields.

```
procedure DepthFirstSearch(G: Digraph);
var v: Vertex;
    val: VertexVal;
begin
  v := FirstVertex(G);
  while v ≠ NilVertex do
    GetVertexVal(v, val);
    val.visited := false;
    SetVertexVal(v, val);
    v := NextVertex(v, G);
  end;

  v := FirstVertex(G);
  while v ≠ NilVertex do
    GetVertexVal(v, val);
    if not val.visited then
      Dfs(G, v);
    end;
    v := NextVertex(v, G);
  end;
end DepthFirstSearch;
```

Depth-first search can be used to construct a *depth-first spanning forest F* for *G*, simply by adding the edge *e* to *F* immediately before the recursive call to *Dfs(G, w)* in procedure *Dfs*. For example, given the undirected graph

$G =$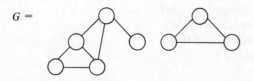

one depth-first spanning forest is

$F =$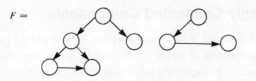

Whether or not G is directed, it is conventional to direct the edges of F the way the search went. There are, of course, many different depth-first spanning forests, since their shape is affected by which node is chosen to begin the search, and the order in which the edges leading out of each node are explored.

The edges of F are called *tree edges*, and if G is undirected, the non-tree edges are called *back edges*. The back edges are characterized by the following theorem.

Theorem 10.5: Let G be an undirected graph, let F be a depth-first spanning forest for G, and let $\{v, w\}$ be any back edge. Then either v is an ancestor of w in F, or w is an ancestor of v.

Proof: by contradiction. Suppose neither vertex is an ancestor of the other. Without loss of generality, it may be assumed that v was visited before w:

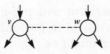

When v was first entered by the search, w was unvisited. Since w is not a descendant of v, when the search left v for the last time, w was still unvisited. But this contradicts the fact that depth-first search visits every unvisited vertex adjacent to v before leaving v for the last time. ∎

Depth-first search thus imposes a degree of structure on a graph – the tree edges forming a forest, the back edges pointing strictly to ancestors:

$G =$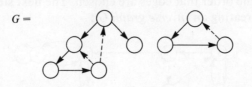

This regularity has proven to be very useful in a number of applications, such as the test for biconnectivity given in Section 10.8. A similar, but more complicated, result holds in directed graphs (Exercise 10.18). Tarjan (1972) contains several applications of depth-first search.

10.7 Strongly Connected Components

Recall from Section 10.3 that two vertices of a directed graph are said to be strongly connected if each is reachable from the other, and that a strongly connected component of a digraph G is a maximal subgraph of G whose vertices are all strongly connected with each other. For example, the following digraph is shown with each of its strongly connected components enclosed in a dashed circle:

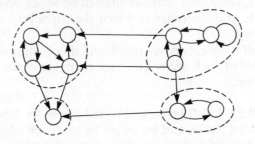

The problem of finding the strongly connected components of a digraph is a good example of the power of depth-first search. The algorithm which will be described is given by Aho *et al.* (1983), who attribute its ideas to R.Kosaraju (unpublished), and to Sharir (1981).

The first step is to perform a depth-first traversal of the given digraph G, numbering its vertices in postorder. For the digraph shown above, the result of this step might be

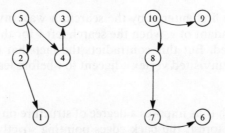

depending on the order that edges are chosen. The next step is to reverse all the edges, creating an *inverse graph* G_r:

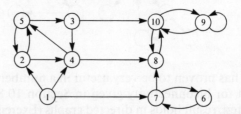

Finally, a depth-first traversal of G_r is performed, beginning at the highest-numbered vertex. If this search does not visit all the vertices of G_r, the highest-numbered unvisited vertex is chosen and the search is resumed there, carrying on in this way until all the vertices have been visited:

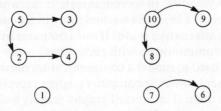

In the resulting forest, each tree contains exactly the vertices of one strongly connected component of G. The reader may verify this startling fact for the example just given.

In order to prove that this algorithm is correct it must be shown that two vertices v and w lie in the same strongly connected component of G if and only if they lie in the same tree of the depth-first spanning forest of G_r constructed by the algorithm.

Suppose first that v and w lie in the same strongly connected component of G. Then there are paths in G_r from v to w and from w to v, which implies immediately that v and w must lie in the same tree of any depth-first spanning forest of G_r, since otherwise the depth-first search would have failed to explore all the paths open to it. This part of the proof is nicely illustrated by the first depth-first traversal shown above, in which each strongly connected component appears within one tree, but the tree may contain more than one component.

Conversely, assume that v and w lie in the same tree T of the depth-first spanning forest of G_r. It must be shown that they are strongly connected in G. In the following discussion, a node is said to be *initiated* when the search reaches it for the first time, and *terminated* when the search leaves it for the last time.

Let x be the root of T. Since v lies in T, there is a path in G_r from x to v. Therefore there is a path in G from v to x.

During the first depth-first traversal, x was terminated later than v. This is so because v was not visited when the second depth-first traversal initiated x, implying that x's number must have been larger than v's number.

Furthermore, during the first depth-first traversal, x was initiated before v. For suppose, on the contrary, that x was initiated after v. From the existence of the path in G from v to x established above, it may be concluded that x must be a descendant of v and hence that x was terminated before v, which contradicts the previous paragraph.

So x was initiated before v and terminated after v. It follows that x is an ancestor of v in the first depth-first spanning forest, and hence that there is a path from x to v in G. So v and x are strongly connected in G.

This same argument may be used to show that w and x are strongly connected in G, and so conclude that v and w are strongly connected in G (via paths through x). So the algorithm is correct.

10.8 Biconnectivity

The problem of *reliability* in communication networks is of great practical importance. If a bridge is washed away in a flood, does the road network provide an alternative route? If one computer in a network fails, can the others still communicate with each other?

Graphs can be used to model a communication network in the usual way: vertices represent towns or computers, edges represent the roads or cables that connect them. Undirected graphs may as well be used, since most communication networks are two-way. The above questions are equivalent to asking whether a graph remains connected whenever a single edge or vertex is deleted (when a vertex is deleted, its associated edges are deleted also). Only vertex failures will be discussed here; Exercise 10.19 looks at edge failures.

For example, if the graph is a tree:

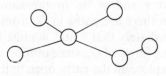

then deletion of any vertex of degree greater than one will disconnect the tree; so this network is not very reliable. If the graph is a *ring*:

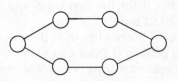

it will tolerate any single failure, assuming that the network is able to re-route its messages along the alternative path.

A graph is said to be *k-connected* if the removal of any $k - 1$ vertices leaves the remaining subgraph connected. So to be 1-connected is to be connected; to be 2-connected (or *biconnected*) means that one vertex failure can be tolerated, as in the ring above.

If a graph is connected but not biconnected, it has *articulation points*: vertices whose removal would disconnect the graph. For example, the articulation points of the graph

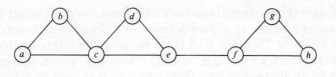

are c, e, and f. The obvious way to find the articulation points of a graph is to take each vertex in turn, delete it, and check whether the remaining subgraph is connected. Since a connectedness check takes $O(n + m)$ time, finding all the articulation points of a graph is $O(n(n + m))$ using this method.

A much faster algorithm has been developed by J.E.Hopcroft (see Aho *et al.*, 1974), who showed how to find all the articulation points during the course of a single depth-first traversal of the graph. The method is based on the following theorem.

Theorem 10.6: Let G be a connected graph with depth-first spanning tree T. Then v is an articulation point of G if and only if

(1) v is the root of T, and v has at least two children; or
(2) v is not the root of T, and for some child w of v in T there is no back edge from any descendant of w to any proper ancestor of v.

Proof: Suppose first that v is the root of T. If v has no children or one child, deleting v will clearly not disconnect G. If v has at least two children, w and x, then deletion of v must disconnect them, since by Theorem 10.5 there is no cross edge connecting T_w with T_x.

If v is not the root, then the following situation applies:

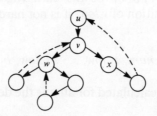

If, as is shown, there is no back edge from any descendant of w to a proper ancestor of v, then deletion of v clearly disconnects w from u, since by Theorem 10.5 there are no other edges leaving T_w. If there is such a back edge, as there is within T_x above, that edge provides an alternative path from u to x, so that v can be deleted without disconnecting u from x.   ∎

The first step in applying this theorem to a graph G is to perform a depth-first search, numbering the vertices from 1 to n in the order they were first visited by the search (that is, in preorder). The number assigned to vertex v is stored in the field $v.num$. If $\langle v, w \rangle$ is any tree edge, then clearly v was first visited before w, so $v.num < w.num$; while for any back edge $\langle v, w \rangle$, Theorem 10.5 says that w is an ancestor of v, so $v.num \geq w.num$, with equality only if we are allowing self-loops.

Let $\langle v, w \rangle$ be a tree edge like the one shown above in the proof of the theorem. It is required to know whether or not there is a back edge from some descendant of w to some proper ancestor of v. So $v.low$ is defined to be the number of the smallest-numbered vertex reachable from v by following down zero or more tree edges, then up at most one back edge. For example, here is the graph of the diagram above; for each vertex v, the value of $v.num$ is shown inside the vertex, and $v.low$ adjacent to it:

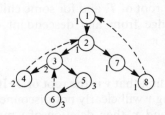

If $w.low \geq v.num$, then by following zero or more tree edges down from w, then at most one back edge, an ancestor of v cannot be arrived at, therefore, by Theorem 10.6, v must be an articulation point. Conversely, if $w.low < v.num$ for all children w of v, then v is not an articulation point. Thus, if $v.low$ can be found for all v, the problem is solved.

Let $\langle v, t_1 \rangle, \langle v, t_2 \rangle, \ldots, \langle v, t_i \rangle$ be the tree edges leading down from v, and let $\langle v, b_1 \rangle, \langle v, b_2 \rangle, \ldots, \langle v, b_j \rangle$ be the back edges leading up from v. By considering the definition of $v.low$, it is not hard to see that it satisfies the recurrence equation

$$v.low = \min(v.num, t_1.low, \ldots, t_i.low, b_1.num, \ldots, b_j.num)$$

and so $v.low$ may be calculated for all v as the depth-first search proceeds:

all the quantities on the right-hand side are known by the time the search finally leaves v.

The following algorithm performs a depth-first search of G, beginning at vertex v. The second parameter u equals the parent of v, or *NilVertex* if v has no parent. The algorithm calculates $v.low$ according to the recurrence equation just given, and uses it to set $v.articulationpt$ to **true** if and only if v is a non-root articulation point of G.

```
var count: integer;

procedure FAP(v, u: Vertex; G: Graph);
var w: Vertex;
    val, wval: VertexVal;
    e: Edge;
begin
    count := count + 1;
    GetVertexVal(v, val);
    val.num := count;
    val.low := count;
    val.childcount := 0;
    val.articulationpt := false;
    val.visited := true;
    SetVertexVal(v, val);
    e := FirstEdge(v, G);
    while e ≠ NilEdge do
      w := Endpoint(e, G);
      GetVertexVal(w, wval);
      if not wval.visited then
        FAP(w, v, G);
        GetVertexVal(w, wval);
        val.low := Min(val.low, wval.low);
        if (wval.low ≥ val.num) and (u ≠ NilVertex) then
          val.articulationpt := true;
        end;
        val.childcount := val.childcount + 1;
      elsif w ≠ u then
        val.low := Min(val.low, wval.num);
      end;
      e := NextEdge(v, e, G);
    end;
    SetVertexVal(v, val);
  end FAP;
```

The test $w \neq u$ ensures that no tree edge is traversed backwards. The algorithm also calculates the number of children of v in T, for use in determining whether the root of T is an articulation point. The following procedure makes this determination, and also provides the appropriate initialization:

```
procedure FindArticulationPoints(G: Graph);
var v: Vertex;
    val: VertexVal;
begin
  if FirstVertex(G) ≠ NilVertex then
    v := FirstVertex(G);
    while v ≠ NilVertex do
      GetVertexVal(v, val);
      val.visited := false;
      SetVertexVal(v, val);
      v := NextVertex(v, G);
    end;
    count := 0;
    v := FirstVertex(G);
    FAP(v, NilVertex, G);
    GetVertexVal(v, val);
    if val.childcount ≥ 2 then
      val.articulationpt := true;
      SetVertexVal(v, val);
    end;
  end;
end FindArticulationPoints;
```

It is assumed that G is connected, so there is no need to look for unvisited vertices after executing $FAP(v, NilVertex, G)$. Since this algorithm is a simple elaboration of depth-first search, it is clearly $O(n + m)$ in the worst case.

10.9   Minimum Spanning Trees and Kruskal's Algorithm

Consider the following problem. There are a number of cities, and it is desired to connect them by an electric power network, in such a way as to minimize the cost of the network. As described by Graham and Hell (1985), this problem was first studied by O. Borůvka, who learnt of it from friends employed in the electrification of Southern Moravia (now part of Czechoslovakia).

Borůvka's solution involved an assumption that will also be made here: that junctions in the network may occur only within cities. This allows the problem to be represented as a graph. Each city is a vertex, and whenever a direct link between two cities is feasible, the corresponding vertices are connected by an edge e, labelled with a non-negative number $c(e)$, equal to the cost of the link. For example,

$G =$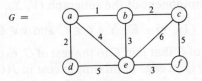

represents six cities; the cost of a direct link between a and d is 2, and so on.

The desired electric power network is a subgraph of G that connects all of the vertices of G together, using edges whose total cost is minimum. No cycles are needed, since one edge of a cycle can always be deleted without increasing the total cost of the network, or disconnecting any vertices. So the network is a spanning tree of minimum total cost: a *minimum spanning tree*. For example,

$T =$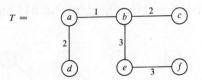

is a minimum spanning tree of the graph G above, and its total cost is 11. The total cost of T is denoted by $c(T)$. If G is not connected, a minimum spanning tree of each connected component can be found. Taken together, these trees form a *minimum spanning forest*.

There are a variety of algorithms for finding minimum spanning forests, but in general terms they all work in the same way. Two sets of edges, which will be called X and Y, are used. The sets are initially empty, and are gradually enlarged while maintaining the loop invariant

'There exists a minimum spanning forest of G which contains all of the edges of X, and none of the edges of Y.'

Initializing X and Y to empty establishes this invariant. If $X \cup Y = E$ at termination, the invariant implies that $F = \langle V, X \rangle$ is a minimum spanning forest of G. The following theorem shows how to add one edge to X while maintaining this invariant:

Theorem 10.7:   Let $G = \langle V, E \rangle$ be a graph, and suppose there are two subsets of E, called X and Y, that obey the following condition: there exists a minimum spanning forest F of G which contains all of the edges of X, and none of the edges of Y. Let C be any connected component of the subgraph $\langle V, X \rangle$, and let

$$J(C) = \{ \{u, v\} \in E - Y \mid u \in C \text{ and } v \notin C \}$$

be the edges of G that join C to the rest of G, excluding any edges of Y. Suppose e is an edge of minimum cost in $J(C)$. Then there exists a minimum spanning forest F' of G which contains all of the edges of $X \cup \{e\}$, and none of the edges of Y.

Proof: Looking first at an example, consider

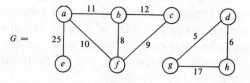

and suppose that $X = \{ \{b, f\}, \{d, g\}, \{d, h\} \}$ and $Y = \{ \}$. Then

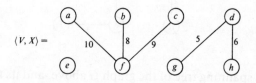

C could be the connected component of $\langle V, X \rangle$ whose vertices are b and f, in which case $J(C) = \{ \{b, a\}, \{b, c\}, \{f, a\}, \{f, a\}, \{f, c\} \}$. Since the edge $\{f, c\}$ has minimum cost among the edges of $J(C)$, the theorem says that $\{f, c\}$ may be added to X.

Now for the proof. For convenience of notation, F and F' are treated as sets of edges. If $e \in F$, then $F' = F$ and the proof is done. So assuming that $e \notin F$, let $e = \{u, v\}$. Since u and v are connected by e, there must be some path in F connecting u with v. This path begins at u in C and ends at v outside C, and it contains no edges from Y; so it must contain at least one edge $e' \in J(C)$:

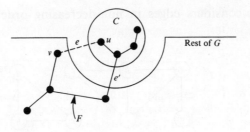

Since e is of minimum cost in $J(C)$, $c(e) \le c(e')$. Now let

$$F' = F \cup \{e\} - \{e'\}$$

Then F' is a spanning forest of G, and $c(F') = c(F) + c(e) - c(e')$ $\le c(F)$. But F was a minimum spanning forest, so $c(F) \le c(F')$. It can be concluded that $c(F) = c(F')$, $c(e) = c(e')$, and F' is also a minimum spanning forest. Clearly F' contains all of the edges of $X \cup \{e\}$ and none of the edges of Y. ∎

It is not hard to use this theorem to build minimum spanning trees by hand: choose any component C, which will initially be a single vertex, add a smallest incident edge, and repeat. A simple implementation of this method will now be considered.

Kruskal's algorithm.   The following algorithm for finding a minimum spanning forest of a graph $G = \langle V, E \rangle$ is due to Kruskal (1956):

```
procedure Kruskal(⟨V, E⟩: graph): graph;
var Q, X, Y: set of edges;
begin
  X := { }; Y := { };
  Q := E;
  while not Empty(Q) do
    Delete an edge {v, w} of minimum cost from Q;
    if v and w lie in different components of ⟨V, X⟩ then
      Insert({v, w}, X);
    else
      Insert({v, w}, Y);
    end;
  end;
  return ⟨V, X⟩;
end Kruskal;
```

The algorithm considers edges in non-decreasing order by cost. For example, if

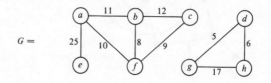

then the first edges considered, with costs 5, 6, 8, 9, and 10, can all be accepted into X, giving

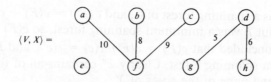

After that, the algorithm considers and rejects the edges with costs 11, 12, and 17, finally accepting the last edge with cost 25, and returning

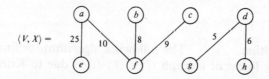

With the help of the theorem given above, Kruskal's algorithm is easy to prove correct:

Theorem 10.8 (Loop invariant of Kruskal's algorithm): At the beginning of the kth iteration of the loop in $Kruskal(G)$, where $G = \langle V, E \rangle$,

(1) there exists a minimum spanning forest of G which contains all of the edges of X, and none of the edges of Y; and

(2) $Q = E - X - Y$.

Proof: The invariance of $Q = E - X - Y$ is obvious, since it is true initially and, during each iteration, one edge is deleted from Q and inserted into X or Y. It remains to prove (1) by induction on k.

Basis step: Initially, X and Y are empty, so any minimum spanning forest satisfies the condition.

Inductive step: The inductive hypothesis is as given above; it must be shown that it is true for $k + 1$. Let $e = \{v, w\}$ be the edge extracted at the beginning of the kth iteration.

First, suppose that v and w lie in different components of $\langle V, X \rangle$. Then it must be the case that $e \in J(C)$ for some C. Since e is of minimum cost among the edges of $Q = E - X - Y$, and $J(C) \subset E - X - Y$, e is of minimum cost in $J(C)$. By Theorem 10.7, e may be added to X.

Second, suppose that v and w lie in the same component of $\langle V, X \rangle$. This means there is a path $\langle v, \ldots, w \rangle$ in $\langle V, X \rangle$, and the minimum spanning forest F which exists by the inductive hypothesis also contains this path, since F contains all the edges of X. Therefore e cannot be in F, since if it was, F would contain the cycle $\langle v, \ldots, w, v \rangle$. Thus e may be added to Y.   ∎

When the algorithm terminates, every edge is either in X or in Y, and so (1) gives an assurance that $\langle V, X \rangle$ is a minimum spanning forest of G.

Implementation and analysis of Kruskal's algorithm.   Clearly, the edges of G should be stored in a priority queue ordered by cost. The vertices fall into disjoint sets, one set for each connected component of $\langle V, X \rangle$, and the *DisjointSets* ADT from Chapter 9 is appropriate for them. For example, if

then the disjoint sets structure is $\{ \{a\}, \{b, f\}, \{c\}, \{d, g, h\}, \{e\} \}$. To determine whether v and w lie in different components of $\langle V, X \rangle$, the test $Find(v, D) \neq Find(w, D)$ can be performed; and when two components of $\langle V, X \rangle$ are merged into one by the insertion of an edge into X, a *Union* operation merges the corresponding sets of vertices. There is no need to maintain Y, since its value is never used.

Kruskal's algorithm does not traverse its graph in the usual way, and so the *Graph* ADT is not helpful here. In the following implementation, the value of each edge is a record containing a *cost* field containing its cost, and a boolean flag *inforest* which will be set to **true** in each edge which is included in the minimum spanning forest. The procedure *Endpoints*$(e, v1, v2)$ sets $v1$ and $v2$ to the two endpoints of e; it is not provided by the *Graph* ADT normally used. The value of each vertex is a record containing a pointer to its entry in the disjoint sets structure.

```
procedure Kruskal(G: KGraph);
var D: DisjointSets; Q: PriorityQueue;
    v, v1, v2: Vertex; val, val1, val2: VertexVal;
    e: Edge; eval: EdgeVal; Set1, Set2: SetType;
begin

  (* initialize disjoint sets of vertices *)
  Initialize(D);
  v := FirstVertex(G);
  while v ≠ NilVertex do
    GetVertexVal(v, val);
    val.entry := New( );
    MakeSet(val.entry, D);
    SetVertexVal(v, val);
    v := NextVertex(v, G);
  end;

  (* initialize priority queue of edges *)
  Initialize(Q);
  e := FirstEdge(G);
  while e ≠ NilEdge do
    GetEdgeVal(e, eval);
    Insert(New(eval.cost, e), Q);
    eval.inforest := false;
    SetEdgeVal(e, eval);
    e := NextEdge(e, G);
  end;

  (* build minimum spanning forest *)
  while not Empty(Q) do
    e := ValueOf(DeleteMin(Q));
    EndPoints(e, v1, v2);
    GetVertexVal(v1, val1);
    GetVertexVal(v2, val2);
    Set1 := Find(val1.entry, D);
    Set2 := Find(val2.entry, D);
    if Set1 ≠ Set2 then
      Union(Set1, Set2, D);
      GetEdgeVal(e, eval);
      eval.inforest := true;
      SetEdgeVal(e, eval);
    end;
  end;

end Kruskal;
```

The disjoint sets operations may be implemented so as to be virtually $O(1)$ each, according to Section 9.4, and the initialization is $O(n + m)$, so the time complexity is dominated by the m *Insert* and *DeleteMin* operations. Their total complexity is $O(m\log m)$ using any one of a variety of priority queue implementations from Chapter 7.

10.10 Prim's Algorithm

A second algorithm for finding a minimum spanning forest is due to V. Jarník (see Graham and Hell, 1985); it was rediscovered and implemented by Prim (1957), and independently by Dijkstra (1959).

Theorem 10.7 allows the freedom to choose any component C of the growing forest $\langle V, X \rangle$, when deciding which edge to include next. Kruskal's algorithm jumps from component to component; the idea of Prim's algorithm is to stay with one component throughout. For example, if this approach is applied to the graph

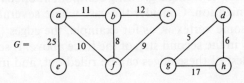

and C is initially the component of $\langle V, X \rangle$ which contains the single vertex a, the following trace would be obtained. The edges of C are shown as solid, and those of $J(C)$ as dashed. A dashed edge of minimum cost is made solid at each stage:

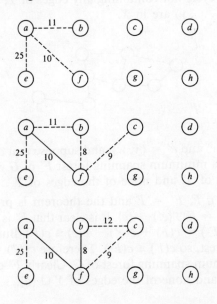

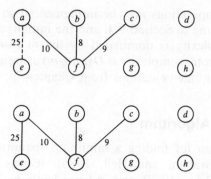

Now $J(C)$ is empty and the algorithm must be restarted on another component of G. The correctness of this algorithm follows in the same way as Kruskal's algorithm: the included edges are justified by Theorem 10.7, and the others would cause a cycle so must be excluded.

This restriction to a single growing component opens the way for an interesting optimization. Consider the case where several edges in $J(C)$ lead from C to some vertex w, as for example, the edges $\{a, b\}$ and $\{f, b\}$ lead from C to b in the second step of the trace above. It seems likely that all but the smallest of these edges can be ruled out, and in fact this is so:

Theorem 10.9: Let $G = \langle V, E \rangle$ be a graph, and suppose there are two subsets of E, called X and Y, that obey the following condition: there exists a minimum spanning forest F of G which contains all of the edges of X, and none of the edges of Y. Let $\langle w, x, \ldots, y, w \rangle$ be a simple cycle not containing any edges of Y, and such that the edges of $\langle x, \ldots, y \rangle$ are in X:

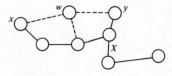

Let $e = \langle x, w \rangle$ and $e' = \langle y, w \rangle$, and suppose that $c(e) \geq c(e')$. Then there exists a minimum spanning forest F' of G which contains all of the edges of X, and none of the edges of $Y \cup \{e\}$.

Proof: If $e \in F$, $F' = F$ and the theorem is proven. So assume $e \in F$. Let $F' = F \cup \{e'\} - \{e\}$. It is clear that F' is a spanning forest of G, and $c(F') = c(F) + c(e') - c(e) \leq c(F)$. But F is a minimum spanning forest, so $c(F) \leq c(F')$. Therefore $c(F') = c(F)$, and F' is also a minimum spanning forest of G. Clearly F' contains all of the edges of X, and none of the edges of $Y \cup \{e\}$. ■

Incidentally, this theorem can be generalized (Exercise 10.27).

Prim's algorithm, then, combines the growing of a single component C from a start vertex a, with the optimization of remembering only a smallest edge leading from C to any vertex w. For convenience in the following code, these remembered edges are directed: $\langle v, w \rangle \in Q$ implies that $v \in C$ and $w \notin C$.

```
procedure Prim(⟨V, E⟩: Graph; a: Vertex): Graph;
var X, Y: set of edges;
    Q: set of directed edges;
begin
    X := { }; Y := { }; Q := { };
    for each vertex w adjacent to a do
        Insert(⟨a, w⟩, Q);
    end;
    while not Empty(Q) do
        Delete an edge ⟨u, v⟩ of minimum cost from Q;
        Insert({u, v}, X);
        for each vertex w adjacent to v do
            if w has not been visited previously then
                Insert(⟨v, w⟩, Q);
            elsif w is connected to a in ⟨V, X⟩ then
                do nothing;
            else (* there must be an edge ⟨x, w⟩ in Q *)
                if c(v, w) < c(x, w) then
                    Replace ⟨x, w⟩ in Q by ⟨v, w⟩;
                    Insert({x, w}, Y);
                else
                    Insert({v, w}, Y);
                end;
            end;
        end;
    end;
    return ⟨V, X⟩;
end Prim;
```

For example, consider again the graph

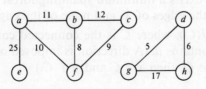

Executing Prim's algorithm on this graph, and taking a as the start vertex, gives the following trace. As usual, the edges of X are shown as solid, and those of Q as dashed:

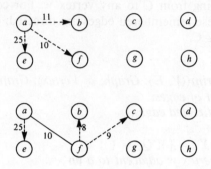

Here the edge $\langle a, b \rangle$ has been discarded from Q, in favour of the shorter edge $\langle f, b \rangle$. The next step is

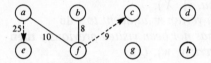

At this point, the edge $\langle b, c \rangle$ might be expected to enter Q; but since $\langle f, c \rangle$ has smaller cost, $\langle b, c \rangle$ is discarded. Also note that $\langle b, a \rangle$ is not inserted into Q. In two more stages then

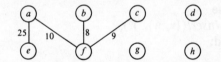

and now the algorithm must be started again at some vertex in the other component.

Theorem 10.10 (Loop invariant of Prim's algorithm): At the beginning of the kth iteration of the main loop in $Prim(G, a)$, where $G = \langle V, E \rangle$ and a is any vertex of G,

(1)   There exists a minimum spanning forest of G that contains all of the edges of X, and none of the edges of Y;

(2) $Q = J(C)$, where C is the connected component of $\langle V, X \rangle$ that contains a. (A direction is imposed on the edges of Q: if $\langle x, y \rangle \in Q$, then $x \in C$ and $y \notin C$.)

Proof: by induction on k. A definition of $J(C)$ is given within Theorem 10.7. Note that $J(C)$ excludes the edges of Y.

Basis step: When the main loop is entered for the first time, X and Y are empty, so (1) is true. The connected component C of $\langle V, X \rangle$ that contains a is $\langle \{a\}, \{\} \rangle$, and $J(C)$ is just the set of edges adjacent to a. These have been correctly inserted into Q.

Inductive step: It is assumed that the two conditions hold at the beginning of the kth iteration, and it must be proved that they hold at the beginning of the $(k + 1)$st iteration.

Since $Q = J(C)$, the edge $\{u, v\}$ of minimum cost in Q may be added to X, by Theorem 10.7, and this the algorithm does. But now C has changed and Q must be updated to equal the new value of $J(C)$. All edges $\{v, w\}$ leading out of v are now potential members of $J(C)$, but they cannot all simply be inserted into Q, because there are a number of special cases.

First of all, if w has never been visited, then $\{v, w\}$ is now in $J(C)$, and must be added to Q. This the algorithm does.

Next, if w already lies in C, then $\{v, w\}$ is not in $J(C)$ and must not be added to Q. The reader is left the task of verifying that $\{v, w\} \in X$ or $\{v, w\} \in Y$ already in this case, so that nothing should be done with this edge.

Finally, w must be the endpoint of an edge $\langle x, w \rangle$ in $J(C)$. By Theorem 10.9 applied to the cycle $C = \langle w, x, \ldots, v, w \rangle$, the larger of $\{v, w\}$ and $\{x, w\}$ may be inserted into Y, thereby deleting it from $J(C)$, while the smaller one goes into $J(C)$. Again, the algorithm does this.

It is concluded that the algorithm correctly re-establishes both parts of the loop invariant.   ■

At termination, Q is empty, implying that $\langle V, X \rangle$ is a minimum spanning tree of the connected component of G that contains the start vertex a.

Implementation and analysis of Prim's algorithm.   The executable implementation of Prim's algorithm given below follows the high-level code quite closely. The major difference is that, instead of inserting the edge $\langle v, w \rangle$ into Q, its endpoint w is inserted, and v is stored in w's *parent* field as a record of which edge leading into w is intended. At termination, the set X consists of all edges $\{w.parent, w\}$ except for $w = a$; the set Y is not explicitly represented.

The *visited* and *intree* flags of each vertex indicate respectively that the vertex has been visited previously, and that it is in C; the *visited* flags must be initialized to false. The *entry* field points to the vertex's entry in the priority queue.

```
procedure Prim(G: Graph; a: Vertex);
var Q: PriorityQueue; v, w: Vertex;
val, wval: VertexVal; e: Edge; eval: EdgeVal;
begin
  v := FirstVertex(G);
  while v ≠ NilVertex do
    GetVertexVal(v, val);
    val.visited := false;
    SetVertexVal(v, val);
    v := NextVertex(v, G);
  end;
  GetVertexVal(a, val);
  val.visted := true; val.intree := false;
  val.parent := NilVertex; val.entry := New(0, a);
  SetVertexVal(a, val);
  Initialize(Q); Insert(val.entry, Q);
  while not Empty(Q) do
    v := ValueOf(DeleteMin(Q) );
    GetVertexVal(v, val);
    val.intree := true;
    SetVertexVal(v, val);
    e := FirstEdge(v, G);
    while e ≠ NilEdge do
      w := Endpoint(e, G);
      GetEdgeVal(e, eval);
      GetVertexVal(w, wval);
      if not wval.visited then
        wval.visited := true;
        wval.intree := false;
        wval.parent := v;
        wval.entry := New(eval.cost, w);
        SetVertexVal (w, wval);
        Insert(wval.entry, Q);
      elsif wval.intree then
        (* do nothing *)
      elsif eval.cost < KeyOf(wval.entry) then
        wval.parent := v;
        SetVertexVal(w, wval);
        DecreaseKey(wval.entry, eval.cost, Q);
      end;
      e := NextEdge(v, e, G);
    end;
  end;
end Prim;
```

As explained above, if this algorithm fails to visit all the vertices of G, an unvisited vertex must be selected and the algorithm restarted there, repeating until all vertices are visited, in the manner we saw for *DepthFirstSearch* at the end of Section 10.6.

The reader has probably noticed a strong resemblance between this code for Prim's algorithm and the code given in Section 10.5 for Dijkstra's shortest path algorithm. The only difference between them is that Dijkstra's algorithm chooses a vertex as close as possible to the start vertex at each stage, while Prim's algorithm chooses a vertex as close as possible to the growing tree. Their correctness proofs seem very different, so too much should not be made of this connection; but it makes the task of analysis very easy.

As for Dijkstra's algorithm, Prim's algorithm makes n *Insert* and n *DeleteMin* calls, and at most $m - (n - 1)$ *DecreaseKey* calls, for a worst-case complexity of

$$W(n, m) = O(n \cdot \text{cost of } Insert + n \cdot \text{cost of } DeleteMin + m \cdot \text{cost of } DecreaseKey)$$

assuming that the graph traversal operations are $O(1)$ each. This leads to an $O(n^2)$ implementation using an unsorted linked list for the priority queue, or $O(n \log n + m)$ using Fibonacci heaps.

Unlike Dijkstra's algorithm, however, this implementation can be bettered. By growing many small components C, and keeping each $J(C)$ in a Fibonacci heap, it is possible to build minimum spanning trees in almost linear time (Fredman and Tarjan, 1987; Gabow *et al.* 1984).

10.11 The Travelling Salesperson Problem

This chapter concludes with a problem that has never been satisfactorily solved, despite the ingenious efforts of researchers over many years: the *travelling salesperson problem*. The problem is to arrange the itinerary of a travelling salesperson, who wants to visit some widely scattered towns in an order which minimizes the total amount of travelling.

Despite this somewhat whimsical description, the travelling salesperson problem has important applications. Consider, for example, a computer-controlled spot welding machine. Its task is to make a number of spot welds on a metal plate. The welder begins in a rest position away from the plate and ends in the same position, so that the plate can be removed and the next one loaded. Here is a typical plate and a path which seems to visit all the welding sites economically:

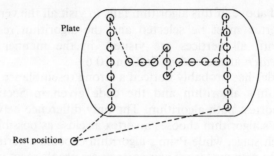

By minimizing the total distance the welder has to travel, the time taken to complete the job is minimized. Similar situations arise frequently in manufacturing and inspection processes.

An instance of the travelling salesperson problem can be represented in the usual way: each town is a vertex of an undirected graph; edge e of cost $c(e)$ joins two vertices when there is a road of length $c(e)$ between the corresponding towns. In the spot welding case, every pair of weld points (including the rest position) would be connected with an edge whose cost equals the distance between the two points.

A *Hamiltonian cycle* of a graph G is a cycle which visits every vertex of G exactly once. (The name honours the mathematician W.R. Hamilton.) Our problem is to find a Hamiltonian cycle whose total cost is minimum. For example, if

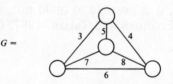

there are three different Hamiltonian cycles:

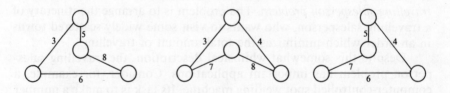

Curiously, they all happen to have cost 22, so they are all minimum.

The travelling salesperson problem is hard, as this example tries to show:

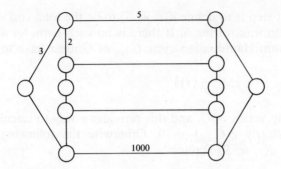

The edge of cost 2 must be included in any minimum spanning tree, by Theorem 10.7. However, if it is rashly decided to include it in a Hamiltonian cycle, the reader can verify that the edge of cost 1000 must be included as well. There seems to be no clever theorem which will help in choosing the right edges.

The travelling salesperson problem is just one of a large number of problems, from all fields of computer science, which are known to be equally hard, and for which no efficient algorithms are known. They are the *NP-complete problems* (although technically the travelling salesperson problem is called *NP-hard*). The theory of these problems is regrettably beyond the scope of this book (see Garey and Johnson, 1979).

The problem can be solved by 'brute force search', which means generating all the permutations of the n vertices, checking each permutation to see if it defines a Hamiltonian cycle, and if so what its cost is, and remembering the smallest. Unfortunately, there are $n!$ permutations, so this algorithm is ruled out for all but small n. For example, if it takes one microsecond to process one permutation, the algorithm will take about 3.6 seconds if $n = 10$, about six months if $n = 15$, and about one million years if $n = 20$.

An interesting improvement to this method has been made by Held and Karp (1962), who noticed some duplication in the brute force algorithm and were able to eliminate it using dynamic programming. Let $S = \{x_1, x_2, \ldots, x_k\}$ be a subset of the vertices of $G = \langle V, E \rangle$. A path P goes from v to w *covering* S if $P = \langle v, x_1, \ldots, x_k, w \rangle$, where the x_i may appear in any order, but each must appear exactly once. For example, the path

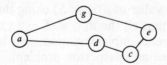

goes from a to a, covering $\{c, d, e, g\}$.

The next step is to define $d(v, w, S)$ to be the total cost of a shortest path from v to w, covering S. If there is no such path, let $d(v, w, S) = \infty$. A minimum Hamiltonian cycle C_{min} of G must have total cost

$$c(C_{min}) = d(v, v, V - \{v\})$$

where v is any vertex of G, and this provides a way to calculate C_{min}. If $|V| = 1$, clearly $c(C_{min}) = 0$. Otherwise the following recurrence equation for $d(v, w, S)$ applies:

$$d(v, w, \{\}) = c(v, w)$$
$$d(v, w, S) = \min_{x \in S} [c(v, x) + d(x, w, S - \{x\})]$$

where $c(v, w)$ is the cost of the edge $\{v, w\}$ if it exists, or ∞ otherwise. The second line applies only to non-empty S; it says that a shortest path from v to w covering S first goes to some vertex x in S, then follows a shortest path from x to w, covering $S - \{x\}$.

The recursive evaluation of this recurrence equation is straightforward, and by keeping track of the value of x which minimized $d(v, w, S)$ at each stage, a minimum Hamiltonian cycle can be found along with its cost. Unfortunately, it can be shown that $d(v, w, \{\})$ is evaluated $(n - 1)!$ times, where n is the number of vertices in G, during the evaluation of $d(v, v, V - \{v\})$ (Exercise 10.29). The recurrence equation searches through all possible Hamiltonian cycles, and there is not yet any improvement over brute force search.

But now, observe that $d(x, y, \{\})$ can only take on $n(n - 1)$ values – one for each pair of vertices x and y. There must be a great deal of repeated evaluation of subproblems going on, so the situation calls for dynamic programming – solving the subproblems where $|S| = 0$ first, then $|S| = 1$, and so on.

How many subproblems $d(x, y, S)$ are there? Well, S could be any one of the 2^{n-1} distinct subsets of $V - \{v\}$, while x could be any one of the n vertices of G. A careful look at the recurrence equation above will show that y must always equal v; so this gives $n2^{n-1}$ subproblems, and in fact there are somewhat fewer than this, since the restriction $x \notin S$ has not been taken into account.

To determine the value of $d(v, w, S)$ using the recurrence equation above, and assuming that all the $d(x, w, S - \{x\})$ are known, requires $O(n)$ time. With a careful implementation, this leads to an $O(n^2 2^{n-1})$ algorithm for the travelling salesperson problem.

Although this algorithm is still hopelessly impractical for large n – and there is the added problem of a huge memory requirement for the table – it is very much faster than brute force search. For example, if it takes one microsecond for each of the $n^2 2^{n-1}$ steps, then $n = 20$ can be solved in about three minutes.

An approximate solution to the travelling salesperson problem.

Since all known algorithms for the travelling salesperson problem are impractical, it becomes worthwhile to ask whether the problem can be solved efficiently on the average, or whether a good but non-minimum Hamiltonian cycle can be found quickly, and so on. The remainder of this section is devoted to a method which is guaranteed to produce a Hamiltonian cycle of reasonably low cost.

An assumption is needed about G that fortunately is justifiable in nearly all applications. It is the *triangle inequality*: for every three vertices u, v, w, the condition $c(u, w) \le c(u, v) + c(v, w)$ must hold. For example, the triangle inequality holds if the vertices represent points in space, and costs are distances between points:

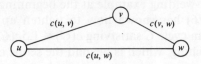

Here is the method. First, find a minimum spanning tree T of G:

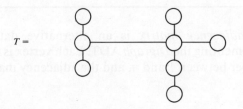

Next, construct a cycle P by a clockwise traversal of T:

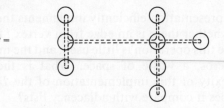

Finally, transform P into a Hamiltonian cycle C by cutting corners to avoid revisiting any vertices:

$$C = $$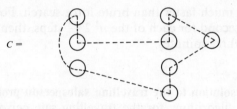

By the triangle inequality, $c(C) \leq c(P) = 2c(T)$.

Now consider a minimum Hamiltonian cycle C_{min}. If any edge e of C_{min} is deleted, the result is a spanning tree of G, which happens to be skew. Since T is a minimum spanning tree,

$$c(T) \leq c(C_{min} - \{e\})$$
$$\leq c(C_{min})$$

and so $c(C) \leq 2c(C_{min})$. In other words, Hamiltonian cycle C has no more than twice the minimum possible cost. The reader is urged to try out this algorithm on the spot-welding example at the beginning of this section.

Christofides (1976) has shown how to tighten up this method to produce a Hamiltonian cycle C satisfying $c(C) \leq 1.5c(C_{min})$. His method uses a minimum matching, which is beyond the scope of this text.

EXERCISES

10.1 The *adjacency matrix* is an alternative data structure for implementing the *Digraph* ADT. Each vertex is represented by a number between 1 and n, and the adjacency matrix A is defined by

$$A(i, j) = 1 \qquad \text{if there is an edge from vertex } i \text{ to vertex } j;$$
$$= 0 \qquad \text{otherwise.}$$

This representation efficiently implements the operation 'determine whether there is an edge from vertex i to vertex j', but in practice this operation is little used; and the matrix is often filled with zeros, a waste of space. What is the worst-case time complexity of this implementation of the *Digraph* ADT, and how does it compare with adjacency lists?

10.2 Let $d(v, w)$ be the length of (number of edges on) a shortest path between v and w in a graph G. If v and w are not connected, let $d(v, w) = \infty$. Define a relation 'v is close to w' to hold when

$d(v, w) \leq 10$. Which of the five properties (reflexivity, irreflexivity, symmetry, antisymmetry, and transitivity) hold in all graphs G?

10.3 Let G be a graph, and let a be a fixed vertex of G. Define a relation $R(v, w)$ between vertices of G to hold when there exists a shortest path from a to w which contains v. Which of the five properties holds in all graphs G? Be careful with antisymmetry.

10.4 It was observed in Section 10.4 that a directed acyclic graph may have many distinct topological orderings. Which dag with n nodes has the minimum possible number of topological orderings? Which has the maximum number?

10.5 Verify the statement made in Section 10.4 that the directed acyclic graph

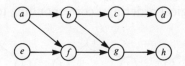

has 47 topological orderings.

10.6 Design an algorithm to list all the topological orderings of a given directed graph.

10.7 (This question requires expertise with binomial coefficients.) Let T be an arbitrary non-empty binary tree:

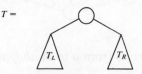

Show that $f(T)$, the number of topological orderings of T, satisfies the recurrence equation

$$f(T) = \binom{s(T) - 1}{s(T_L)} f(T_L) f(T_R)$$

where $s(T)$ is the number of internal nodes of T. Solve this recurrence equation by repeated substitution to obtain the formula

$$f(T) = \frac{s(T)!}{\displaystyle\prod_{x \in I(T)} s(T_x)}$$

for the number of topological orderings of T, where $s(T_x)$ is the size of the subtree rooted at x. A good way to approach this problem is to notice that the number of topological orderings of an n-node tree T is equal to the number of ways to place the numbers $1, 2, \ldots, n$ in its nodes such that the tree is heap-ordered. For example, the tree

has 3 topological orderings, corresponding to

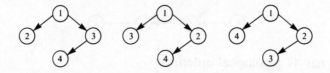

10.8 Find a recurrence equation which computes the number of paths between two vertices of a directed acyclic graph. For example, in the dag

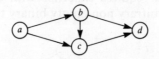

there are three paths from a to d: *abd*, *abcd*, and *acd*.

10.9 The critical path algorithm of Section 10.4 finds the earliest possible time that a project could finish. Now suppose that it is necessary to know the latest time at which each subproject could begin, without jeopardising the earliest possible finish time that has been determined. For example, in the project

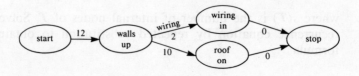

the subproject *wiring* could be started as late as time 20. Adapt the critical path algorithm to find these times.

10.10 Let G be a directed graph with non-negative edge costs, and let $\langle v, w \rangle$ be any edge of G. Show that $d(a, w) - d(a, v) \le c(v, w)$.

10.11 Show that, if $\langle a, \ldots, x, \ldots, b \rangle$ is a shortest path from a to b, then $\langle a, \ldots, x \rangle$ is a shortest path from a to x, and $\langle x, \ldots, b \rangle$ is a shortest path from x to b.

10.12 The *single-source bottleneck path problem* is defined as follows. Given non-negative edge costs, define the cost of a path to be the maximum of the costs of its edges, with the cost of an empty path being 0. The problem is to find 'shortest' paths under this new definition of cost. Can Dijkstra's algorithm be adapted to this problem? *explain.*

10.13 A region contains a number of towns connected by roads:

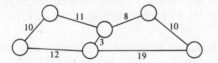

A hospital is to be built in one of these towns to service them all. Its site must be chosen to minimize the maximum distance from any town to the hospital. Devise an algorithm to solve this problem, given an arbitrary road map which is a graph with non-negative edge costs.

10.14 Consider the edges of an undirected graph G which are not included in a breadth-first spanning forest F. Show that these edges never connect a vertex to one of its proper ancestors in F.

10.15 Let $G = \langle V, E \rangle$ be an arbitrary graph, and let T be any depth-first spanning tree for G. Show that

$$|E| \le i(T)$$

where $|E|$ is the number of edges in E, and $i(T)$ is the internal path length of T. Hence show that any depth-first spanning tree for a complete graph (that is, a graph containing all possible edges) must be skew.

10.16 Find an $O(n + m)$ algorithm which, given a graph or digraph, either prints a cycle of the graph or else prints a message stating that no cycle exists.

10.17 Give a non-recursive implementation of *DepthFirstSearch*, using a stack as defined in Section 3.2 to hold the pending vertices. Compare your algorithm with *BreadthFirstSearch*.

10.18 Use depth-first search to classify the edges of a directed graph, in a manner similar to Theorem 10.5 for undirected graphs.

10.19 Find an $O(n + m)$ algorithm for determining which edges of a connected graph, when deleted, cause the graph to become disconnected.

10.20 Show that the relation 'v and w lie in the same biconnected component of G' is not an equivalence relation.

10.21 Prove that any triconnected graph with n vertices has at least $3n/2$ edges, assuming $n \geq 4$. Find a family of triconnected graphs with exactly this many edges, for all even n.

10.22 Show that the strongly connected components algorithm given in Section 10.7 can be implemented in $O(n + m)$ time.

10.23 Your company is planning to install a new microwave network to connect major cities together. One link of the network connects two cities, and its cost is proportional to the distance between the cities. The problem is to write a program to find the cheapest possible network, which is, of course, a minimum spanning tree.

Your input begins with a list of the cities to be connected. Each line contains one city name with its latitude and longitude in degrees:

⟨cityname⟩ ⟨latitude⟩ ⟨longitude⟩

The list is terminated by an empty line. When this point is reached your program is to calculate and print the minimum spanning tree as a list of pairs of cities with the distance between them in kilometres. According to Pythagoras' theorem, the distance between City1 and City2 is approximately

$$\text{sqrt}((\text{Lat1} - \text{Lat2})^2 + (\text{Long1} - \text{Long2})^2)\,\frac{40\,075}{360}\,\text{kilometres}$$

since the equatorial circumference of the earth is $40\,075$ kilometres.

Next, your program continues reading the file, where it finds a short list of pairs of cities, one pair per line (the cities must have been mentioned in the first part of the file). For each pair of cities found, your program is to print

⟨city1⟩ to ⟨city2⟩ direct: ⟨number⟩ km
via network: ⟨number⟩ km

where the first number is the direct distance between the cities, and the second is the distance via the minimum spanning tree.

10.24 Suppose you are asked to find a minimum spanning forest, under the restriction that a specified subset E' of the edges must be included. Can Kruskal's or Prim's algorithm be adapted to handle this?

10.25 How can you be sure that the loop invariant of Prim's algorithm, plus termination, implies that every edge in the connected component of G containing a has been inserted into X or Y? Could the algorithm have overlooked or lost any edges?

10.26 The analysis of Prim's algorithm says that there are at most $m - (n - 1)$ *DecreaseKey* operations. Since G is undirected, each edge is represented by two edge records. So shouldn't this be $2m - (n - 1)$?

10.27 Prove the following generalization of Theorem 10.9.

Theorem: Let $G = \langle V, E \rangle$ be a graph, and suppose there are two subsets of E, called X and Y, that obey the following condition: there exists a minimum spanning forest F of G which contains all of the edges of X, and none of the edges of Y. Let C be any simple cycle of G not containing any edges from Y, and let e be an edge of maximum cost among the edges of C not in X. Then there exists a minimum spanning forest F' of G which contains all of the edges of X, and none of the edges of $Y \cup \{e\}$.

10.28 Investigate algorithms for the minimum spanning tree problem based primarily on the theorem from the preceding question. How efficiently can you implement them?

10.29 Show that, during the obvious recursive evaluation of the recurrence equation given in Section 10.11, $d(v, w, \{\})$ is evaluated $(n - 1)!$ times.

10.30 Let us call a path which visits every vertex exactly once a *salesperson path*. For example,

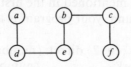

is a salesperson path. Here is an attempt at an algorithm for the *travelling salesperson path* problem; that is, the algorithm attempts to construct a minimum salesperson path:

```
procedure FindPath(⟨V, E⟩: graph): graph;
var Q, X: set of edges;
begin
    Q := E; X := { };
    while not Empty(Q) do
        Delete an edge {v, w} of minimum cost from Q;
        if the degree of v in ⟨V, X⟩ is ≤ 1 and
        the degree of w in ⟨V, X⟩ is ≤ 1 and
        v and w are not connected in ⟨V, X⟩ then
            Insert({v, w}, X);
        end;
    end;
    return ⟨V, X⟩;
end FindPath;
```

The algorithm is quite closely modelled on Kruskal's minimum spanning tree algorithm.

(a)   Trace the algorithm on the following graph. It turns out that the algorithm does find a minimum salesperson path in this graph.

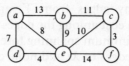

(b)   There are graphs, even connected graphs, for which no salesperson path exists. For example,

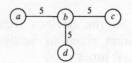

is such a graph. Find a graph which shows that the algorithm may fail to find *any* salesperson path, even when such a path exists.

(c)   Find a graph which shows that the algorithm may fail to find a minimum salesperson path, even if it does find a salesperson path.

10.31 Let T be an undirected tree with edge costs, and define the *diameter* of T to be the cost of the longest simple path in T. For example, the diameter of

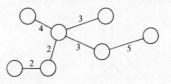

is 12. Devise a linear algorithm for finding the diameter of a tree.

10.32 Consider the problem of finding the unique path between two specified vertices of an undirected tree T. For example, if

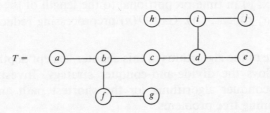

then the path from a to g is $\langle a, b, f, g \rangle$.

One way to solve this problem is to perform a search (depth-first or breadth-first) beginning at one of the two given vertices. When the other one is reached, the search may be halted; parent pointers give the path. Unfortunately, this method may visit every vertex in the tree, even if the path itself contains only a few nodes.

If many such paths through a single tree must be found, it may be worthwhile to do some preprocessing. For example, each vertex could be assigned a number in the range 1 to n, and an array constructed:

next: **array** $[1..n]$, $[1..n]$ **of** $[1..n]$

where $next[v, w]$ is the first vertex on the path from v to w. This would guarantee that a path could be found in time proportional to its length, but it requires $O(n^2)$ storage, which may be prohibitive both in size and in the time it takes to initialize.

Find a method which solves this problem efficiently, yet employs only a modest amount (say, $O(n)$) of precomputed information.

10.33 Let T be a rooted tree, and let $nca(x, y)$ be the *nearest common ancestor* of x and y. For example, in

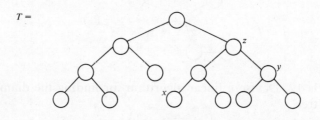

$nca(x, y) = z$. Find an algorithm which, without any preprocessing of T except for the construction of parent pointers, calculates $nca(x, y)$ in time proportional to the length of the path $\langle x, \ldots, nca(x, y), \ldots, y\rangle$. Can $O(n)$ preprocessing reduce this?

10.34 None of the algorithms of this chapter, except depth-first search, employs the divide-and-conquer strategy. Investigate divide-and-conquer algorithms for the shortest path and minimum spanning tree problems.

Implementation Module 10.1   Adjacency lists implementation of the *Digraph* ADT. If undirected edges are required, *InsertEdge* must be modified to add an edge record to *w*'s list as well as to *v*'s.

```
implementation module Digraph;

    from System import Allocate;
    from SYSTEM import CAST;

    type Digraph    = pointer to vertexnode;
    type Vertex     = pointer to vertexnode;
    type Edge       = pointer to edgenode;

    type vertexnode =
    record
        nextvertex: Vertex;
        firstedge: Edge;
        value: VertexVal;
    end;

    type edgenode =
    record
        nextedge: Edge;
        endpoint: Vertex;
        value: EdgeVal;
    end;

    procedure InitDigraph (var G: Digraph);
    begin
        G := nil;
    end InitDigraph;

    procedure InsertVertex(val: VertexVal; var G: Digraph): Vertex;
    var v: Vertex;
    begin
        Allocate(v, SIZE(v^));
        v^.nextvertex    := CAST(Vertex, G);
        v^.firstedge     := NilEdge;
        v^.value         := val;
        G                := CAST(Digraph, v);
        return v;
    end InsertVertex;
```

```
procedure InsertEdge(v, w: Vertex; val: EdgeVal;
var G: Digraph): Edge;
var e: Edge;
begin
  Allocate(e, SIZE(e^));
  e^.nextedge    := v^.firstedge;
  e^.endpoint    := w;
  e^.value       := val;
  v^.firstedge   := e;
  return e;
end InsertEdge;

procedure GetVertexVal(v: Vertex; var val: VertexVal);
begin
  val := v^.value;
end GetVertexVal;

procedure SetVertexVal(v: Vertex; val: VertexVal);
begin
  v^.value := val;
end SetVertexVal;

procedure GetEdgeVal(e: Edge; var eval: EdgeVal);
begin
  eval := e^.value;
end GetEdgeVal;

procedure SetEdgeVal(e: Edge; val: EdgeVal);
begin
  e^.value := val;
end SetEdgeVal;

procedure FirstVertex(var G: Digraph): Vertex;
begin
  return CAST (Vertex, G);
end FirstVertex;

procedure NextVertex(v: Vertex; var G: Digraph): Vertex;
begin
  return v^.nextvertex;
end NextVertex;

procedure FirstEdge(v: Vertex; var G: Digraph): Edge;
begin
  return v^.firstedge;
end FirstEdge;
```

```
procedure NextEdge(v: Vertex; e: Edge; var G: Digraph): Edge;
begin
    return e^.nextedge;
end NextEdge;

procedure Endpoint(e: Edge; var G: Digraph): Vertex;
begin
    return e^.endpoint;
end Endpoint;

begin
    NilVertex  := nil;
    NilEdge    := nil;

end Digraph.
```

Chapter 11

Lower Bounds

Enjoyable as it is to study elegant and efficient algorithms, such as Quicksort or Dijkstra's algorithm for shortest paths, the very ingenuity that is so admirable in these algorithms raises a disturbing question: to what extent does the brilliant idea, the lucky guess, play a part in algorithm design?

Even more disturbing are problems for which no efficient algorithm is known. The travelling salesperson problem (Section 10.11), for example, has not been efficiently solved – and it is of great practical importance in manufacturing. Has a brilliant idea been missed, or is no efficient algorithm possible?

After a problem has been solved, new and better algorithms and implementations may still be found. Dijkstra's algorithm began in 1959 with an $O(n^2)$ implementation based on an unsorted array, then progressed through $O(m\log n)$ and $O(m\log_{2+m/n}n)$ implementations to the current best, $O(n\log n + m)$ using Fibonacci heaps, in 1983. Will today's algorithms be superseded by more efficient ones in the future? For which problems is it worth trying to find better algorithms?

Ultimately, such questions can only be answered by a theorem of the form, 'All algorithms for problem P have complexity $T(n) \geq f(n)$'. A function $f(n)$ appearing in such a theorem is called a *lower bound on the complexity of* P. If the fortunate situation arises that there is an algorithm of complexity $f(n)$ for P, that algorithm is *optimal*: it cannot be bettered.

This chapter develops the techniques used to find lower bounds, and applies them with some success. It will be shown, for example, that under certain conditions, *Mergesort* is very close to optimal (that is, as efficient as possible), and that the $O(n\log n + m)$ implementation of Dijkstra's algorithm is asymptotically optimal (that is, to within a constant factor).

11.1 Models of Computation

When a certain characteristic operation is declared to be realistic (Section 2.1), the belief is based on some idea of the class of physical machines on which algorithms will be run. For example, in the analysis of binary search it was declared that one comparison between keys was realistic. This ruled out physical machines whose memory consists of a single magnetic tape, because on those machines the complexity of binary search is dominated by the cost of winding the tape backwards and forwards.

Whenever $f(n)$ is asserted to be a lower bound on the complexity of a problem P, the assumptions about the physical machines on which algorithms may run must be specified. Presumably a machine which implements the operation 'solve P' for arbitrary instances of P in $O(1)$ time would be excluded, for example, unless P was very trivial. (Here there will be no attempt to use the laws of physics to exclude such machines.)

This set of assumptions about the physical machine is called a *model of computation*, and it can be clearly described by an ADT defining the permitted assembly level operations:

    definition module *TypicalMachine*;

        type *DataAddress*;
        type *InstructionNumber*;
        type *MachineInteger*;
        . . .

        procedure *AddInteger*(*x*, *y*: *DataAddress*);
        procedure *JumpIfZero*(*x*: *DataAddress*; *a*: *InstructionNumber*);
        . . .

    end *TypicalMachine*.

By definition, each operation has a certain cost, which at this low level is usually $O(1)$. Only algorithms which are expressed as a numbered sequence of these operations are considered; the complexity of such an algorithm is the total cost of the operations it executes.

The study of lower bounds is now on firm ground, because which algorithms are permitted and how their cost is measured have been precisely specified. Our theorems may now take the form, 'With respect to model of computation M, $f(n)$ is a lower bound on the complexity of problem P.'

The model of computation may be taken to be a real, physically existing machine, in which case the ADT, the meaning of each operation, and the costs may all be obtained from the manufacturer's documentation. When this is done, a problem is always encountered: the types *DataAddress* and *MachineInteger* have fixed upper limits, typically $2^{32} - 1$ at the time of writing. To remove this restriction, which prevents the solution of truly arbitrary instances of problems, it is necessary to construct a *virtual machine*, which is just a second ADT implemented using the operations of the first, whose data types do not carry this restriction. There is no difficulty in doing this – arbitrary-length arithmetic, for example, is quite easy to implement – but the price is an increase in the cost of each operation from $O(1)$ to $O(\log N)$, where N is the largest number or address needed to solve the particular instance. A few operations, like multiplication, become more expensive still.

The analyses of this book have all been based on a somewhat unrealistic model of computation, in which arbitrary instances may be solved, yet only $O(1)$ is charged per operation. This model is useful because in practice integers or addresses larger than $2^{32} - 1$ are never needed, and it is preferable not to clutter up analyses with allowances for them. Readers who are uncomfortable with this model should have no difficulty in redoing the analyses, charging $O(\log N)$, or whatever is appropriate, per operation.

11.2   Adversary Bounds

Consider the problem of finding the sum of the elements of the array $A[1 .. n]$. Every element contributes something to the result, so every element must be examined. But, under any reasonable model of computation, only a fixed number of elements can be examined in $O(1)$ time. Therefore any algorithm for this problem is $\Omega(n)$; that is, its complexity is bounded below by some constant times n.

This argument is called an *input lower bound*. It is extremely general, and it can be used to derive an $\Omega(n)$ bound for most problems. Not every algorithm examines all of its input, however: one example is binary search.

Another, quite useful, way to express this argument is to use an *adversary*: someone who watches as the algorithm runs, and tries to break it. For the summing problem, this version of the argument is as follows. Suppose some algorithm does not examine every element. The adversary watches and, when the algorithm terminates, it moves in and changes the value of some unexamined element. The algorithm is run again, and it gives the same result as before, since it does not see the change. But the true result has changed, so the algorithm is incorrect. It can be concluded that any correct algorithm examines every element, and so is $\Omega(n)$.

If something more specific than an asymptotic bound is required, the model of computation must be more specific. Consider the problem of finding the index of a minimum element of the array $A[1 .. n]$, under the assumption that

if $A[i] < A[j]$ **then** *jump to* x

is the only operation capable of examining A in any way. (Recall that assembly level operations are being used here.)

Hashing the values or comparing sums of values, for example, have been ruled out; and it is reasonable to ask what point there is in finding a lower bound under such a restrictive model. The answer is that there is already one algorithm that obeys this model, and it makes $n - 1$ comparisons (Section 2.1); it is desirable to know whether it can be improved, without getting side-tracked into difficult questions about the usefulness of comparing sums of elements.

Clearly at least $\lceil n/2 \rceil$ of these comparisons must be made, for otherwise some element is left unexamined. But an adversary can do better than this. Represent the elements of A by nodes of a directed graph, and whenever the algorithm discovers that $A[i] < A[j]$, draw an edge from $A[i]$ to $A[j]$. When the algorithm terminates, mark the element that it declares to be a minimum with an m:

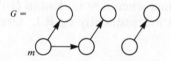

Now the adversary examines this graph. If it is not connected, take any component C not connected to m. The values in C may all be made smaller than m, without contradicting what the algorithm discovered. Run the algorithm again: it declares m to be a minimum element, which is incorrect. It can be concluded that G must be connected, hence that at least $n - 1$ comparisons are necessary, and that the algorithm from Section 2.1 is optimal.

Consider the problem of merging two sorted sequences, containing n and m elements respectively, into one sorted sequence:

$$\langle 2.8, 3.5, 5.0, 6.2 \rangle + \langle 1.1, 4.5 \rangle \Rightarrow \langle 1.1, 2.8, 3.5, 4.5, 5.0, 6.2 \rangle$$

This problem was studied in Section 8.3, where an algorithm of worst-case complexity $W(n, m) = n + m - 1$ was presented. Is this optimal?

If n and m are very different, the algorithm is certainly not optimal. Consider the case $m = 1$:

$$\langle 2.8, 3.5, 5.0, 6.2 \rangle + \langle 4.5 \rangle \Rightarrow \langle 2.8, 3.5, 4.5, 5.0, 6.2 \rangle$$

The algorithm degenerates to linear search, with worst-case complexity $W(n) = n$. Binary search would solve the problem much more efficiently. This suggests that it would be better to store the larger sequence in a binary search tree and insert the elements of the smaller sequence into it, but this approach won't be examined now.

Merging is most often done on sequences of equal length, so it should be seen what can be done with the assumption $n = m$. Suppose the two sorted sequences are $\langle a_1, \ldots, a_n \rangle$ and $\langle b_1, \ldots, b_n \rangle$. Let the adversary choose the values to ensure that

$$a_1 < b_1 < a_2 < \ldots < a_n < b_n$$

Every correct algorithm must compare a_1 with b_1, b_1 with a_2, $\ldots$, a_n with b_n at some stage. For suppose, on the contrary, that some merging algorithm does not compare b_i with a_{i+1} (the case of a_i not compared with b_i is similar). Since no elements lie between b_i and a_{i+1}, the adversary is free to exchange their values without contradicting what the algorithm discovered. Thus the algorithm is incorrect.

It is thus shown that at least $2n - 1$ comparisons between elements must be made in the worst case, which means that the merging algorithm of Section 8.3 is optimal when $n = m$. Knuth (1973b) reports that this result was discovered independently by R.L. Graham and R.M. Karp about 1968.

11.3   Decision Trees

Suppose that a problem specification says that, in certain circumstances, the result is to be 0, otherwise the result is to be 1. It seems intuitively clear that any algorithm for this problem must decide at some point whether the circumstances hold or not: the algorithm must make a test with a boolean outcome. If more than two distinct values for the result are possible, more tests must be made.

Unfortunately for this argument, an algorithm can produce a large number of distinct results without making any tests, just by echoing its input:

```
procedure Echo(n: integer): integer;
begin
    return n;
end Echo;
```

It turns out, though, that by adopting a model of computation that severely restricts the ways in which an algorithm may access its input, some valuable lower bounds can be derived.

Let I be an instance of some problem P. Divide I into two parts, the *free part f*, and the *restricted part r*, so that $I = \langle f, r \rangle$. Adopt a model of computation which allows an algorithm to use f in any way it wishes, but restricts all access to r to operations of the form

if $b(v, f, r)$ **then** *jump to* x;

where $b(v, f, r)$, hereafter called a *restricted test*, is an arbitrary boolean function of v (the working variables of the program), f, and r. The restricted tests must be free of side-effects. The number of restricted tests performed is taken as the measure of complexity; this is called the *decision tree* model of computation, for reasons that will become clear shortly.

For example, let P be the problem of sorting the array $A[1 .. n]$ into non-decreasing order. Let n itself be free, but the values within A be restricted. That is, these values may only be accessed in boolean tests like

if $A[i] < A[j]$ **then** . . .

or

if $A[i]/i + A[j]/j > n$ **then** . . .

for example. Notice that this model prohibits assignments of restricted input, so the sorted sequence can never be written to output. Instead, the output is required to be a permutation of the numbers 1 to n, which indicates how to rearrange A into sorted order.

It is easy to verify that all of the sorting algorithms of Chapter 8 except radix sort can be implemented using this model of computation. (They must be modified to manipulate an array of indices of A, not the elements of A itself. *Mergesort* already does this.) Another example is the problem of finding a shortest path spanning tree in a directed graph G with edge costs. Here it is appropriate to let G itself be free, but make the edge costs restricted. An algorithm may access the edge costs, for example, in tests like

if *length of path* P_1 < *length of path* P_2 **then** . . .

which is a comparison of sums of edge costs, selected by the working variables P_1 and P_2. Dijkstra's algorithm can be implemented under this model, a fact which will be exploited in Section 11.5 to derive a lower bound on its complexity.

As a simple example of an algorithm implemented under the decision tree model of computation, consider this algorithm for finding the index of a minimum element of the array $A[1 \ldots n]$:

```
procedure MinIndex(var A: AType; n: integer): integer;
var i, m: integer;
begin
    m := 1;
    for i := 2 to n do
        if A[i] < A[m] then
            m := i;
        end;
    end;
    return m;
end MinIndex;
```

Let n be free and the contents of A be restricted. The algorithm obeys the model because the only access to the contents of A is in the test $A[i] < A[m]$. The algorithm is now traced on the input $A = \langle 3.5, 1.8, 7.6 \rangle$. The trace is presented in a graphical form that emphasises the restricted tests:

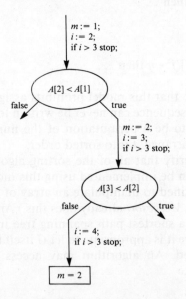

The algorithm's output has been written in the square node at the end, but it may be generated at any intermediate point. Clearly, this diagram is one path through a binary tree, from the root to an external node. If the free part of the input is kept fixed (in this example, fix $n = 3$), and the restricted part varied, the whole tree comes into view:

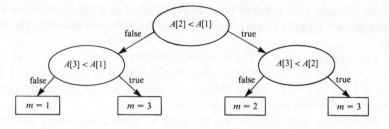

This is a *decision tree*, and it is clear that any algorithm implemented under the decision tree model of computation can be expressed as such a tree, simply by tracing it as here. Let $R(f)$ be the set of all possible results of problem P, for a given f. For example, if P is the minimum-finding problem, then $R(3) = \{'m = 1', 'm = 2', 'm = 3'\}$.

Theorem 11.1:   Let A be any algorithm for problem P implemented under the decision tree model of computation, and consider only instances of P whose free part is f. Let T be the corresponding decision tree, and let $R(f)$ be the set of all possible results. Then T has at least $|R(f)|$ external nodes.

Proof: Every element of $R(f)$ is the result of some instance $\langle f, r \rangle$ of P, and so must appear in at least one of the external nodes of T. If it can be shown that any two distinct results never appear in the same external node of T, the theorem will follow.

Let o_1 be the result produced by instance $\langle f, r_1 \rangle$, let o_2 be the result of $\langle f, r_2 \rangle$, and suppose that $o_1 \neq o_2$. The algorithms are deterministic (that is, for a given input there is only one output), but this implies immediately that o_1 and o_2 lie in different external nodes. ∎

By Theorem 5.4, any binary tree with at least $|R(f)|$ external nodes has height at least $\lceil \log_2 |R(f)| \rceil$, so it can be concluded that the worst-case complexity of any decision tree algorithm for problem P is

$$W(f) \geq \lceil \log_2 |R(f)| \rceil$$

if the measure of complexity is the number of restricted tests performed. By $W(f)$ is meant the worst case over all instances I whose free part is f. Similarly, if the $|R(f)|$ outputs have equal probability of occurring, the average complexity is

$$A(f) \geq \lceil \log_2 |R(f)| \rceil - 1$$

again by Theorem 5.4. The great value of these results is that they apply to any decision tree algorithm, yet $R(f)$ depends only on the problem P.

Notice, though, that if lower bounds are needed as a function of the size of the instance (as is usual), then the size must be included in the free part.

For example, if P is the minimum-finding problem, it is clear that $R(f) = \{'m = 1', 'm = 2', \ldots, 'm = n'\}$, and so $W(n) \geq \lceil \log_2 n \rceil$, and $A(n) \geq \lceil \log_2 n \rceil - 1$. These results are inferior to the adversary bound developed for this problem in Section 11.2.

A decision tree bound can be used to show that binary search is optimal. Let P be the following problem: given a number x and a sorted sequence of numbers $\langle x_1, x_2, \ldots, x_n \rangle$, determine the value of i, if any, such that $x = x_i$; or else determine the value of i such that $x_i < x < x_{i+1}$ (or the obvious variant when $i = 0$ or $i = n$). Since this has $2n + 1$ distinct outcomes, the decision tree bound is $W(n) \geq \lceil \log_2(2n + 1) \rceil$.

Unfortunately, this does not fit comfortably with the analysis of binary search in Section 2.2, because there 1 per comparison was charged, yet the comparison was allowed to have a *three-way* result. The bound could be changed to $W(n) \geq \lceil \log_3(2n + 1) \rceil$, but it is probably better to proceed as follows. Assume that $x \neq x_i$, for all i. For this restricted problem, the comparisons of binary search have two-way results. Now there are only $n + 1$ distinct outcomes, and the bound is $W(n) \geq \lceil \log_2(n + 1) \rceil$, which is achieved by binary search. In this sense, then, binary search is optimal.

If P is the problem of sorting n numbers, $R(f)$ is the set of all permutations of the numbers $1, \ldots, n$. Therefore the worst-case complexity of any decision tree sorting algorithm is at least $\lceil \log_2 n! \rceil$, and the average complexity is at least $\lceil \log_2 n! \rceil - 1$. Since $n! \approx (n/e)^n$ by Stirling's approximation, $\log_2 n! \approx n \log_2 n - 1.44n$, and the lower bounds are a very satisfactory $\Omega(n \log n)$. *Mergesort*, then, whose worst-case complexity is $n \log_2 n - (n - 1)$ comparisons between keys in the worst case, for n a power of 2, is very close to optimal.

11.4 Entropy

In the last section, a lower bound on the average complexity of decision tree algorithms was found, under the assumption that each outcome was equally likely. A fascinating theory, due to Shannon (1949), arises when this restriction on the probabilities is dropped.

Let $p_1, p_2, \ldots, p_k$ be a probability distribution; that is, $p_i \geq 0$ for all i, and $\sum_{i=1}^{k} p_i = 1$. Define the *entropy* of the distribution by

$$H(p_1, p_2, \ldots, p_k) = -\sum_{i=1}^{k} p_i \log_2 p_i$$

Since $p_i \leq 1$ for all i, then $\log_2 p_i \leq 0$, and so $H(p_1, p_2, \ldots, p_k) \geq 0$. If $p_i = 0$, $\log_2 p_i$ is undefined; however, since $\lim_{x \to 0} x \log_2 x = 0$, $0 \log_2 0$ may be defined to be equal to 0. In effect, zero probabilities are ignored.

The entropy of a probability distribution is a measure of how uniform the distribution is. Its minimum value is 0, which occurs when one of the p_i is 1 and the others are 0; its maximum value, $\log_2 k$, occurs when the probabilities are all equal. The general shape of the entropy function can be seen in the following graph of $H(p, 1 - p)$:

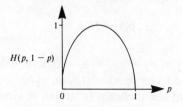

In a moment it will be shown how entropy arises in lower bounds. But first, a basic property of entropy is developed.

Theorem 11.2 (Decomposition of entropy): Let $p_1, p_2, \ldots, p_k$ be a probability distribution, and suppose that $k \geq 2$. Divide the distribution into two non-empty parts, $p_1, p_2, \ldots, p_j$ and $p_{j+1}, p_{j+2}, \ldots, p_k$, and let $u = \sum_{i=1}^{j} p_i$ and $v = \sum_{i=j+1}^{k} p_i$. Then

$$H(p_1, p_2, \ldots, p_k) = uH(p_1/u, p_2/u, \ldots, p_j/u) + \\ vH(p_{j+1}/v, p_{j+2}/v, \ldots, p_k/v) + H(u, v)$$

Proof: To begin with, assume that both u and v are non-zero. Then

$$uH(p_1/u, p_2/u, \ldots, p_j/u) = -u \sum_{i=1}^{j} (p_i/u) \log_2(p_i/u)$$

$$= -\sum_{i=1}^{j} (p_i \log_2 p_i - p_i \log_2 u)$$

$$= -\sum_{i=1}^{j} p_i \log_2 p_i + u \log_2 u$$

Similarly,

$$vH(p_{j+1}/v, p_{j=2}/v, \ldots, p_k/v) = -\sum_{i=j+1}^{k} p_i \log_2 p_i + v \log_2 v$$

and the result follows quickly from adding these two equations together:

$$uH(p_1/u, p_2/u, \ldots, p_j/u) + vH(p_{j+1}/v, p_{j+2}/v, \ldots, p_k/v)$$

$$= -\sum_{i=1}^{j} p_i\log_2 p_i + u\log_2 u - \sum_{i=j+1}^{k} p_i\log_2 p_i + v\log_2 v$$

$$= -\sum_{i=1}^{k} p_i\log_2 p_i + u\log_2 u + v\log_2 v$$

$$= H(p_1, p_2, \ldots, p_k) - H(u, v)$$

If $u = 0$, then $p_1 = p_2 = \ldots = p_j = 0$, and $-\sum_{i=1}^{j} p_i\log_2 p_i + u\log_2 u$ has been defined to be 0, so $uH(p_1/u, p_2/u, \ldots, p_j/u)$ may be taken to be 0 also, and the theorem is trivial. A similar argument applies if $v = 0$; and since both cannot be 0 because $u + v = 1$, the theorem is proved.   ∎

The next step is to use this theorem to relate entropy to the weighted external path length of a binary tree. Let T be a binary tree with a *weight* (a non-negative real number) attached to each external node. If there are k external nodes and k weights $w_1, w_2, \ldots, w_k$, define

$$wepl(T) = \sum_{i=1}^{k} w_i d_i$$

where d_i is the depth of the external node to which w_i is attached. For example, if

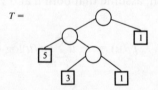

then $wepl(T) = 5\cdot 2 + 3\cdot 3 + 1\cdot 3 + 1\cdot 1 = 23$. Note that $wepl(T)$ has been defined previously, when studying Huffman trees (Section 5.4).

The significance of weighted external path length for decision trees is as follows. If T is a decision tree with k external nodes, and w_i is the probability that an instance occurs which leads to the ith external node, then, since d_i is the time complexity of that instance, the average complexity $A(n)$ of the decision tree algorithm is $wepl(T)$.

In order to get a lower bound on the average complexity of a problem under the decision tree model, a lower bound is needed for $wepl(T)$ that holds for all T yet depends only on the probabilities $w_1, w_2, \ldots, w_n$ of the instances, not on the shape of T. This is what entropy provides.

Theorem 11.3 (Entropy lower bound):   Let T be a binary tree with k external nodes, and suppose that non-negative weights $w_1, w_2, \ldots, w_k$ are attached to these external nodes in any order. Then

$$wepl(T) \geq wH(w_1/w, w_2/w, \ldots, w_k/w)$$

where $w = \Sigma_{i=1}^{k} w_i$ is the total weight.

Proof: If $w = 0$, the right-hand side is taken to be 0 in the usual way, and the result is trivial. The remainder of the proof is by induction on k.

Basis step: $k = 1$. Then $H(w_1/w) = 0$, and the result is again trivially true.

Inductive step: $k \geq 2$. Define $p_i = w_i/w$ for all i, so that $p_1, p_2 \ldots, p_k$ is a probability distribution. Let T' be T with w_1 replaced by p_1, w_2 replaced by p_2, etc. Since T' has at least two external nodes, we may put

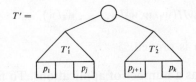

for some j. Although the p_i are shown in order from left to right, this argument will work for any ordering of the p_i. Now, if d_i is the depth of the external node containing p_i,

$$wepl(T') = \sum_{i=1}^{k} p_i d_i$$

$$= \sum_{i=1}^{k} p_i(d_i - 1) + 1$$

$$= \sum_{i=1}^{j} p_i(d_i - 1) + \sum_{i=j+1}^{k} p_i(d_i - 1) + 1$$

$$= wepl(T'_1) + wepl(T'_2) + 1$$

$$\geq uH(p_1/u, p_2/u, \ldots, p_j/u) + vH(p_{j+1}/v, p_{j+2}/v, \ldots, p_k/v) + 1$$

by the inductive hypothesis applied to T'_1 and T'_2, where $u = \sum_{i=1}^{j} p_i$ and $v = \sum_{i=j+1}^{k} p_i$ have been set. Now $H(u, v) \le \log_2 2 = 1$, so

$$
\begin{aligned}
wepl(T') &\ge uH(p_1/u, p_2/u, \dots, p_j/u) + \\
&\quad vH(p_{j+1}/v, p_{j+2}/v, \dots, p_k/v) + H(u, v) \\
&= H(p_1, p_2, \dots, p_k)
\end{aligned}
$$

by Theorem 11.2. Now, recalling the definitions of T' and the p_i,

$$
\begin{aligned}
wepl(T) &= \sum_{i=1}^{k} w_i d_i \\
&= w \sum_{i=1}^{k} p_i d_i \\
&= w \cdot wepl(T') \\
&\ge wH(p_1, p_2, \dots, p_k) \\
&= wH(w_1/w, w_2/w, \dots, w_k/w),
\end{aligned}
$$

and the theorem is proved. ∎

This theorem has a number of applications. To find a lower bound on the average complexity of decision tree sorting, for example, $k = n!$, $w_i = 1/n!$ for all i, and so

$$
\begin{aligned}
A(n) &\ge wH(w_1/w, w_2/w, \dots, w_k/w) \\
&= H(1/n!, 1/n!, \dots, 1/n!) \\
&= -n! \cdot \frac{1}{n!} \log_2 \frac{1}{n!} \\
&= \log_2 n!
\end{aligned}
$$

which is a slight improvement on the lower bound obtained in the last section.

The entropy bound is most interesting, however, in cases where the probabilities differ. It is now known, for example, that the weighted external path length of a Huffman tree built from the weights $w_1, w_2, \dots, w_n$ is at least $wH(w_1/w, \dots, w_k/w)$. Since this wepl is the length of the encoded message, the possibility of the message being very short exists only when the weights differ significantly from each other.

11.5   Transformations

When two problems are closely related, it may be possible to transfer a lower bound from one problem to the other.

Let P and P' be two problems. Suppose an arbitrary instance I of P can be solved by converting I into an instance I' of P', solving I', and converting the solution S' thus obtained back into a solution S of I:

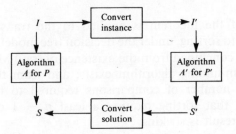

If algorithms exist for converting I into I' and S' into S, it is said that *there is a transformation from P to P'*, written $P \propto P'$. For example, the problem of finding the median of a set of n numbers (that is, the $\lceil n/2 \rceil$th smallest) transforms to sorting:

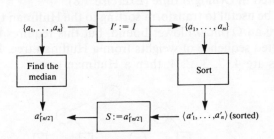

The two conversion algorithms are trivial, since $I' = I$ and S is just the $\lceil n/2 \rceil$th element of the sorted sequence S'.

The consequences of the relationship $P \propto P'$ for the worst-case complexity of the two problems are expressed by the following theorem.

Theorem 11.4 (Transformation lower bound):   Suppose that $P \propto P'$, and that the worst-case complexities of the algorithms that convert I into I' and S' into S are $f_1(n)$ and $f_2(n)$ respectively, where n is the size of I. Then

(a) For every algorithm for P' of worst-case complexity $W'(n)$, there is an algorithm for P of complexity $f_1(n) + W'(n) + f_2(n)$.

(b) If $g(n)$ is a lower bound on the complexity of P, then $g(n) - f_1(n) - f_2(n)$ is a lower bound on the complexity of P'.

Proof: It is assumed that all algorithms and bounds are with respect to a single model of computation. The proof of (a) is obvious; the proof of (b) is by contradiction: if an algorithm for P' of complexity less than $g(n) - f_1(n) - f_2(n)$ existed, then by (a) an algorithm for P of complexity less than $g(n)$ would exist, contradicting the assumption that $g(n)$ was a lower bound on the complexity of P.   ∎

For example, if the theorem is applied to the transformation from median-finding to sorting, under the decision tree model, $f_1(n) = f_2(n) = 0$, and it can be concluded from the existence of (say) Mergesort that an $O(n\log n)$ median-finding algorithm exists; and from the lower bound $n - 1$ on the number of comparisons required to find the median (Exercise 11.1), that sorting requires a least $n - 1$ comparisons. Of course, neither result is striking.

The transformation from median-finding to sorting is a natural one; the two problems are closely related. Not all transformations are so clear.

Consider finding a lower bound for the *Huffman tree problem*: given n weights $w_1, w_2, \ldots, w_n$, find a Huffman tree for them. Huffman trees were presented in Section 5.4, and an algorithm was given there that can be implemented in $O(n\log n)$ time (Exercise 7.8).

It would be useful to transform sorting to the Huffman tree problem, so as to prove an $\Omega(n\log n)$ lower bound, but this requires the ability to read off a sorted sequence of weights from a Huffman tree. For example, if the weights are 4, 7, 3, 2, 4, then a Huffman tree is

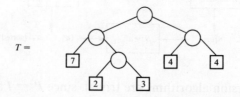

and it is not clear how to retrieve the sorted sequence $\langle 2, 3, 4, 4, 7 \rangle$ from this tree. It is known that smaller weights appear deeper in the tree, however, so there is hope. In fact, if the Huffman tree turns out to be skew, then the weights are sorted with the largest at depth 1, the second largest at depth 2, etc.

Define, therefore, the following problem, which will be called Sort*. Given a set of n positive numbers $w_1, w_2, \ldots, w_n$ suppose there is a permutation $w'_1, w'_2, \ldots, w'_n$ of these numbers such that

$$w'_i > \sum_{j=1}^{i-1} w'_j$$

for all i. The problem is to sort the numbers.

It is easy to see that the $\Omega(n\log n)$ decision tree bound for sorting applies equally well to Sort*, since the new condition does not change the number of external nodes in the decision tree. Now transform Sort* to the Huffman tree problem:

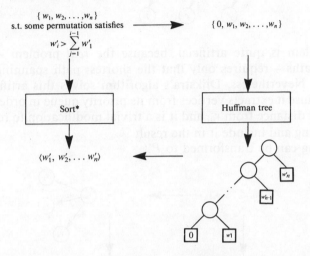

The Huffman tree must be a skew tree like the one shown, as will now be shown. Since $w'_n > \sum_{j=1}^{n-1} w'_j$, clearly w'_n contains over half the total weight and must appear at depth 1. The same argument applies to the remaining weights within their subtree. But now the transformation back to the sorted sequence $\langle w'_1, w'_2, \ldots, w'_n \rangle$ is easily accomplished by an $O(n)$ traversal of the tree. It may be concluded that any decision tree algorithm for constructing Huffman trees is $\Omega(n\log n)$, and therefore that Huffman's algorithm is asymptotically optimal: there is no substantially faster algorithm.

This section concludes with a proof that the Fibonacci heaps implementation of Dijkstra's algorithm is optimal to within a constant factor, under the decision tree model. The result is interesting in that it shows that there are only two possible ways in which some new algorithm for the shortest path problem can be made asymptotically faster than Dijkstra's.

Consider the following problem, which will be called P'. Given an edge-weighted directed graph G with distinguished vertex v_0, the problem is to determine a shortest-path spanning tree for G, rooted at v_0, *and* a sequence of all the vertices of G, ordered by non-decreasing distance from v_0. For example, given the instance

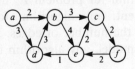

with $v_0 = a$, the result is to be

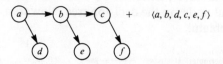

This problem is quite artificial, because the *real* problem – finding shortest paths – requires only that the shortest path spanning tree be produced. Nevertheless, Dijkstra's algorithm solves this artificial problem, because it extracts vertices from its priority queue in order of non-decreasing distance from v_0, and it is a trivial modification to remember this ordering and include it in the result.

Sorting can be transformed to P':

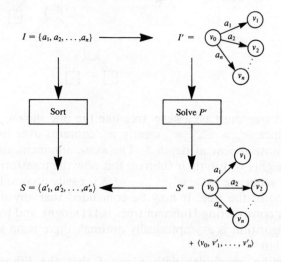

Given a set of numbers to sort, they can be used as costs in the directed graph I' shown, thus producing an instance of P'. The solution to this instance is a shortest path spanning tree which is identical with I', plus the sequence $\langle v_0, v'_1, \ldots, v'_n \rangle$ of vertices in non-decreasing order of distance from v_0; in other words, in non-decreasing order of the a_i. Dropping v_0 from the sequence and replacing each v'_i with its corresponding a'_i yields the original numbers in non-decreasing order.

It is easy to see that the two conversion algorithms are both $O(n)$, and indeed under the decision tree model, $f_1(n) = f_2(n) = 0$. So it can be deduced from Theorem 11.4 and the $\Omega(n\log n)$ sorting lower bound, that any decision tree algorithm for problem P' must be $\Omega(n\log n)$. By the usual adversary argument, any algorithm for problem P' must be $\Omega(n + m)$, where m is the number of edges. It can be concluded that, under the decision tree model, any algorithm for problem P', including any implementation of Dijkstra's algorithm, must be $\Omega(n\log n + m)$.

The argument shows clearly that there are only two possible ways to improve on Dijkstra's algorithm implemented using Fibonacci heaps. The first is to go outside the decision tree model. For example, Dijkstra's algorithm might be used, but the priority queue implemented with methods analogous to radix sorting.

The second way is to devise a shortest path spanning tree algorithm which is not capable of generating the sequence of vertices in non-decreasing order of distance from v_0. In fact, such an algorithm has already been studied. It was based on topological sort, and it ran in linear time (Section 10.4); but unfortunately it works only on directed *acyclic* graphs.

These remarks show the great practical value of lower bound results in guiding the search for better algorithms. There are a large number of problems, such as matrix multiplication, minimum spanning trees, and the travelling salesperson problem, where the lower bounds that are known are not strong enough to show that any existing algorithm is asymptotically optimal. Our knowledge of algorithms and data structures, therefore, is very far from complete.

EXERCISES

11.1 Use the adversary argument for minimum-finding given in Section 11.2 to show that the problem of finding the kth smallest of a set of n numbers requires at least $n - 1$ comparisons for any k, under the model of computation employed for minimum-finding.

11.2 Using an adversary argument and induction, prove that any algorithm for the Towers of Hanoi problem must make at least $2^n - 1$ disk moves, and so conclude that the algorithm given in Section 2.2 is optimal.

11.3 Use an adversary argument to prove that any algorithm which finds the kth smallest of a set of n numbers must also find which of the remaining numbers are smaller, and which are larger.

11.4 (This question requires expertise with binomial coefficients.) Using the result of the previous question, find a decision tree lower bound on the cost of finding the median of a set of $2k + 1$ distinct numbers. How does this bound compare with the adversary bound of Question 1?

11.5   Draw a decision tree for the *Mergesort* of the array $A[1 .. 3]$. Is *Mergesort* optimal for $n = 3$?

11.6   *Mergesort* will sort five numbers in eight comparisons in the worst case, but since $\lceil \log_2 5! \rceil = 7$, it is possible that some other algorithm, requiring at most seven comparisons, exists. Find one.

11.7   Show how to simulate the r-way branch of radix sort by a decision tree of depth $O(\log r)$, and use this to produce a decision tree lower bound for radix sorting.

11.8   (This question requires expertise with binomial coefficients). Find a decision tree bound on the complexity of merging a sorted list of n numbers with a sorted list of m numbers. Investigate the special cases $n = m$ and $m = 1$.

11.9   Find an $\Omega(n \log n)$ decision tree bound for the problem solved by Huffman's algorithm.

11.10   Show that the problem of finding a longest common subsequence of two sequences (as discussed in Section 4.4) has

$$\sum_{k=0}^{\infty} \binom{n}{k}\binom{m}{k} = \binom{n+m}{n}$$

distinct outcomes, where n and m are the lengths of the two sequences. The right-hand side is a well-known simplification of the left. Use it to find a decision tree bound for this problem.

11.11   What is the set of all outcomes of the problem solved by Dijkstra's algorithm? What can you say about the decision tree bound for this problem?

11.12   Prove that $H(p_1, p_2, \ldots, p_n)$ achieves its maximum value when $p_1 = p_2 = \ldots = p_n = 1/n$, and show that this value is $\log_2 n$.

11.13   In this question the binary trees of minimal weighted external path length are characterized, and it is shown that the entropy bound cannot be improved in general.

(a) Let T be a binary tree with k external nodes, containing weights $w_1, w_2, \ldots, w_k$, and let $w = \sum_{i=1}^{k} w_i$. Show that $wepl(T) = wH(w_1/w, w_2/w, \ldots, w_k/w)$ if and only if, for every internal node x of T, the total weight of the left and right subtrees of T_x is equal.

(b) Show that $wepl(T) = wH(w_1/w, w_2/w, \ldots, w_k/w)$ if and only if $w_i/w = 2^{-d(x_i)}$ for all i, where x_i is the external node containing w_i, and $d(x_i)$ is its depth.

11.14 What does the $\Omega(n\log n)$ sorting bound imply about the complexity of the priority queue and ordered symbol table ADTs?

11.15 Show that the binary relation $\propto$ is reflexive ($P \propto P$ for all problems P) and transitive (that is, if $P \propto Q$ and $Q \propto R$, *then* $P \propto R$).

Recommended Further Reading

Aho, A.V., Hopcroft, J.E. and Ullman, J.D. (1974). *The Design and Analysis of Computer Algorithms*. Reading, MA: Addison-Wesley
A seminal book of extraordinary breadth and depth, which collects together areas as diverse as data structures, arithmetic, pattern-matching, and complexity theory.

Cohen, D.I.A. (1978). *Basic Techniques of Combinatorial Theory*. Chichester, UK: Wiley
A clear account of binomial coefficients, generating functions, permutations, graphs, and other topics, with many captivating examples and exercises.

Dijkstra, E.W. (1976). *A Discipline of Programming*. Englewood Cliffs, NJ: Prentice-Hall
An influential and much-discussed book presenting formal correctness as a design method.

Garey, M.R. and Johnson, D.S. (1979). *Computers and Intractability: A Guide to the Theory of NP-completeness*. San Francisco: Freeman
The standard reference for the profound theory of the NP-complete problems.

Knuth, D.E. (1973). *The Art of Computer Programming* Vol.1: *Fundamental Algorithms* 2nd ed. Reading, MA: Addison-Wesley
This pioneering volume, first published in 1968, is still the best introduction to the advanced techniques of combinatorial algorithm analysis.

Knuth, D.E. (1973). *The Art of Computer Programming* Vol.3: *Sorting and Searching*. Reading, MA: Addison-Wesley
A thorough and inspirational treatment of symbol table data structures and sorting. Essential reading.

Manber, U. (1989). *Introduction to Algorithms — A Creative Approach*. Reading MA: Addison-Wesley
A unified algorithm design method, with many interesting case studies.

Sedgewick, R. (1988). *Algorithms* 2nd edn. Reading, MA: Addison-Wesley
An excellent reference for a broad range of algorithms, including sorting, searching, string matching, parsing, cryptology, computational geometry, graph algorithms, and mathematical algorithms.

Tarjan, R.E. (1983). *Data Structures and Network Algorithms*. Society for Industrial and Applied Mathematics.
A study of four classical graph problems (minimum spanning trees, shortest paths, network flows, and matchings) and associated data structures.

References

Adel'son-Vel'skii, G.M. and Landis, E.M. (1962). An algorithm for the organization of information. *Dokl. Akad. Nauk SSSR* **146**, 263-6 (in Russian). English translation in *Soviet Math.* **3** (1962), 1259-63.

Aho, A.V., Hopcroft, J.E. and Ullman, J.D. (1974). *The Design and Analysis of Computer Algorithms.* Reading, MA: Addison-Wesley

Aho, A.V., Hopcroft, J.E. and Ullman, J.D. (1983). *Data Structures and Algorithms.* Reading, MA: Addison-Wesley

Allen, B. and Munro, I. (1978). Self-organizing binary search trees. *Journal of the ACM* **25**, 526-35.

Bayer, R. and McCreight, E. (1972). Organization and maintenance of large ordered indexes. *Acta Informatica* **1**, 173–89.

Bitner, J.R. (1979). Heuristics that dynamically organize data structures. *SIAM Journal on Computing* **8**, 82-110.

Blum, M., Floyd, R.W., Pratt, V., Rivest, R. L. and Tarjan, R.E. (1973). Time bounds for selection. *Journal of Computer and System Sciences* **7**, 448-61.

Brown, R. (1988). Calendar queues: a fast $O(1)$ priority queue implementation for the simulation event set problem. *Communications of the ACM* **31**, 1220-7.

Christofides, N. (1976). *Worst-case Analysis of a New Heuristic for the Travelling Salesman Problem.* Technical Report, Graduate School of Industrial Administration, Carnegie-Mellon University, Pittsburgh PA

Dijkstra, E.W. (1976). *A Discipline of Programming.* Englewood Cliffs, NJ: Prentice-Hall

Dijkstra, E.W. (1959). A note on two problems in connexion with graphs. *Numerische Mathematik* **1**, 269-71

Driscoll, J.R., Gabow, H.N., Shrairman, R. and Tarjan, R.E. (1988). Relaxed heaps: an alternative to Fibonacci heaps with applications to parallel computation. *Communications of the ACM* **31**, 1343-54.

Floyd, R.W. (1967). Assigning meanings to programs. In *Proceedings of the 19th Symposium in Applied Mathematics*, American Mathematical Society, 19–32.

Floyd, R.W. (1964). Algorithm 245 – Treesort 3. *Communications of the ACM* **7**, 701

Fredman, M.L. and Tarjan, R.E. (1987). Fibonacci heaps and their uses in improved network optimization algorithms. *Journal of the ACM* **34**, 596–615.

Fredman, M.L., Sedgewick, R., Sleator, D.D. and Tarjan, R.E. (1986). The pairing heap: a new form of self-adjusting heap. *Algorithmica* **1**, 111–29.

Gabow, H.N., Galil, Z. and Spencer, T.H. (1984). Efficient implementation of graph algorithms using contraction. In *Proc. 25th Annual IEEE Symposium on Foundations of Computer Science*, 347-57.

Galler, B.A. and Fischer, M.J. (1964). An improved equivalence algorithm. *Communications of the ACM* **7**, 301–3.

Garey, M.R. and Johnson, D.S. (1979). *Computers and Intractability — A Guide to the Theory of NP-completeness.* San Franciso: Freeman.

Graham, R.L. and Hell, P. (1985). On the history of the minimum spanning tree problem. *Annals of the History of Computing* **7**, 43–57.

Gries, D. (1981). *The Science of Programming*. New York: Springer-Verlag

Held, M. and Karp, R.M. (1962). A dynamic programming approach to sequencing problems. *J. Society for Industrial and Applied Mathematics* (since renamed *SIAM Journal on Applied Mathematics*) **10**, 196–210.

Hoare, C.A.R. (1969). An axiomatic basis for computer programming. *Communications of the ACM* **12**, 576–83.

Hoare, C.A.R. (1962). Quicksort. *Computer Journal* **5**, 10–15

Hopcroft, J.E. and Ullman, J.D. (1973). Set merging algorithms. *SIAM Journal on Computing* **2**, 294-303.

Huffman, D.A. (1952). A method for the construction of minimum-redundancy codes. *Proceedings of the IRE* **40**, 1098-101.

Hunt, J.W. and Szymanski, T.G. (1977). A fast algorithm for computing longest common subsequences. *Communications of the ACM* **20**, 350-3.

Jones, D.W. (1986). An empirical comparison of priority-queue and event-set implementations. *Communications of the ACM* **29**, 300–11.

Karatsuba, A. and Ofman, Y. (1962). Multiplication of multidigit numbers on automata. *Dokl. Akad. Nauk SSSR* **145**, 293–4 (in Russian).

Knuth, D.E. (1973a). *The Art of Computer Programming* Vol.1: *Fundamental Algorithms* 2nd edn. Reading, MA: Addison-Wesley

Knuth, D.E. (1973b). *The Art of Computer Programming* Vol.3: *Sorting and Searching*. Reading, MA: Addison-Wesley

Kruskal, J.B. Jr. (1956). On the shortest spanning subtree of a graph and the travelling salesman problem. *Proceedings of the American Mathematical Society* **7**, 48–50.

Liskov, B. and Guttag, J. (1986). *Abstraction and Specification in Program Development*. Cambridge, MA: MIT Press.

Paterson, M.S. and Wegman, M.N. (1978). Linear unification. *Journal of Computer and System Sciences* **16**, 158–67.

Perlis, A.J. and Thornton, C. (1960). Symbol manipulation by threaded lists. *Communications of the ACM* **3**, 195–204.

Peterson, G.L. (1987). *A Balanced Tree Scheme for Meldable Heaps with Updates*. Tech. Rep. GIT-ICS-87-23, School of Information and Computer Science, Georgia Institute of Technology, Atlanta, GA

Prim, R.C. (1957). Shortest connection networks and some generalizations. *Bell System Technical Journal* (since renamed *AT&T Technical Journal*) **36**, 1389-401.

Purdom, P.W. Jr. and Brown, C.A. (1985). *The Analysis of Algorithms*. New York: Holt, Rinehart and Winston

Sedgewick, R. (1988). *Algorithms* 2nd edn. Reading, MA: Addison-Wesley

Shannon, C.E. (1949). Communication in presence of noise. *Proceedings of the IRE* **37**, 10-21.

Sharir, M. (1981). A strong-connectivity algorithm and its applications in data flow analysis. *Computers and Mathematics with Applications* **7**, 67-72.

Singleton, R.C. (1969). Algorithm 347: an efficient algorithm for sorting with minimal storage. *Communications of the ACM* **12**, 185-7.

Sleator, D.D. and Tarjan, R.E. (1985a). Amortized efficiency of list update and paging rules. *Communications of the ACM* **28**, 202-8.

Sleator, D.D. and Tarjan, R.E. (1985b). Self-adjusting binary search trees. *Journal of the ACM* **32**, 652–86.

Stanat, D.F. and McAllister, D.F. (1977). *Discrete Mathematics in Computer Science*. Englewood Cliffs, NJ: Prentice-Hall

Strassen, V. (1969). Gaussian elimination is not optimal. *Numerische Mathematik* **13**, 354–6.

Szpilrajn, E. (1930). Sur l'extension de l'ordre partiel. *Fundamenta Mathematicae* **16**, 386–9.

Tarjan, R.E. (1985). Amortized computational complexity. *SIAM Journal on Algebraic and Discrete Methods* **6**, 306–18

Tarjan, R.E. (1983). *Data Structures and Network Algorithms*. Philadelphia, PA: Society for Industrial and Applied Mathematics

Tarjan, R.E. (1975). Efficiency of a good but not linear set union algorithm. *Journal of the ACM* **22**, 215–25.

Tarjan, R.E. (1972). Depth-first search and linear graph algorithms. *SIAM Journal on Computing* **1**, 146–60.

Vuillemin, J. (1978). A data structure for manipulating priority queues. *Communications of the ACM* **21**, 309-15.

Williams, J.W.J. (1964). Algorithm 232: heapsort. *Communications of the ACM* **7**, 347–8.

Index

abstract data type 37 *see also* Data abstraction
abstract value of ADT 45
abstraction function 45
AddLeaf 145
AddRoot 145
Adel'son-Vel'skii G. M. 93, 111, 116, 130.
adjacency lists 223
adjacency matrix 272
adjacent vertices 221
ADT specifications
  BlockHandlen 134
  BlockTable 135
  Boolean 38
  Digraph 222
  DisjointSets 202
  FifoQueue 42
  Graph 223
  Integer 37
  LineSeq 132
  List 40
  ParserStack 50
  PriorityQueue 142
  SimpleSet 38, 43
  Stack 41
  SymbolTable 96
  SymbolTable (ordered) 97
ADT implementations
  of *Digraph*
    adjacency lists 223, 281
    adjacency matrix 272
  of *DisjointSets*
    Galler-Fischer representation 206, 217

    path compression 210, 217
    union by size 208, 217
  of *FifoQueue*
    circular array 43
    circularly linked list 43
  of *List*
    doubly linked list 41
  of *ParserStack*
    linked list 50
  of *PriorityQueue*
    binomial queue 153
    Fibonacci heap 156, 171
    heap 147, 168
    heap-ordered tree 144
    sorted linked list 47
    unsorted linked list 47
  of *Stack*
    array 42
    singly linked list 42
  of *SymbolTable*
    B-tree 116, 139
    binary search tree 103, 136
    hashing 122, 140
    linked list 97
    self-adjusting list 99
    splay tree 110
    threaded binary tree 127
adversary argument 100, 286
Aho, A.V. 66
algorithm, definition of 2
algorithm, incremental (first kind) 64
  BinaryInsertionSort 194
  Horner 10
  insertion sorting 176
  largest k elements, finding 39

309

LinearSearch 10, 15
MinIndex 14
MinMax 33
RadixSort 190
StringSearch 34
summing an array 5, 65
algorithm, incremental (second kind) 65
BreadthFirstSearch 244
BubbleSort 22
CriticalPath 235
Dijkstra 242
Heapsort 149
Huffman's algorithm 89, 166
Kruskal (minimum spanning tree) 257
Merge (of sorted sequences) 183
Prim (minimum spanning tree) 263
TopologicalSort 232
selection sorting, 181
SelectionSort (recursive) 9
StraighSelectionSort 33
Algorithm divide-and-conquer 66
BinarySearch 4, 7, 11
convex hull 68
DepthFirstSearch 246
Factorial 3
Fib (Fibonacci numbers) 30, 71
FindArticulationPoints 254
Hanoi 17
InorderTraversal 19
matrix multiplication (Strassen) 69
Mergesort 184
Quicksort 187
Select (median finding) 196
algorithm, dynamic programming 71
CriticalPath 235
Fib (Fibonacci numbers) 73
Lcs (longest common subsequence) 76
Mergesort 195
TopologicalSort 232
for travelling salesperson 269
Allen, B. 111
amortized analysis 50
of binary number increment 57
of binomial queues 167
of·convex hull algorithm, 57
of Fibonacci heap 157

of inorder traversal 53
of *ParserStack* 52
of path compression 210
of self-adjusting lists 100
of splay trees 113
analysis
of ADT implementations 47
of algorithms 13
see also amortized analysis
see also average analysis
see also recurrence equations
ancestor 83
antisymmetric relation 225
articulation point 250
asymptotic time complexity 27
average analysis 15
of binary search tree insertions 105
of chained hash table 124
of *LinearSearch* 15
average time complexity
of ADT implementations 47
of algorithms 15
see also average analysis
AVL tree 93, 116, 130
axiomatic semantics 1

B-tree 116
back edges 247
batch file update 199
Bayer, R. 116
best-fit memory allocation 132
biconnectivity 250
bill-splitting 11
bin packing 81
binary encoding 88
binary relation 224
binary search 3
analysis of 19, 93
correctness of 3
non-recursive version 7
optimized version 30
position returning version 11
binary search tree 103
binary tree 82 *see also* complete tree
see also skew tree
BinaryInsertionSort 194
binomial queue 153
binomial tree 153
Bitner, J. R. 111

block cache 134
BlockHandler 134
BlockTable 135
Boolean 38
Borůvka, O. 254
BreadthFirstSearch 244
Breadth-first search 243
Brown, C. A. 215
Brown, R. 164
brute force search 269
BubbleSort 22
buckets 124

cache memory 99, 134
Cartesian product 223
Catalan numbers 94
ceiling function 20
celebrity problem 77
chaining 124
characteristic operation 14
child 83
Christofides, N. 272
closed form 18
collision in hash table 122
complete tree 86
  connection with binary search 93
  use in decision trees 289
  use in heap, 148
concrete value of ADT 45
connected graph 221
connected vertices 221
k-connectivity 250
convex hull 67
correctness of ADT implementations 44
correctness of algorithms 1
  BinarySearch (iterative) 7
  BinarySearch (recursive) 3
  Dijkstra's algorithm (shortest paths) 240
  Factorial 2
  Huffman's algorithm 90
  Kruskal (minimum spanning tree) 258
  Partition (in *Quicksort*) 189
  Prim (minimum spanning tree) 264
  strongly connected components 249
  summing an array 5
critical path 233

CriticalPath 235
cycle 220

dag 228
data abstraction 36
  see also ADT specifications
  see also ADT implementations
  see also amortized analysis
  see also analysis of ADT implemlentations
  see also correctness of ADT implementations
  see also design of ADT implementations
data structures *see* ADT implementations
decision tree 289
decomposition of entropy 293
DecreaseKey 143
definition module of Modula-2 37
degree of a vertex 221
depth of node in binary tree 84
DepthFirstSearch 246
depth-first search 245
depth-first spanning forest 246
descendant 83
design
  of algorithms 62
  of ADT implementations 49
diameter of a tree 279
digraph 220
Digraph 222
  use in *BreadthFirstSearch* 244
  use in *CriticalPath* 235
  use in *DepthFirstSearch* 246
  use in Dijkstra's algorithm 241
  use in *FindArticulationPoints* 254
  use in *TopologicalSort* 232
Dijkstra (shortest paths) 242
Dijkstra, E. W., 1 238, 261
Dijkstra's algorithm 238
  lower bound on complexity of 299
directed acyclic graph 228
directed graph 220
DisjointSets 202
  use in *Kruskal* 259
divide-and-conquer *see* Algorithms, divide-and-conquer
document analysis 200

doubly linked list 41
Driscoll, J. R. 164
dynamic programming *see* Algorithms, dynamic programming

edge 220
edge-traverse 24
entropy 292
entry 96
equivalence classes 225
equivalence relation 225
   disjoint sets 205
error checking 46
Euclid's algorithm 31
evaluation of algorithm efficiency 26
exponential search 77
extended binary tree 83
external node 83
external path length 84

Factorial 3
fast Fourier transform 66
feasible problems 27
Fibonacci heap 156
   use in Dijkstra's algorithm 243
   use in Prim's algorithm 267
Fibonacci numbers
   in AVL tree analysis 130
   divide-and-conquer algorithm for 30
   dynamic programming algorithm for 73
   in Fibonacci heap analysis 162
   magnitude of 30
   matrix recurrence equation for 77
FifoQueue 42
   use in *BreadthFirstSearch* 244
   use in *Merge* (of sorted sequences) 183
   use in *RadixSort* 192
FindArticulationPoints 254
finite automation 202
Fischer, M. J. 206
floor function 20
Floyd, R. W. 1, 150, 165
For loops, analysis of 21
forest 90
Fredman, M. L. 156, 164, 267
free tree 221

frequency count heuristic 99

Gabow, H. N. 164, 267
Galil, Z. 267
Galler, B. A. 206
Garey, M. R. 63, 269
Graham, R. L. 254, 261, 288
graph 221
Graph 223
   use in *Prim* 263
greatest common divisor algorithm 30
greedy algorithms *see* algorithms, incremental (second kind)
Gries, D. 1
Guttag, J. 45

Hamilton, W. R. 268
Hamiltonian cycle 268
Hanoi 17
Harmonic numbers 110
hash function 122
hashing 122
headers, for linked lists 43
heap 147
heap invariant 144
heap-ordered tree 144
Heapsort 149
height of binary tree 83
height-balanced tree *see* AVL tree
Held, M. 269
Hell, P. 254, 261
heuristic, 99
Hoare, C. A. R. 1, 187
Hopcroft, J. E. 66, 215, 251
Horner 10
Horner, William G. 10
Huffman, D. A. 89
Huffman's algorithm 89, 166
   lower bound on complexity of, 298
Huffman tree 88
   lower bound on *wepl* of 296
Hunt, J. W. 77

incremental algorithms (first kind) *see* algorithms, incremental (first kind)
incremental algorithms (second kind) *see* Algorithms, incremental (second kind)
indegree 220

infeasible problems 28
inorder traversal of binary tree 19, 23, 103
InorderTraversal 19
  non-recursive version 23
input lower bound 286
insertion sorting 176
instance of a problem 2
Integer 37
internal node 83
internal path length 84
inversion 101, 179
irreflexive relation 224
iterated logarithm 215

Jarnik, V. 261
Johnson, D. S. 63, 269
Jones, D. W. 164

Karatsuba, A. 80
Karp, R. M. 269, 288
knapsack packing 65
Knuth, D. E. 126
Kosaraju, R. 248
Kruskal, J. B. Jr. 257
Kruskal (minimum spanning tree) 257

Landis, E. M. 93, 111, 116, 130
largest *k* elements, finding 38
LCS (longest common subsequence) 76
left-justified tree 147
length of path 220, 221
linear extension of partial order *see* topological ordering
linear probing 123
LinearSearch 10, 15
LineSeq 132
linked list 41
Liskov, B. 45
List 40
Liverpool-Manchester Railway 204
local minimum 78
locality of reference 98
longest common subsequence 74
  lower bound 302
loop invariant 5
lower bounds 284
LSD Radix sorting *see RadixSort*

mathematical entity 36
matrix multiplication
  MatrixMultiply 32
  of sparse matrices 57
  Strassen's algorithm 69
McAllister, D. F. 225
McCormack, J. 11
McCreight, E. 116
McIlroy, M. D. 208
median finding 195
  lower bound 301
MedianQuicksort 196
memory allocation 132
MemoryAllocator 132
Mergesort 184
merging 182
  lower bound 287
minimum spanning tree 254
MinIndex 14
MinMax 33
model of computation 285
move-to-front heuristic 99, 124
move-to-root heuristic 111
MSD radix sort 191
multiplication of integers 13, 80
multiplication of matrices *see* Matrix multiplication
multiset 37
multiway search tree 116
Munro, I. 111

nearest common ancestor 280
NP-complete problems 269
NP-hard problems 63, 269
O-notation 27
Ofman, Y. 80
Ω-notation 27
optimal algorithm 284
optimization of code
  use of dynamic programming for 73, 195
outdegree 220

parallel edges 220
parent 83
ParserStack 50
partial order 227
partially ordered trees *see* heap-ordered trees

Partition (in *Quicksort*) 189
path 220, 221
path compression 210
path length 84
pending event 143
Perlis, A. J. 127
Peterson, G. L. 164
postcondition 2
postorder traversal
  of binary tree 19
  connection with topological ordering
  229
potential function 51
powering 77
precondition 2
predecessor 220
prefix encoding 89
preorder traversal of binary tree 19
Prim (minimum spanning tree) 263
Prim, R. C. 261
PriorityQueue 142
  use in Dijkstra's algorithm 241
  use in finding *k* largest elements 40
  use in Huffman's algorithm 166
  use in *Kruskal* 259
  use in *Prim* 263
  use in selection sorting 182
problem 1
proper path 220, 221
Purdom, P. W. Jr. 215

Quicksort 187

RadixSort 190
reachable vertex 220
realistic characteristic operation 14
recurrence equation 17
  for *BinarySearch* 20
  for *Build* (binary search tree insertions) 108
  for critical paths 233
  for Fibonacci numbers 71
  for Fibonacci numbers (matrix form)
  77
  for *gcd* (greatest common divisor) 31
  for *Hanoi* 18
  for longest common subsequence algorithm 75
  for matrix multiplication 70

for *Mergesort* 186
for *MinIndex* 29
for shortest paths 234
for travelling salesperson 270
solution of 18
red-black trees 126
reduced digraph 226
reflexive relation 224
rehashing 124
relation 223
reliability of networks 250
repeated substitution 18
representation invariant 45
restricted test 289
rooted tree 220
rotation in binary tree 93, 110

Sedgewick, R. 69, 126, 164
Select (median finding) 196
selection sorting 181
self-adjusting lists 98
self-loop 220
sentinel 28
sequence 37
set 36
Shannon, C. E. 292
Sharir, M. 248
shortest paths 236
shortest path spanning tree 237
Shrairman, R. 164
simple cycle 220
simple path 220, 221
SimpleSet 38, 43
  use in *TopologicalSort* 231
simulation 143
single source bottleneck path problem
  275
size balance 93
size of an ADT 48
skew tree 85
Sleator, D. D. 52, 112, 164
sorting 175
  BinaryInsertionSort 194
  Bubblesort 22
  Heapsort 149
  Insertion sorting 176
  StraightInsertionSort 178
  lower bound 292
  MedianQuicksort 196

Mergesort 184
Quicksort 187
Selection sorting 181
SelectionSort (recursive) 9
StraightSelectionSort 33
RadixSort 190
spanning tree 220, 221
sparse matrix 56
specification *see* Correctness
Spencer, T. H. 267
splay tree 110
spot welding 267
spread, in radix sorting 190
stability
    of priority queue implementations 165
    of sorting algorithms 194
Stack 41
Stanat, D. F. 225
state of ADT implementation 50
Steiner tree 63
StraightInsertionSort 178
StraightSelectionSort 33
Strassen, V. 69
StringSearch 34
strongly connected component 227
strongly connected vertices 220
subgraph 220, 221
subset sum problem 80
successor 220
suffix 75
summing an array 5
SymbolTable 96
    use in insertion sorting 176
symmetric relation 224
Szpilrajn, E. 230
Szymanski, T. G. 77

tail recursion 11

Tarjan, R. E. 52, 112, 156, 164, 215, 247, 267
termination, proof of 6
text editor 132
Θ-notation 27
Thornton, C. 127
threaded binary tree 127
time complexity 14
topological ordering 228, 73
TopologicalSort 232
Towers of Hanoi 17
    lower bound 301
transformation lower bound 297
transitive relation 225
transpose heuristic 99
travelling salesperson 267
traversal of binary tree 19
tree, free 221 *see also* binary tree
triangle inequality 271
Tritter, A. 210

Ullman, J. D. 66, 215
undirected graph 221
unification 202
union by size 208
union-find algorithms *see* DisjointSets

vertex 220
virtual machine 286
Vuillemin, J. 153

weighted external path length 89, 294
Williams, J. W. J. 150
window manager 56
worst case analysis *see* analysis
worst case time complexity
    of ADT implementations 47
    of algorithms 15